A History of Higher Education Exchange

Weakened by two Opium Wars and a succession of internal rebellions in the mid-1800s, China made a historic decision—to break a tradition of isolation and seek education outside the homeland's borders. In time, an acquisition of science and technology from the rapidly-industrializing West would enable China to modernize its still-feudal economy and antiquated military, thus restoring stability and establishing protection from future foreign encroachment. Today almost 200,000 Chinese are enrolled in colleges and universities across the United States and the number of Americans choosing to study in China is quickly rising.

As we approach mid-century China is assuming a lofty position of world leadership. This book does not attempt to debate or determine the extent to which higher education exchange with the United States has impacted China's rise. Instead it focuses on the story itself—highlighting the people, programs, trials and triumphs that have wrought its extraordinary history. It offers the first sequential book-length review of Sino-American education exchange that takes the story from its origins to the present day.

Teresa Brawner Bevis is Adjunct Professor at Crowder College and holds an EdD from the University of Arkansas. Works include *A Fieldbook for Community College Online Instructors* (2006) and *International Students in American Colleges and Universities* (2007) co-authored with Christopher J. Lucas.

Routledge Research in International and Comparative Education

This is a series that offers a global platform to engage scholars in continuous academic debate on key challenges and the latest thinking on issues in the fast growing field of International and Comparative Education.

Books in the series include:

Teaching in Primary Schools in China and India
Contexts of Learning
*Nirmala Rao and Emma Pearson
with Kai-ming Cheng and
Margaret Taplin*

A History of Higher Education Exchange
China and America
Teresa Brawner Bevis

A History of Higher Education Exchange
China and America

Teresa Brawner Bevis

Routledge
Taylor & Francis Group
NEW YORK   LONDON

First published 2014
by Routledge
711 Third Avenue, New York, NY 10017

Simultaneously published in the UK
by Routledge
2 Park Square, Milton Park, Abingdon, Oxon OX14 4RN

*Routledge is an imprint of the Taylor & Francis Group,
an informa business*

© 2014 Taylor & Francis

The right of Teresa Brawner Bevis to be identified as the author of this work has been asserted in accordance with sections 77 and 78 of the Copyright, Designs and Patents Act 1988.

All rights reserved. No part of this book may be reprinted or reproduced or utilised in any form or by any electronic, mechanical, or other means, now known or hereafter invented, including photocopying and recording, or in any information storage or retrieval system, without permission in writing from the publishers.

Trademark Notice: Product or corporate names may be trademarks or registered trademarks, and are used only for identification and explanation without intent to infringe.

Library of Congress Cataloging-in-Publication Data
Bevis, Teresa Brawner.
  A history of higher education exchange : China and America / Teresa Bevis.
    pages cm. — (Routledge research in international and comparative education)
  Includes bibliographical references and index.
  1. Educational exchanges—China. 2. Educational exchanges—United States. 3. China—Relations—United States. 4. United States—Relations—China. I. Title.
  LB2376.3.C6B48 2013
  370.116—dc23
  2013013553

ISBN13: 978-0-415-83930-3 (hbk)
ISBN13: 978-0-203-77272-0 (ebk)

Typeset in Sabon
by IBT Global.

Printed and bound in the United States of America
by IBT Global.

To my husband David and my children, Thomas and Elizabeth, you make my life and my work worthwhile, and I love you always and forever.

Contents

List of Figures		ix
Preface		xi
1	The Back Story	1
2	The Runaway	23
3	The Chinese Educational Mission	45
4	Righteous and Harmonious Fists	79
5	A Random Grafting of Twigs	106
6	The Mao Years	117
7	A Third Wave	132
8	China's New Academic Face	154
9	Leaning Toward Mid-Century	174
	Appendex A	191
	Appendex B	195
	Appendex C	197
	Notes	203
	Bibliography	221
	Index	229

Figures

1.1	First Opium War, bombardment of Canton, circa 1840.	18
2.1	Anson Burlingame and the Chinese Embassy, circa 1868.	36
2.2	Chinese Educational Mission students before leaving for America, 1872.	43
3.1	Chinese Educational Mission students arrive in San Francisco, 1872.	47
3.2	Y. T. Woo.	69
4.1	Theodore Roosevelt, circa 1910.	86
5.1	John Dewey, circa 1925.	108
6.1	Mao Zedong's student Red Guards, circa 1965.	129
7.1	Jimmy Carter and Deng Xiaoping 1979.	135
8.1	Secretary of State Hillary Clinton and American exchange students during the U.S.-China Consultations on People-to-People Exchange in Beijing, 2012.	160

Preface

Yiting Liu's parents' methods for turning out an Ivy League-bound child were, from the perspective of most Americans, unconventional. When she was a baby her toys were taken away, to make her work for the privilege of playing with them. As a toddler she was challenged to hold ice in her hand for as long as she possibly could, to increase her endurance. And when she competed against playmates in a sports event she was made to practice jumping rope every day, for longer and longer periods, until she won the contest. After she reached school age her parents insisted she do homework in the noisiest and busiest part of the family home, to improve her ability to focus and concentrate. "It's a very Chinese kind of method. It's hard for Americans to understand" observed Zhongrui Yin, a sophomore at Harvard.

Liu's upbringing and her subsequent academic success was the subject of the book *Harvard Girl*, a controversial best-seller published about a dozen years ago. It has since sold millions, a substantial portion to Chinese parents hoping to raise Ivy League-bound children. Since the 1870s, graduating from a prestigious Western university, especially an American one, has been a national obsession in China. And since the government's enforcement of China's one-child policy, parental pressure to ensure the success of their only offspring has taken on a special urgency. But the task of earning an American degree, given the added trials of intergovernmental rifts, political interventions, oppressive regulations and vacillating border policies, has since imperial times been a special challenge for the Chinese.

* * *

It was late in the summer of 1872 when the Qing imperial court broke with China's policy of isolation to dispatch its first group of 30 bright boys, some as young as ten, on a voyage that would begin an extended and volatile collaboration of higher learning exchange with the United States of America. Given the abiding philosophical differences between the two cultures, few might have envisioned such a prolonged association. Indeed, what events had led to this union? Certainly the growing presence of American missionaries, government envoys and traders who worked in China during the eighteenth and nineteenth centuries had resulted in many friendships and diplomatic alliances—and a shared interest in intercultural understanding. However the inducements for China's educational allegiance to the United States can be more closely linked to the waning Chinese economy and the imperial court's growing worries about national security.

The academic migration introduced by the Qing leaders could scarcely have paired two more philosophically-opposed cultures and from the beginning it was a challenge to keep the channels of exchange open. Over the years, sporadic episodes of discord between China and the United States have produced a roster of wildly fluctuating enrollment levels. Even so, since China first opened its doors to outside education many more Chinese students have traveled to America for college degrees than to any other country.

The impact of Western education on China has by all accounts been immense. By the opening years of the twenty-first century, according to a survey reported in Asian Perspective, the influence of study abroad had permeated the inner workings of China. Of the 356 full and alternate members of the 2006 Chinese Communist Party's Central Committee for example, 32 had studied or worked abroad. Fifty-four percent of the members of the Chinese Academy of Engineering and more than 80 percent of the members of the Chinese Academy of Sciences had studied abroad, chiefly in the West; in Shanghai, about 80 percent of the presidents of its universities held foreign degrees, and the list goes on.

The ever-growing presence of American-educated professionals in China has given rise to a number of social networks—websites, directories, newsletters and so forth—put in place for the purpose of keeping the so-called *haigui* population connected. (Haigui are indigenous turtles that go out to sea but then return to lay eggs, thus the term is sometimes used in "popular culture" and in the Chinese media as a reference to the Western-educated population.) Ironically perhaps, these social networking forums are routinely monitored and restricted by the Chinese "Golden Shield" project, an organization that manages firewalls to block information not approved by the government—a system for censorship based on Western computer science and administered by Chinese technicians, many of whom received their training in the United States.

China's thousands of American-educated scientists, engineers, professors, business leaders, physicians and politicians have shared a collective thread of experience. From the beginning most were inspired by a desire to use their American education to help modernize China. The students who sought those degrees had in common some special challenges, among them learning English, adapting to a foreign academic approach and establishing financial backing. Adjusting to a very different social and political culture added to the confusing transformation the students had to undergo—all the while allaying concerns of folks back home who were apprehensive about the possibly detrimental effects of prolonged exposure to the West.

* * *

"Higher education", Fareed Zakaria remarked in *The Post-American World*, "is America's best industry" and for more than two centuries its loyal customers have included a legion of foreign students. A substantial portion of those enrollments have been Chinese. Especially since World War II, institutions of higher learning in the United States have been in the business of seeking out, recruiting, transporting, admitting, assimilating, housing, feeding and educating foreign (international) students. Among the motivations for welcoming these students and scholars into American colleges and universities has been a monetary return for the United States that, according to some estimates, now approaches 20 billion dollars annually.

Even so there are those who argue that the overall cost of sustaining international students, combined with the possibility of increased risks to border security, in the long run may outweigh the net gain for the United States. Some vehemently disagree with the largely indiscriminate transfer of American science and technology to countries such as China that have had historically unsteady relationships with America—a point seldom brought up outside academic or political confines.

Therefore many American viewers were surprised in 1994 when Connie Chung, news anchor for CBS, broadcast that "planeloads of Chinese students arrive legally in the United States . . . but to the Chinese government, some of them may be future spies, who a few years down the road will be activated to steal America's military and technological secrets . . . " Chung's report had been prompted by the publication of a book by CIA intelligence officer Nicholas Eftimiades, titled *Chinese Intelligence Operations*. Eftimiades charged that China's espionage activities in America were more developed than in any other country. He estimated that aside from 11,500 diplomats and trade officials who were suspected of espionage, there were also thousands of Chinese students and Chinese Americans who were functioning as spies for the Chinese government.

Chung's report was instantly attacked as sensational and inflammatory. A letter of apology was deployed five months later by CBS chief executive officer Eric Ober in response to several protests by Chinese students. But as it turns out, the student protesters were not disagreeing that international students from China have been routinely used as "spies" for the government—the truth of the report was not the issue. It was the timing of the announcement to the American public that they objected to, as it could prevent recent Chinese graduates from finding jobs in the United States. Who will hire a potential spy?

Skeptics of the long-range benefits of education exchange have further charged that the many costly programs launched after World War II, inspired by a widely held belief that cultural understanding and interaction would surely lead to world peace, have yet to reap such a result. No one disagrees that many valuable friendships, programs and partnerships have resulted from intercultural interaction through education exchange, but successfully arguing that world peace has been advanced could present a challenge. Incidents of violence between countries, particularly those with divergent religious ideologies, appear instead to be on the rise as threats against America seem increasingly ominous in tone and urgency.

Yet in spite of continuing terrorist threats, border control concerns, evidence of espionage and questions about the true cost-effectiveness of student exchange for American taxpayers, the overwhelming majority of educators and policymakers in the United States hold fast to the conviction that the benefits of cultural interaction and knowledge-sharing outweigh the risks. Today on the agenda of almost every American college and university is the goal of increasing foreign student enrollments. According to the Institute for International Education, the United States currently hosts nearly 800,000 foreign students from about 100 countries and continues to be the top educational destination for globally-mobile students worldwide, in spite of aggressive competition from other countries. International enrollments are predicted to continue to rise over the next several years, with China remaining at or near the top of the list of leading senders.

China has consistently ranked among the top senders since 1979, when Deng Xiaoping eased Maoist restrictions and re-opened China's borders to education exchange—a resolution Henry Kissinger credits in his book *On China* as being a turning point in its quest for modernization. Since that decision China has experienced a remarkable period of accelerated growth (in the seven to ten percent range) that "seems to defy the laws of economic gravity", said Zakaria. China now exports more in a single day than it did in all of 1978.

In a report published by the Carnegie Endowment, deputy director of the U.S. Treasury's Office of East Asian Nations Albert Keidel said China's economy could surpass that of the United States by 2035, and may double it by mid-century. China's rapid growth, Keidel argues, is driven not by exports but by domestic demand and therefore may avoid potential stumbling blocks to sustained growth. Export concerns, domestic economic instability, inequality and poverty, pollution, social unrest or even corruption and slow social reform are unlikely to undermine China's long-term success.

It has been only a few years since China's epic rise was first displayed on the world-wide stage, as the opening ceremonies of the 2008 Olympics in Beijing exploded in a spectacular parade of technology. Images of a new and exciting city were broadcast on television and computer screens worldwide to the delight and amazement of millions, and many traveled to China to witness the historic event first-hand. "If Westerners feel dazed and confused upon exiting the plane at the new international airport terminal here (Beijing), it's understandable", wrote Nicolai Ouroussoff in the *New York Times*. "It's not just the grandeur of the space. It's the inescapable feeling that you're passing through a portal to another world, one whose fierce embrace of change has left Western nations in the dust."

The world was dazzled by the fantastic woven exteriors of the new National Stadium (the so-called "bird cage"), the aura of the brilliant and translucent National Aquatics Center, and the CCTV television authority headquarters with its impossibly oblique and interconnected architectural forms. The look of twenty-first century Beijing, combined with the extravagant theatrical and technological feats performed in the opening Olympic ceremonies, was an exhibit of cutting-edge innovation beyond almost anyone's expectations.

Other feats of engineering were quick to follow—the completion of the colossal Three Gorges Dam spanning the Yangtze River, then in 2011 the inauguration of a 300-kilometer per hour bullet train between Beijing and Shanghai (a $32.5 billion project and the crowning achievement of a system that already stretched nearly 5,000 miles). China's launch of a lunar probe in 2013, setting loose a rover on the moon, anticipates a manned landing and the opening of a space station sometime after 2020—the same year the International Space Station is scheduled to close. How could these staggering models of futuristic science and technology spring from a country that only a few decades ago was regarded by most of the world as "backward?"

China's security and prosperity and a commitment to forever erasing "backward" from its image have motivated Sino-American education exchange from the beginning. Economic advancement and national security were at the core of the Qing leaders' nineteenth century decision to break with China's penchant for isolation and to allow the acquisition of American technology. And despite centuries of fluctuating political relations and occasional rifts between the two countries, China's commitment to educational exchange with the United States remains steadfast.

Just as persistent have been China's worries about the effects of Western exposure on the ever-increasing numbers of Chinese students enrolled in American universities. However by most accounts those fears have not been realized—in fact an enduring sense of national pride has remained alive and well in China in spite of Western influences, and in the last few years even appears to be gaining new strength.

A provocative *YouTube* video that exposed this more recent swell of Chinese nationalism was the subject of an article published just a few years ago in *The New Yorker*. The six-minute video, according to the article's author, attracted more than one million "hits" in only ten days and laid bare the indignation of Chinese youth following the Tibetan uprising in March 2008. Media coverage of the conflict that ensued had drawn new attention to Chinese policies regarding Tibet, sparking international criticism of its aggressive response to the uprising, and renewed controversy over China's human rights policies. Moreover, condemnation of China's actions by an assortment of world leaders, among them U.S. Speaker of the House Nancy Pelosi, even brought into question the appropriateness of China's role as host of the Olympic games that year.

Chinese reaction to the criticism, as the *YouTube* video graphically revealed, was furious, immediate and aimed squarely at the offending countries. *Xinhua*, China's official news service, referred to Pelosi's comments as disgusting. Other and more overt retaliations included a massive demonstration in France, accompanied by a call for a boycott of French goods by Charles Zhang, founder and C.E.O. of one of China's leading web portals (and graduate of the Massachusetts Institute of Technology).

The video, it turns out, had been produced by a soft-spoken, twenty-eight-year-old graduate student in Shanghai named Tang Jie. "It appears I have expressed a common feeling, a shared view," said Tang when asked why he thought his video had caused such a sensation. Like many of his friends, Tang had been drawn to Western thought during his upbringing in China. However his loyalties and those of his peers, as the video seemed to attest had remained firmly fixed in support of China and its government's direction.

According to the Pew Research Center this has been a view consistent with the Chinese mainstream. In its report from the same year, almost nine out of ten Chinese indicated approval of the way things were going in China, the largest share of any of the twenty-four countries surveyed—never mind a legacy of economic struggles and despite what many view as excessive governmental control over its citizens. Devotion to China's interests, for most Chinese, has remained resolute. "China had been viewed as backward in the modern world", remarked Tang's young associate Liu Chengguang. "We learned from the West. All of us who are educated have this dream: Grow strong by learning from the West."

* * *

This book draws from a broad spectrum of sources and perspectives. Accounts of early trade, which led to the Opium Wars, are drawn from historical archives as well as from trade publications and military documentation. Also referenced are classic works such as Y.C. Wang's *Chinese Intellectuals and the West: 1872–1949*, which provided the world with the first comprehensive story of Sino-American education exchange, and Joseph Needham's *Science and Civilization in China*. Important sources for the early history of exchange also include Thomas Lafarge's *China's First Hundred*, and Edward J. M. Rhoads' *Stepping into the World*, which house rich and personal accounts of the individual and collective experiences of the first American-educated Chinese. More recent core sources include David Lampton's *A Relationship Restored*, Stacy Bieler's *Patriots or Traitors: A History of American Educated Chinese Students* (2004) and Fairbank and Goldman's (2006) comprehensive historical review, *China: A New History*—texts used in combination with hundreds of professional writings on the subject, from both American and Chinese sources.

The purposes that have guided the production of this book are similar to those employed by Y.C. Wang. The first is to give readers a historical backdrop for understanding the vast philosophical differences that influenced the development of sciences in the East and the West. Next the book examines the unique circumstances which ultimately led to China's nineteenth century decision to emerge from isolation and pursue education exchange with the United States. Third, the text offers an overview of the people and programs that influenced the student exchanges that followed and fourth, it examines individual and collective accomplishments of American-educated Chinese. The reader is provided a review of recent trends, such as the growing number of Americans studying in China, and finally a cross-section of forecasts regarding Sino-American education exchange from professionals in the field.

The extent to which Sino-American education exchange has impacted China's rise is impossible to accurately determine. But from a qualitative viewpoint it is safe to suggest that the effort has contributed substantially to China's modernization and that many *haigui* have served their country well. Of course not all Chinese students who studied in America completed their degrees or achieved far-reaching accomplishments toward China's modernization, but thousands have done so. In the past century-and-a-half, a host of American-educated Chinese have returned to their homeland to become engineers, inventors, transformational educators, scientists, technologists, economists, physicians, policy-makers, entrepreneurs, business leaders and government officials. Some built railroads while others reformed schools, built telegraph systems, improved mining operations, advanced medical practices, developed communication systems, shaped governmental policies or helped upgrade the military. China has proven to be remarkably skillful in its ability to adapt and apply Western technology to its modernization. The Qing imperial court's decision to begin sending Chinese youth to learn in the United States, most now agree, was not only far-sighted and prudent but perhaps even essential to China's current ascension.

Nevertheless this book does not attempt to quantify or qualify the extent to which education exchange with America has impacted China's rise. It simply endeavors, with as much unbiased historical accuracy and authenticity as possible, to tell the story of higher learning exchange between two powerful and dynamic countries. It is a tale of ancient traditions, religious zeal, greed, addiction, war, rebellion, ambition, hope and transformation; but at the center it is the story of a legion of students and scholars who, individually and collectively, have served as brilliant cogs in the revolution of a giant educational wheel.

* * *

Where possible and appropriate, Chinese translations or equivalents of names and terms are included in this text. In the Romanization of Chinese personal names and place names, the simplified spelling is used, however when relying on older sources that utilizes Wade-Giles or some other Romanization system, the original spelling has been retained. In cases where an older form has become the accepted standard, like "Hong Kong", the popular term is applied.

1 The Back Story

> "Let China sleep, for when China wakes, it will shake the world."
>
> Napoleon Bonaparte

By accident or by design, conditions in the mid-1800s linked China and the United States, two countries with divergent perspectives on just about everything, in what would be a historic and abiding collaboration of academic exchange. Whether or not this unlikely union could accomplish China's long-range objective of realizing economic and military security was a question only the future could answer.

Why did nineteenth-century China find itself in need of Western education? After all, China was hardly lacking in its own triumphs—in the 1200s, for example, in the time of the Southern Song dynasty, China led the world in nautical expertise.[1] Early Daoists (Taoists) added to China's technology through the practice of alchemy and centuries of research on herbs, and their development of elixirs led to a massive pharmacopoeia upon which the world still draws. Chinese alchemy contributed to the technology of porcelain, dyes, alloys, and even the invention of gunpowder. Writing in the 1600s, philosopher Francis Bacon declared that nothing in the history of civilization had changed the world more than the invention of gunpowder, printing, and the compass. All three (as Joseph Needham pointed out three centuries later) were invented by the Chinese.[2]

Few in the West were apprised of the astounding array of technological "firsts" credited to Chinese ingenuity until the publication of Needham's landmark text, *Science and Civilization in China,* in the mid-twentieth century. This exhaustively researched work celebrated two thousand years of Chinese invention and accomplishment and at the same time exposed China's failure to bring those inventions into utility for the industrialized age. Before the twentieth century China's technology had remained largely embryonic, Needham explained. Contrariwise, eighteenth- and nineteenth-century Americans witnessed an unprecedented period of scientific discovery and technological development.

Why had China and America progressed so differently in the pursuit and development of science and technology? Professor He Zhao-wu believed he knew the answer. In 1991, Professor He presented a paper at Tsinghua University in Beijing on "Chinese Intellectual Tradition and Modern Science," in which he attempted to describe the dissimilarities between the fundamental productive forces of China and the West.[3] The emergence of modern science during the European Renaissance, explained He Zhao-wu, had required particular prerequisites: that those in power have an urgent need for sciences; and that the sciences are promoted by the social and political orders to encourage participation by the best intellectuals. Prior to the nineteenth century, He explained, the only road open to intellectuals in China was promotion through becoming an official by means of traditional Confucian-centered civil-service examinations. Further, while Western culture sought knowledge for its own sake, Chinese culture focused on virtuous action; moreover, "atomism and mechanicism" were prerequisites for modern science and neither, Professor He explained, existed in China.[4]

In harmony with He's assessment were noted intellectuals such as Carl Jung, who addressed the question of Chinese scientific development in his own writings.[5] Writer Chen Xuanling (who translated J.P. Sartre's *L'Être et le néant*) concluded in his monograph "On the Question of Transcendence in China" that the principles of science and democracy were channeled by the Christian belief that God is both the origin and the end of mankind. No such notion of a transcendent deity existed in traditional Chinese culture, Chen explained, and therefore China was void of "idealists."[6]

Astrophysicist Fang Lizhi, in an article published in 1990, joined in the assertion that the influence of Christian ideology had been a powerful springboard for the development of the sciences in the West. While China's astronomers were fixed on the extraordinary or irregular aspects of the heavens, Western scientists went further to give an explanation for irregularities, according to Fang. Standing on the principle that the universe was the creation of one intelligent deity, Christianity presupposes that uniformity exists in the universe, and moreover that everything is intelligible.[7]

Evidence of similar views can be found in early documents from the West. From the perspective of twelfth-century Christian Europe, a place and time that gave birth to the modern concept of universities, Adelhard of Bath wrote of "Quaestiones naturales":

> I do not detract from the power of God, for all that exists does so from Him and by means of His power. However, this is not to say that nature itself is chaotic, irrational, or made up of discrete elements. Therefore it is possible for men to achieve an understanding of this rational order inherent in nature, an understanding as complet as the sextent that human knowledge (*scientia*) progresses.... Consequently, since we do not turn pale before our present state of ignorance about nature, let us return then, to the method of reason.[8]

Writing in 1612, Thomas Tymme declared that God "hath set before our eyes two most principal books: the one of nature, the other of his written Word."[9] For Tymme, science and the observation of nature were a part of divine service, and research a quest for God. By contrast, the

Chinese were historically bound not to divine service, but to a very different perspective.

In a document written well before the birth of Confucius there exists a lengthy and detailed account of "the Great Norm."[10] According to tradition, the nine categories of the Great Norm were said to have come from *T'ien*, whom the ancient Chinese (from the time of the Oracle Bones, 1324–1123 BCE) believed to be the supreme ruler of all natural and human orders. The *Daoi-de-Jing*, which spelled out the principals of Daoism (Taoism), introduced China to the idea of a universal and impersonal "Way" or the "Dao." Daoist philosophers did not seek or trust reason, but instead believed in the random character of natural events. Thus Daoist thinking did not share the fervor of Western Christian researchers, who devoted much of their energy to discovering the details of "God's work."

As steadfast Chinese remained loyal to time-honored traditions, eighteenth- and nineteenth-century Americans were seeking out the details of natural events with unapologetic enthusiasm. Only when the time was right would China make the decision to acquire modern technology for itself—on its own terms and for its own unique purposes.

UNDERPINNINGS OF AMERICAN DISCOVERY

On the morning of October 28, 1636, a news bulletin was distributed around the colony. The Massachusetts General Court had granted 5 pounds for the loss of an eye to colonist George Munnings, it read. The court had ordered towns in the region to fix wages, ceded an island to Charlestown (on the condition it would be used for fishing), and had passed a legislative act that would be the first step in the creation of Harvard College.[11] Newsworthy indeed was the imminent chartering of Harvard, as it planted an educational seed that would grow to become the world's most advanced system of higher learning.

Townspeople who heard the news were enthusiastic about the prospect of having a center of higher learning in the colonies, because for the first time young American men would be assured a means of earning a college degree without having to journey to one of the faraway universities of Europe. "I beleev a colledg would put noe small life into the plantation . . . ,"[12] declared Lucy Downing. Puritan divine Increase Mather would remark in retrospect, "'Twas therefore a brave and happy thought that first pitched upon this Colledge . . . " As historian Frederick Rudolph later observed, "Both were quite right."[13]

The founding of a college was an important component in the development of America's sense of independence and autonomy. "After God had carried us safe to New England," wrote the author of *New England's First Fruits* in 1640, "and we had built our houses, provided necessaries for our livelihood, reared convenient places for God's worship, and led the civil government, one of the next things we longed for and looked after was to advance learning and perpetuate it to posterity."[14]

America's first college was to take the name of Reverend John Harvard, who had bequeathed half of his sizable estate to the institution, a generous gift that included his library, a collection of more than 400 volumes. Even with the benefit of funding, getting the college "up and running" was not without complications. Limited instruction had begun in 1638 but a few months later the college was obliged to close its doors due to alleged misconduct by its first administrator, Nathaniel Eaton. When the college reopened on August 27, 1640, it was under the presidency of Henry Dunster, alumnus of Magdalene College at Cambridge, and from that point Harvard began its continuous operation.

Between Harvard's opening and the eve of the Revolutionary War, colonial America opened its first nine colleges. Harvard, America's first degree-granting institution of higher education, remained the only college operating in the colonies until 1693, when the College of William and Mary was founded at Williamsburg. The establishment of William and Mary was soon followed by the Collegiate School at New Haven (later renamed Yale College) in 1701. The College of Philadelphia, which would become the University of Pennsylvania, was founded in 1740 and the College of New Jersey (Princeton) opened four years later. King's College, the predecessor of Columbia University, began its operation in New York in 1754, followed in 1764 by the College of Rhode Island, later renamed Brown University. Queen's College was established in 1766 (it would become Rutgers) and then Dartmouth, the last college to be founded before the Revolutionary War, opened its doors to students in 1769.[15]

Before the American Revolution the standard course of study offered in a typical colonial college was, not surprisingly, almost exactly the same as that of English institutions such as Queen's College in Oxford or Emmanuel College at Cambridge. Medieval learning, devotional studies that upheld the preservation of confessionalism and Renaissance arts, made up the generally accepted curricular mix for every young man seeking to become a learned clergyman, gentleman, and scholar.[16] The fundamental disciplines required the study of Greek and Latin, and some proficiency in classical languages was also essential for collegiate admission. Staples of the curriculum during the first year of study included Greek, Latin, Hebrew, logic, and rhetoric, all of which usually continued into the second year with the addition of "natural philosophy." The third year introduced the study of moral philosophy (ethics) and Aristotelian metaphysics. The fourth year added mathematics and advanced philological studies in classical languages, perhaps supplemented by Syriac and Aramaic.

Like their English predecessors, America's colonial colleges embraced a curriculum that served more as a body of absolute truths and much less as an induction to critical thinking or inquiry—a repository of facts to be committed to memory and not questioned.[17] The view that classical learning was essential for success in the professions of law, medicine, or theology was shared by almost everyone involved with higher education at the time.

Less frequently addressed by colonial educators was the issue of childhood academics. Even as American higher learning was on the rise, less-than-higher education in the colonies remained remarkably undeveloped. On the eve of the American Revolution, there was no public provision for elementary education in the colonies outside New England, although there did exist a selection of "charity schools" run by various religious denominations in eastern coastal cities such as Philadelphia and New York. Early grammar schools were the forerunners of the modern high school. Among the most prominent was the Boston Latin School, which was created by the Town of Boston a year before the founding of Harvard. It is still in operation today as a public high school.

However, for the rest of colonial America it was most often up to the parents to see that children were taught to read, write, and do basic mathematics. Preparing to meet the academic requirements to enter the early colleges was a special challenge for those raised in areas far distant from New England or the larger cities. Nevertheless, young men throughout the colonies who did qualify for admission were substantial enough in number to continuously expand colonial college enrollments right up until the onset of the Revolutionary War.[18]

America's war for independence would lead to dramatic enrollment setbacks, however. Just before the outbreak of the fighting in 1771, Harvard had graduated 63 students, its largest class ever. The several years of conflict and recovery that followed put higher education on hold for many aspiring students, and it would take forty years for Harvard to achieve that number again.[19]

RISE OF SCIENCE

Before the American Revolutionary War, a college education in colonial America had for the most part been a means of preparing political leaders and a learned ministry. As a new century approached, however, a now-independent United States turned to higher learning as a means of providing fresh and progressive paths toward a generally better future. New ideas and concepts for learning were being bandied about everywhere, including George Washington's (unrealized) proposal for a national or "federal" university—innovative notions that had in common a focus on independence, progress, prosperity, and the building of a strong national identity.[20]

While the colonial colleges had embraced Christian teachings and classical learning, the sciences that emerged in the infancy of the new nation were not at all incompatible with the existing dogma. Early scientists were for the most part men of religious principle who, in the tradition of the evangelical, saw science not just as empirical study but as an instrument for explaining the ways of God. Science "gained entry into the American college not as a course of vocational study but as a handmaiden of religion."[21]

A few inroads into scientific inquiry had been established early on, well before the American Revolution, such as Harvard's 1727 appointment of its first professor of mathematics and natural philosophy. Substantial changes in the American college curriculum would not take place until after the fighting subsided, however. Higher learning in postwar America gradually refocused on science as colleges took steps to bring this new knowledge to the forefront of scholarship. Columbia was an early postwar champion of the sciences, adding botany to the curriculum in 1792; and in 1795 Princeton's first professor of chemistry, John MacLean, joined its faculty.[22]

By the turn of the century many American colleges were seeking out talented individuals to serve both as innovators and as leaders in the push for scientific progress. One early recruit was Benjamin Silliman, who had received his degree from Yale—an education rumored to have been paid for by the sale of two African slaves from his mother's farm in Fairfax County.[23]

Silliman soon thereafter joined its faculty and with the endorsement of Yale's president Timothy Dwight was appointed its first professor of "chemystry" and natural history in 1802—even before he had witnessed a single chemical experiment. His preparatory study at the University of Pennsylvania in Philadelphia and at John MacLean's laboratory at Princeton qualified Silliman to offer his first course of lectures at Yale, which he followed with a brilliant career of experiments and scientific contributions. Among other things, after amassing a distinguished collection of minerals for use with America's first illustrated course in mineralogy and geology (1818), he was instrumental in founding *The American Journal of Science and Arts*, which provided scientists with a platform and an audience for their research.[24] Later heralded as the "Father of American Scientific Education," Silliman helped found Yale's Sheffield Scientific School and is also credited for being among the first to make other institutions aware, through his visiting lectures and writings, of the importance of instituting a scientific curriculum in America's colleges. Silliman College at Yale University today bears his name.

Silliman's son, a noted chemist in his own right, continued the family legacy at Yale alongside son-in-law James Dwight Dana, another forerunner in the study of mineralogy. These and other talented individuals would soon make Yale the undisputed center for scientific study, attracting aspiring young scholars from around the world.

Offshoots of the Silliman legacy included Amos Eaton, one of Benjamin's former students, who published a pioneering manual on botany. Eaton's writings, as well as his lectures to aspiring scholars, helped to stir nationwide interest in the sciences. One student inspired by his lectures was young Edward Hitchcock, who would become a professor of chemistry and natural history at Amherst and conduct the first state geological survey (for the Commonwealth of Massachusetts) in America. Yet another was Asa

Gray, who became an eminent botanist. As Harvard's first Fisher Professor of Natural History, Gray was one of only three scientists to receive an advance copy of Charles Darwin's *Origin of Species*.[25]

Early-nineteenth-century America was a center of invention. The first permanent astronomical observatory was completed; at Princeton Joseph Henry experimented with uses for electricity and was exploring physics; and at the College of William and Mary, William Barton Rogers was gaining worldwide acclaim for his work in physics and geology. The new sciences and their application to the country's progress and prosperity "fed on the natural enthusiasm and ambition of American youth . . . strengthened by the deepening mood of nationalism which . . . was speaking the language of manifest destiny."[26]

But even as the endorsement of science established acceptance in nineteenth-century nationalism, the implementation of corresponding changes in the American college curriculum was slow to take place. Among the first to lobby for widespread curricular change was American scholar George Ticknor, who attended a German university in 1815 and had returned with an abiding appreciation and admiration of its higher learning approach—particularly the flexibility of course offerings and the opportunities for scientific inquiry.[27] Throughout his career at Harvard, Ticknor actively promoted changes in the American college curriculum that would reflect the German model.

Benjamin Franklin and Thomas Jefferson, two of America's founding fathers, likewise supported comprehensive curricular change in American colleges. Like Ticknor, Franklin had a long-time association with the German "gymnasium" and endorsed the incorporation of some of its components into the American system; and at the University of Virginia, Jefferson was experimenting with a newfangled curriculum that allowed students to choose from a variety of courses offered within eight specialized schools (ancient languages, modern languages, mathematics, natural philosophy, history, anatomy and medicine, moral philosophy, and law).[28]

In concert with Franklin and Jefferson's thinking was Yale's president Jeremiah Day, who in 1827 finally "resolved to meet the issues head-on."[29] Appointing a committee to draw up a persuasive position paper on the topic of curricular change, Day's intention was to once and forever eradicate "dead languages" from the school's required course of studies. The resulting Yale Report was published in 1829 in *The American Journal of Science and Arts,* quickly becoming the most widely circulated and most influential proclamation on higher education of its time. Among other things, the Yale Report addressed public criticism of higher education's failure to adapt to nineteenth-century needs, making a strong case for sweeping change in the American college program. New studies in chemistry, mineralogy, geology, political economy, and other subjects had already been added to older courses at Yale, the report pointed out, and the new curriculum now balanced both classical learning and scientific studies.

Neither the arguments put forth by the Yale Report, nor the convictions of popular figures such as Ralph Waldo Emerson (who endorsed curricular change in his 1837 "American Scholar" address at Harvard) could squelch the curriculum dispute any time soon, however. Ongoing deliberations between those holding to academic tradition and the proponents of curricular change kept the debate going throughout the middle years of the century.

Influential new voices joining in toward the end of the century included president Eliot of Harvard, Brown president Francis Wayland, and A. P. Barnard of Columbia, all of whom likewise rejected the Oxford-Cambridge tradition as unsuited to American purposes and needs. The sciences, they agreed, offered a utilitarian orientation which the ancient studies lacked.[30] The push for curricular change was unrelenting, and before the end of the 1800s the so-called "new" subjects (mathematics, natural philosophy, botany, chemistry, zoology, geology, and mineralogy) were being offered at some level in colleges and universities nationwide.

In addition to growing support from the academics, to some extent a new flow of immigrants from Europe in the mid-nineteenth century also served to shape American college culture. In particular two waves of German immigrants, one early in the century and another in the 1840s, brought with them fresh support for the gymnasium movement—including the component of physical training.[31] German universities not only offered flexibility and choice in academic offerings, but they also differed from American institutions in that they encouraged undergraduates to take part in organized physical activities alongside their studies. American colleges and universities that had embraced the German model of flexible course offerings now also began to mimic the German approach to extracurricular opportunities. Soon many American colleges were sponsoring physical activities such as bowling, boxing, dancing, hunting, swimming, walking, skating, wrestling, and foot races.

Some of the physical education components developed into team activities, among them an early adaptation of English rugby which would evolve into American football, now a mainstay of university culture. Sometimes played with a skull or an inflated cow's bladder, the earliest "football" games were essentially free-for-alls between teams that could take place on the college yard or perhaps in a nearby field. By late century playing and watching impromptu football had become such a popular pastime that it was adopted as a regular activity in some colleges, complete with organized competitions. The Princeton-Rutgers game of 1869, the contest that officially inaugurated American football, was significant not only because it incorporated the sport into the mainstream college experience, but also because it marked the first time since Harvard was chartered that American colleges engaged in any sort of ongoing intercollegiate relations.[32]

Intercollegiate collaborations relating to sports would someday lead to the establishment of America's "Ivy League"—a term officially coined after the formation of the National Collegiate Athletic Association (NCAA) Division One conference, a group that included Brown, Harvard, Yale, Columbia, Princeton, Dartmouth, Cornell, and the University of Pennsylvania. The term "Ivy League" now refers not just to the athletic allegiance but to these eight elite institutions in general.

THE FOUNDING OF MANY COLLEGES

The academic and extracurricular changes taking place in higher education during America's college movement were "undertaken in the same spirit as canal-building, cotton-ginning, farming, and gold-mining . . . [and] in the founding of colleges, reason could not combat the romantic belief in endless progress."[33] America's passion for progress spawned dozens of new colleges and universities in the nineteenth century as institutions of higher learning sprung up everywhere, even in sparsely populated regions.[34] The state of Ohio, for example, with a population of only about three million, at one time was hosting thirty-seven institutes of higher education. (England, with a population of twenty-three million, had only four.) America began the Revolutionary War with nine colleges but entered the Civil War with 250, every one needing steady funding to survive.

Antebellum colleges were neither public nor private, and all appealed for money from every possible source.[35] By far the most active financial supporters of colleges throughout the first half of the nineteenth century were the various religious denominations, as churches across America attended to the business of establishing their own monuments to progress and posterity. Some denominations even joined forces, such as the Presbyterians and Eastern Congregationalists, who in 1843 formed the very successful Society for the Promotion of Collegiate and Theological Education in the West. Baptists and Methodists were busy building colleges too, and, by the onset of the American Civil War, denominationalism had founded dozens of colleges across many states, including eleven in Kentucky, twenty-one in Illinois, and thirteen in Iowa.[36]

During the Civil War years most college building was discontinued, but when the fighting subsided there was an immediate resurgence of interest in higher education development—in particular the advancement of natural and physical sciences. Characterized by accelerating urbanization and expanding industrialization, the period following the war also witnessed the final push west and the settling of a fast-disappearing America frontier.

Development of new sciences for a growing and united nation had become a force upon which American business and industry increasingly relied. There was an expectation of innovation, coupled with the emergence of a more secular society—conditions which served to make institutions that were still preoccupied with the training of clergymen seem obsolete. Critically important in the amalgam of circumstances was the growth in

American surplus capital, enabling higher education's further promotion through generous donations (many designated for the development of the sciences) from the expanded fortunes of industrial entrepreneurs, railroad tycoons, and business magnates. By the 1870s, with the advantage of increasingly available funds, most of America's colleges and universities were soon fully invested in a "new curriculum" that focused on the advance of science and technology.[37]

Alongside the watershed effect of curricular change, the culture and makeup of the American college classroom began to take on a new "face" as increasing numbers of women, and many more foreign nationals, contributed to the mix. As early as 1855 women's names were appearing on rosters in Iowa's colleges and by the mid-1870s most collegiate institutions in the West were accepting women into their programs. Enrollments were slow to increase, however. Social expectations, family obligations, and a lack of independent funds were among the obstacles that bright young women often faced when contemplating college at the time. It is estimated that less than 1 percent of the nation's young women were attending college in 1870 and twenty years later the total was still no more than 2.5 percent.[38]

While few in number, women established their rightful places in the institutions they began to occupy and put to rest any residual concerns about their academic potential. A case in point was Mary Low Carver, the first female ever to enroll at Colby College. She graduated with honors in 1875 and was class valedictorian.

As the numbers of females in American higher education grew, so did enrollments from foreign countries. A few foreigners (mostly from Latin America) had studied in the United States as early as the 1760s but it was not until the mid-1800s that the world took serious notice of the advancing quality and status of American higher education. From that point the United States would find itself hosting ever-increasing numbers of international students and scholars from almost everywhere, even far-distant and exotic lands such as China.

EDUCATION IN IMPERIAL CHINA

In the mid-1800s, as the United States was embracing scientific inquiry in a new industrial age, China was still under Qing (Manchu) rule—the last of a long dynastic tradition. The Qing imperial leaders were actually Manchus who had conquered China in the seventeenth century, their reign marking only the second time in China's long history that it was ruled by foreigners—the first time being the Yuan Dynasty, when China was under the control of the Mongols.

Founded by the Manchu clan in northeast China (Manchuria), the dynasty's influence and control expanded during the mid-1600s into China proper and its territories, establishing the Empire of the Great Qing—a word meaning "clear" or "pure." The Manchurians, although they comprised only about two percent of China's population, had enforced their own system of government and imposed a number of social practices on the Chinese population, including the introduction of Manchu attire and a requirement for men to shave their heads and wear queues. Although the dress of Chinese women remained the same, the Manchus did abruptly and officially abolish foot binding, a practice they considered a barbaric form of child abuse. It proved to be a ruling impossible to enforce, however, and in 1668 the order was reluctantly withdrawn.

The reigns of the first three Qing emperors (the Kangxi emperor ruled from 1662 to 1722; the Yongzheng emperor from 1722 to 1736, and the Qianglong emperor from 1736 to 1796) had been, for the most part, times of peace and prosperity for China. Policies were enforced during these reigns that stimulated agriculture and favored the small farmers of China, who at the time comprised about 80 percent of the population. For example, a change in tax laws implemented by the Yongzheng emperor was designed to help farmers who had only small plots of tillable land. Traditionally, taxes had been calculated according to the number of males residing in each household, but under Yongzheng's revision taxes were now based instead on the amount of land the farmer owned. In some cases, taxes were reduced or even eliminated by the Qing rulers when farmers were unable to produce good crops.[39]

Helpful to China's farmers were the granaries that were established in most of China's 1,282 districts, for the purpose of stabilizing prices. When grain was abundant the government purchased the excess so the prices would not fall, and during poor harvests the stored grain could be released as needed to help balance the supply. Cultivation of land was encouraged by the earliest Qing rulers—hillsides were terraced, marshes were drained, and land was reclaimed, even as new crops were being introduced (corn, sweet potatoes, peanuts, tobacco, among others) as a consequence of seventeenth and eighteenthcentury contacts with the West.

With these early outside contacts came growing foreign demand for goods made in China, such as cotton cloth, porcelain, silk, and tea, and it was the influence of trade that prompted many of China's farmers to stop planting grains and instead begin planting more profitable cash crops such as cotton, peanuts, and tobacco. While the farmers often did profit from these new opportunities, they also became increasingly dependent on the erratic nature of the economy, resulting in a loss of much of their self-sufficiency. Towns and cities at first bustled during the early Qing administration—commerce grew and a banking system was developed—however, the increase in trade and the move away from independent farming began to have unexpected results. Now, food was becoming scarce and growing numbers of Chinese were facing poverty.

Prior to the establishment of the Qing Dynasty in the mid-1600s, the population of China had by most accounts remained under 100 million.

However, by the mid-1800s, in the course of just two centuries, it had expanded to somewhere between 200 and 400 million citizens, a figure that varies depending on the historical source. As a result the amount of cultivated land in China diminished from 1.3 acres to about 0.45 acres per capita, according to one calculation, and the long-term effect was devastating. Between 1500 and 1800, life expectancy in China (for those who had already reached the age of 14) decreased from 62 to 48 years.[40] By the middle of the nineteenth century China was on a destructive course that led to increasing poverty, war, and rebellion—circumstances that finally induced the Chinese intelligentsia to reconstruct and modernize the tottering empire with technology imported from the West.

LITERATI

In the view of historian Y. C. Wang, a study of the changing intelligentsia is the key to understanding China.[41] In ancient times knowledge was a virtue and society a hierarchy of intellect over ignorance, a reflection of Confucian principles that profoundly influenced the actions of the scholar class, and in turn society at large. Nearly every dynasty sponsored the collecting of books. Scholar-officials, the predecessors of the intelligentsia of the twentieth century, constituted an elite group of leaders in various fields and occupied a superior position over other classes of Chinese society.

Higher learning in the United States had over time modified practice and policy to accommodate a newly industrialized nineteenth-century world. In contrast, China emerged into the nineteenth century holding fast to an ancient Confucian tradition that revered knowledge but also vehemently resisted change. For more than two millennia scientific inquiry and learning in China had been guided not with the notion of progress but by moral principle based on Confucian ideals.

Apart from filial piety, wrote Bertrand Russell in his 1922 book *The Problem with China*, Confucianism was in practice a code of civilized behavior. It taught self-restraint, moderation, and, above all, courtesy, a moral code unlike Buddhism or Christianity, which only a few saints "could hope to live up to . . . so much concerned with personal salvation as to be incompatible with political institutions."[42]

As historian Y. C. Wang put it, Chinese thought was "devoted to the realization of true good for all mankind."[43] "True good" referred to the attainment of happiness in one's current life. Furthermore, "Little concern was shown for such questions as the beginning of human life, man's position in the universe, and the relation between the natural and supernatural," Wang explained.[44] Simply said, man was what he was, and the only significant question was how he should live; and for the Chinese masses, a good life maintained harmony and peace with others "through the fulfillment of their role in the perpetuation of social life."[45] Confucianism concerned itself with "mundane happiness, defining the good life as a minimum of material wants and a maximum of moral cultivation . . . recognizing the unequal intellectual capacities of men."[46] The whole Chinese sociopolitical structure could be viewed as "an application of the concept of *jen* (benevolence) . . . that man is by nature good, that he has an inner feeling of sympathy for others, and that as this feeling develops, he will share their joys and sufferings as part of his own experiences."[47] Within this context, the family became the basic unit in the system, and the state an extended form of family.

Buddhism, which had been imported from India in the middle of the first century, coexisted alongside Confucianism from the time of the Tang dynasty and was similar to Confucianism in that it emphasized moral behavior. The "Buddhist Age" (500–850) had witnessed the implementation of clerical exams for both Buddhist and Confucian classical scholars, administered by the Minister of Rites—a system that dominated both education and occupational promotion for several centuries.

The term "intellectual" or "literati" could take on different definitions when applied to the general population of China, but within the realm of the elite, the meaning was clear-cut. Either term simply meant "educated man" and served to indicate a separation between the learned few and the uneducated masses.[48] (Because "intellectual" is a more modern term, "literati" may be a more appropriate application for China's educated elite before the twentieth century.) Within elite society existed two basic levels of intellectuals—higher and lower, indicating men who had substantial or little formal education. China's elite society, comprising about ten percent of the population, was made up of scholars who were charged with the responsibility of preserving traditional ethical values in addition to attending to the tasks of governing.

The official hierarchy had the emperor at the top, followed by the elite. Below them were the imperial clansmen, comprising a small number of officials who had inherited titles. Continuing in descending order were the civil bureaucrats (otherwise known as scholar-officials or mandarins, who had earned their positions by passing the civil-service examinations); then below the civil bureaucrats were wealthy, educated men who had either passed or hoped to pass the civil-service examination, but who held no official position. Further down the hierarchical ladder were farmers and peasants, who made up about 80 percent of China's population, followed by the lowest level of society, which consisted of beggars, actors, butchers, and prostitutes.

While the Chinese greatly valued knowledge, the availability and attainment of education in China was largely dependent on a person's place in society, and for the Chinese mainstream the availability of education in mid-nineteenth century was far removed. In the 1800s only about half of the male population of China had acquired any level of literacy, despite numerous instances of special imperial support for the education of poor boys.[49] Neither schools nor imperial support existed for the education of Chinese girls, however.

FEMALE LITERACY IN IMPERIAL CHINA

In ancient times, from birth to age seven, girls and boys were treated virtually the same, playing together and following very similar daily routines. At age seven they met their first separation as boys began to attend school, where girls were not allowed. By the age of ten, girls were barred from pursuing anything but domestic affairs, and were more or less banished to their boudoirs. They were prepared solely for the roles of wife, mother, and housekeeper.

For centuries females at every level of Chinese society had been groomed for marriage, under the Confucian ideal of the "Three Obediences": to the father before marriage; to the husband after marriage; and to the sons in widowhood.[50] The notion that women who lacked literary talent were virtuous and desirable had been perpetuated for centuries, a social expectation promoted for the purpose of maintaining females in a position of servitude. Even so, an estimated ten percent of intrepid Chinese women managed to find their own means of achieving literacy, usually through the help of an educated family member or friend.

Ancient China witnessed some success among the female literati even in the face of such a rigid society, and talented women managed to contribute to a broad field of arts and poetry. However, as Confucian ideology gained strength after the close of the Song dynasty (960–1279), the repression of women increased. In a publication titled "Wen's Book of Mother Indoctrination" it was recommended that it was sufficient for women to know only a few hundred words such as fuel, rice, fish, and meat for their daily use. To know more could do more harm than good, it claimed. A virtuous woman was defined as "she who hath no talent."[51]

An accurate assessment of female literacy in China before the nineteenth century cannot be provided. A girl's access to education usually depended on external factors such as the family's academic background and geographical location. Families with a literary tradition often provided some rudimentary education for their daughters or nieces, and women residing in certain regions such as the lower Yangtse Delta enjoyed a considerably higher incidence of literacy than females born in other provinces.

A noteworthy influence in the advancement of female literacy was China's invention of the printed book in the ninth century and the subsequent availability of written materials. To some degree social attitudes shifted in favor of women's education as a result of a widespread readership of popular novels, many of which portrayed *ts' ai nu* (literary-talented women) as the acceptable ideal for females.[52]

While educational opportunities for Chinese women were severely limited prior to the very early twentieth century, it would be inaccurate to suggest that they lacked influence in China's academic or governmental history. Renowned Chinese scholar and Columbia University graduate Hu Shi (Hu Shih), in a 1931 essay presented before the American Association of University Women in Tientsin, argued that despite a history of repression and planned ignorance, the Chinese woman had been able to "establish for herself a position that we must regard as a fairly exalted one."[53]

Throughout China's history many women served not only as ruling members of the empire—Empress Dowager Cixi (Tzu-Hsi), for example—but also as contributing members of the literati. In the 1950s Ch'ien Hsun, a woman in her seventies and the wife of a former Chinese minister to Rome, published "Bibliography of Works by Woman Writers During the Last Three Hundred Years," which reported that 2,301 Chinese women had written and published in the field of literature. Another writer, Hsu Chi-yu, later published a collection of 100 complete works of 100 women songwriters covering the same period, in addition to an anthology of 2,045 songs written by 783 Chinese women. The moral of the story, according to Hu, is that "it is simply impossible to suppress women—even in China."[54]

The position of women in the old family was never as low to the casual observer as many believe, Hu claimed. "On the contrary, woman has always been the despot of the family. The authority of the mother and the mother-in-law is very well known . . . no other country in the world can complete with China for the distinction of being the nation of hen-pecked husbands." This was so partly because, according to Hu, "she could not be divorced!"[55]

There was actually no law forbidding divorce. The classics had passed down seven conditions for divorcing a wife, among them jealousy, failure to produce sons, and talking too much. But the classics had also given three conditions under which she could not be sent away. A wife could not be divorced if she had shared a three-year mourning period with her husband over one of his parents or if the husband became rich or attained a high position since the marriage, nor could she be sent away if she had no home to return to—conditions making divorce nearly impossible. But in spite of considerable authority within the home, other rights and privileges such as an equal education had until that time been denied most Chinese women.

It was during the Qing dynasty (1644–1911) that women began to break away from their yoke of educational repression as public opposition to the restrictions increased. Reformers such as Yan Mei and Chen Bichen went so far as to set up private schools that would take in girl pupils.[56] Not until the early 1900s, however, fifty years after the inception of Sino-American education trade, did China begin to afford its women many of the same learning opportunities historically reserved for men.

FROM TEA AND OPIUM

It was the middle of the tumultuous nineteenth century when the imperial government sought its first academic ties with the United States. This was not the first Sino-American collaboration, however. The earliest contacts between China and America developed not from education exchange but through the trading of goods and commodities—Chinese teas and silks in particular.

The *Empress of China* was the first vessel to sail from the United States to China, arriving in Guangzhou (Canton) in August of 1784. The supercargo Samuel Shaw had been appointed as an unofficial consul by the U.S. Congress but he was unable to make contact with Chinese officials or gain diplomatic recognition for the United States. Since 1760 all trade with the West had been administered in Guangzhou through an appointed group of Chinese merchants with official licenses. Some trading between the American colonies and China had occurred prior to 1784, but this diplomatic journey, while it did not accomplish the goal of diplomatic recognition, marked the new nation's entrance into the lucrative China trade in tea, porcelain, and silk.[57]

English settlers had brought their affection for tea-drinking to the American colonies, and by the early nineteenth century tea was a necessity in the United States with an importance "almost equivalent to that of bread," commented Robert Waln in 1820.[58] Most American families, even those of humble means, included tea-drinking in their everyday routine. However, the merchants in the business of providing this popular commodity were afforded little stability, as the world's tea trade was consistently competitive and speculative. Prices and availability could fluctuate unpredictably, depending on market conditions, and the effects on profits and losses for tea merchants, as well as the shop owners who sold tea to the public, were sometimes dramatic.

Several gluts in the tea market occurred in the eighteenth and nineteenth centuries. In 1790, for example, American traders imported two million pounds of tea when consumer demands were only for about one million, and in 1807 a similar imbalance caused tea prices to plummet.[59] In 1826 prices dropped again as a result of an ill-advised marketing scheme. Because tea was the focus of early trade, imbalances such as these could impose a heavy impact, not only on the tea industry itself but on the general economy. To help offset the inevitable fluctuations in the tea market, merchants concluded that efforts should be made to expand and diversify the types of goods being traded.

Prior to Andrew Jackson's presidency, most trade between China and America fell into two general categories—luxury goods (which included fine teas and silks) for Americans in the higher ranks of wealth and lower-priced goods, porcelain and cheaper teas primarily, for the public at large. A third category comprised of fancy but affordable items was added in the early 1830s as a new and expanding American middle class, fortified with increasing disposable income, emerged.[60]

One of the earliest shipments of goods intended for the growing middle class was transported to America on the *Howard*, a vessel owned by traders Nathaniel and Frederick Carne. When the ship returned from Canton and docked in New York's harbor in 1832, it was not loaded with the usual luxury items intended for the wealthy, or the lower-priced teas for the not-so-wealthy. Instead, according to a surviving auction catalog, the ship's cargo was a hodgepodge of affordable but fancy nonessentials that included silk boxes, ivory chessmen, pongee handkerchiefs, fireworks, feather dusters, colored papers, walking canes, shawls, lacquered furniture, window blinds, baskets, and a variety of fans—all designed to appeal to the new American middle class.[61]

Traders such as the Carne brothers, who had for years imported expensive and luxurious goods from France, were now working with Chinese artisans to replicate those same items in China at considerably lower costs. The Chinese, it turns out, were extraordinarily adept at reproducing all sorts of fancy things, quickly and efficiently, for very non-fancy prices. Walter Barrett, who wrote about New York's nineteenth-century merchants, declared that the Chinese silk weavers had not just imitated the European models to perfection but in some cases had even improved on the patterns.[62]

But as Europeans and Americans were purchasing ever-increasing amounts of teas and other goods from China, the Chinese had little interest in purchasing much from the West. Over time the disparity created an imbalance in the flow of silver, which was the accepted means of currency for most international exchange at the time. Simply put, from the perspective of the West, China was reaping too many of the profits, securing too much of the available silver, and merchants wanted to find a way to reverse that trend. The English were first to come up with a plan and their solution to the problem of trade imbalance would include the marketing of opium to the Chinese.

The opium poppy (*Papaver somniferum*), grown and harvested in India, was sold at auction and then taken to China by English and Indian traders, licensed by the British East India Company. There it was aggressively marketed, initially just in the port cities but later expanding to outlying regions, as the disease of addiction spread.

The psychological effects of opium may have been known as early as 4,000 BCE. A number of historical references exist, for example, the Sumerian symbol for poppy was *hul*, "joy" and *gil*, "plant." The word "opium" itself is derived from ancient Greek, and is referred to in Homer's *The Iliad* and *The Odyssey* (850 BCE). The opium poppy was likely introduced to China around the fourth century CE by Arab traders who used it for medicinal purposes. Chinese literature bears reference to its use—noted Chinese physician Hua To of the Three Kingdoms (220–264 CE) gave opium preparations to patients before surgery. Recreational use of opium in China is associated with the introduction of tobacco smoking in pipes by Dutch traders from Java in the seventeenth century. First mixed with tobacco, the practice predictably resulted in increased use of opium, as a mixture or on its own.

By the late seventeenth century the British East India Company had gained control of the prime Indian poppy-growing regions and by 1800 had a monopoly on its sales—much of it now slated for China. Even after the Qing court officially banned its use and importation, ever-greater quantities were routinely smuggled past the port authorities. By the 1830s China's legion of addicts were consuming an estimated 23,570 chests of opium annually, supplied by the so-called country traders.[63] Opium sales at Guangzhou paid for teas shipped to London in what became a thriving India-China-Britain triangle, which at first appeared to help balance the profits for both European and American merchants.

For a while the plan helped slow the eastward flow of silver, but in time the strategy backfired for American manufacturers. Merchants in the United States had for years hoped to export more American-made goods to China, but now the Chinese were spending most of their silver on opium, severely stifling their ability to purchase anything else. Americans, on the other hand, were purchasing more and more products from China. With each passing year, as the Chinese faced increasing levels of drug addiction and growing poverty, American companies seemed to be losing, not gaining, trade opportunities with China.

Opium addiction was reaching epidemic levels across the land and finally the Chinese had had enough. In 1836 the emperor sent imperial commissioner Lin Zexu on a mission to compel the traders to stop importing opium. In a bold act of defiance reminiscent of America's infamous Boston Tea Party fifty years prior, Lin ordered the confiscation and removal of 20,000 containers of opium belonging to British merchants, barricading the foreigners in the factories at Guangzhou until they surrendered their stock.

Figure 1.1 First Opium War, bombardment of Canton, circa 1840.

The response of the British government was immediate and fierce. Sixteen warships and 4,000 troops were quickly dispatched to China's coast to engage in what was essentially an undeclared war.[64] Equipped with the new paddle-wheel steamers, the British proceeded to engage in a half-dozen bloody battles along China's southeast coast, damaging or destroying many of China's naval facilities. The Chinese, ill-prepared to fight their British invaders with their outdated and poorly equipped fleet, were quickly defeated in what is now known as the First Opium War—a conflict that weakened China and its ability to protect itself. France's victories over China during the Second Opium War would weaken it further still. And the series of internal rebellions that followed extended China's era of conflict well past midcentury.

For China, the devastating consequence of this period was a distribution of foreign authority over its ports through several postwar treaties, a humiliating confirmation to the world that China's imperial forces were incapable of protecting its own interests. Confounding the predicament was a rapidly rising population, increasing poverty, and widespread famine, altogether a toxic combination of problems that set the stage for dynastic decline.

It was the awesome display of Western power during the Opium Wars and later during the Taiping Rebellion that squelched any remaining doubt that China must modernize. Even as the battles were being won, the demonstration of Western military technology was making clear China's vulnerability in a newly industrialized world. Scholar-general Li Hongzhang reported that the presence of Western artillery and steamships had revealed an unprecedented change in China's situation. Many Chinese leaders were now convinced that in order to survive China had no choice but to educate itself in the new technologies of the West. Thus it was a succession of situations and events—unstable trade, the weakening of China's economy, Opium Wars, internal rebellion, and the witnessing of Western machines and military power—that moved the imperial leaders to reform and rebuild through the acquisition of American higher education.

SYLVAN HILLS AND OCEAN PEOPLE

In the early 1800s few Americans (with the exception of missionaries, traders, government officials, or seafarers) had ever met anyone from China. The California gold rush and the building of the transcontinental railroads, which would draw thousands of Chinese to the United States at midcentury, were yet to take place. Therefore it was oftentimes commercial imagery, such as advertising produced for the marketing of tea, that formed America's first impression of the Chinese—at the time the general notion was that they were mysterious, elegant, wise, and exotic.

Tea promotions were designed to endorse and glamorize the many alleged benefits of its consumption, and almost without exception American tea merchants illustrated advertisements and packaging with attractive images of China. Chinese people were portrayed in colorful silks, their distant empire idyllic, existing in "sylvan settings of pagoda-topped hills and charming tea fields."[65] Missing were any scenes of famine, blight, poverty, illiteracy, or opium addiction.

A case in point was the Afong Moy promotion, an advertising scheme devised by the aforementioned Carne brothers. It was in the 1830s when one of their ships, the *Washington*, docked in New York's harbor carrying the usual cargo of tea and assorted fancy nonessentials. Also on board was a beautiful nineteen-year-old girl named Juila Foochee Ching-chang King, daughter of Hong Wang-tzang Tzee King—the first (officially recorded) Chinese woman ever to come to the United States.[66]

The young woman's arrival set forth a nineteenth-century media frenzy and the *New-York Daily Advertiser* was among the first to carry the news. Reporters described the mysterious girl as rarified, her complexion transparent and blooming, her clothing elegant. And, she could be viewed by anyone disposed to pay a 25-cent charge. One could witness firsthand the cruel results of foot binding, said the advertisement—an ancient and grotesque practice that caused a Chinese woman to "twaddle about all her life."[67] A detailed description of the procedure was included in the news article. *The New York Sun* claimed that the young woman was a member of China's elite.

Miss Juila Foochee Ching-chang King was an instant sensation and no detail about her was too trivial to print. Her name was changed to Afong Moy because of the difficulty Americans were having writing or pronouncing her real one and she remained on display for many days in the exotically furnished hall, her four-inch feet delicately propped on a cushion.[68] The widespread reports of her idealized image had an immediate effect of popularizing all things Chinese in American fashion and decorating, as new demands for China's exports were created. A successful advertising ploy to be sure, the Afong Moy promotion also served to strengthen many Americans' stilted impressions of China and the Chinese.

America's opinion of the Chinese was influenced too by written and spoken accounts from those few who had spent time in China—usually government or military officials, or Christian missionaries who returned with flamboyant stories, each confirming that China was indeed a mysterious and strange place. Published in a nineteenth-century issue of the *New York Herald* was a lecture by the Honorable Caleb Cushing which began by begging pardon for what might be considered "rambling and desultory" observations of Chinese life:

> The thronging myriads everywhere around—their strange costume—the incessant clash of gongs—the junks with mat sails . . . does he receive a letter, he finds the writing running in lines from top to bottom . . . a family mourning for the death of a relative dresses in white, instead of black; shuttlecock is played with the feet; ladies compress and distort the feet—ours the waist . . . all the boatmen on the river are

women . . . as a substitute for cock-pits and horse races, the Chinese fight a main with two crickets in a bowl. . . . [69]

Tea-drinking Americans in the early 1800s viewed the Chinese as exotic and admirable, their strange customs fascinating. America's crystalline image of the Chinese would begin to cloud around midcentury, however, as legions of poor and uneducated men and women from China came to the United States to seek their fortunes building railroads or to pan for California gold.

It was not long before the growing population of impoverished Chinese became a source of irritation for the local residents, who soon developed a list of grievances against the "yellow peril"—chief among them the loss of jobs for Americans. The spread of discontent slowly led to pervasive nationwide discrimination against the Chinese, attitudes that would soon steer the United States toward its first immigration laws—policies enforced as a means of legal exclusion, aimed right at China.

To some extent, in the mid-1800s an American's attitude toward the Chinese depended on whether they lived in the East or the West. The harshest backlash against the Chinese was concentrated in the western United States, particularly in San Francisco and other areas of California where many of the penniless immigrants had settled as their dreams of finding fortune through gold-mining or railroad-building began to vanish.

In the eastern states, where far fewer of the disenfranchised Chinese laborers had settled, some of the old illusions promoted by the trading companies still prevailed. Therefore when the first Chinese students arrived in Connecticut at midcentury they encountered a mingling of public opinion—acceptance and even admiration in the local community, an attitude soon to be swayed by quickly approaching scorn from the West.

Of course, misinterpretations regarding foreigners were also common in China. In the early nineteenth century very few Chinese had visited the outside world or actually knew any "barbarians," China's generally accepted term for all foreigners. Even fewer had met anyone from America. It was rumored that Westerners or "red hair men" came from the sea, spoke an unintelligible language, and exhibited strange and even diabolical behaviors. In a letter to Emperor Guangxu, written by viceroys Zhang Zhidong and Liu Kunyiin, the ruler was apprised of these popular misimpressions. "Even last summer there were still some officials, both in and outside the capital," the letter advised the emperor, "who claimed that the ocean people (Westerners) could not walk on land . . . "[70]

GOD'S PROVIDENCE

When the Chinese first decided to send students to the United States, their singular goal was the acquisition of technology for China's modernization.

For many Americans, however, the prospect of Sino-American academic exchange offered a unique evangelical opportunity. The arrival of new students from China promised nothing less than a convenient and expedient means of spreading Christianity. Zealots eagerly promoted the notion that the mission of the church (thus assumedly America's mission) was "not to teach mechanics and civil engineering, but to Christianize them . . . "[71]

Evangelists rationalized that the devastation to China and the hundreds of thousands of deaths inflicted by the Opium Wars must have been "God's providence to inaugurate a new era . . . for the opening of China for the free promulgation of his blessed Gospel."[72] Some were convinced that learning about Christianity and becoming Christians while studying in American institutions were necessary if China was ever to become a "civilized society." Arthur Smith, a dean of missionary education, stated publicly that in his opinion the Chinese lacked character and conscience, insisting that "the forces which have developed Character and Conscience in the Anglo-Saxon race . . . came with Christianity . . . What China needs is righteousness . . . it is absolutely necessary that she have a knowledge of God. . . . "[73]

Not surprisingly, China's imperial court saw things differently. The Celestial Kingdom, after all, was civilized centuries before Christianity came into existence and the Chinese people had from the beginning believed their own values to be vastly superior to anyone else's. China had no interest whatsoever in distancing its youth from traditional beliefs and ideals. Quite the contrary, higher learning exchange with the West was viewed as a means of forever securing and protecting institutionalized Confucianism.

And so it came to be that China and America, motivated by different goals, emerging from seemingly incompatible historical paths and equipped with distorted perceptions of each other, signed on to a long-term "marriage" of academic exchange. A succession of circumstances—trade imbalances, wars, and rebellions—had moved China to send its students to the universities it judged to be the best in the world. But leadership was needed to give the undertaking impetus and direction. That leadership would come from a few visionaries: Zeng Guofan and Li Hongzhang, who mentored the initial exchange programs; Anson Burlingame, the diplomat who championed legislation to strengthen Sino-American relations; and a rebellious runaway from Zhuhai named Yung Wing.

2   The Runaway

> We were half way across the channel when . . . I saw a boat chasing us, making fast time . . . our two oars against their four made it impossible for us to win out . . . and the whole party was captured. Then came the punishment. We were marched through the whole school and placed in a row . . . I was placed in the center . . . with a tall foolscap mounted on my head . . . I had pinned on my breast a large square placard bearing the inscription, "Head of the Runaways."[1]

The escape had failed and Mrs. Gutzlaff, to the delight of the other children, was busy overseeing the punishment. The humiliation of wearing the foolscap must have been judged insufficient reparation, because to make matters worse the headmistress also denied the eight-year-old his midday snack of gingersnaps and oranges. Such as they were, the events foreshadowed the adventurous and influential life the child would come to lead. The enterprising Chinese boy who led a team of schoolmates in a nearly-successful escape from the missionary school would someday become a driving force behind U.S.-China education exchange.

Yung Wing (Rong Hong) was born on the 17th of November, 1828, in the village of Zhuhai near the Portuguese colony of Macao. When he was seven years old his parents broke with Chinese tradition by enrolling him in the nearby Christian missionary school instead of the Confucian school where his older brother had attended. Their unorthodox choice would come to bear unforeseen results—among other things, their son would become the first Chinese citizen ever to have a "completely Western" education, extending from primary school through college.

The little missionary school was run by the flaxen-haired Mrs. Gutzlaff, a robust English lady and wife of Reverend Charles Gutzlaff. When Yung Wing was first introduced to the headmistress he was " . . . no less puzzled than stunned." As he recalled much later in his autobiography, "I actually trembled all over with fear at her imposing proportions."[2]

The parents' decision to send their youngest son to the American missionary school turned out to be a practical one. An ability to speak English, they correctly predicted, would someday afford their son unique occupational advantages. Yung Wing spent four years learning English and other subjects at the little missionary school before the unhappy news of his father's death brought with it a mandate to return home to his village. His mother, left without a means of support, needed everyone's help to survive and all of the children were put to work. The oldest son helped provide food by fishing and a sister was able to earn money doing housework. Yung Wing, the youngest in the family, took on the job of hawking candy throughout his village, rising at three o'clock every morning and often working late into the evening—an exhausting routine that netted the equivalent of about 25 cents a day.

When a more lucrative opportunity to glean rice in a nearby field was advertised, Yung quit the candy-hawking job to work as a reaper and it was in this situation that his English skills first came to his rescue. Yung Wing's new boss, the head gleaner, had heard rumors about the new employee's ability to speak English, a language few in the village had ever heard spoken. Curious, the boss summoned the boy to demonstrate "red hair men" talk for him and the crew of gleaners and in return Yung would be rewarded with as many sheaves of rice as he could carry home. The twelve-year-old lost no time claiming the opportunity. Standing in a paddy field and up to his knees in water, Yung began reciting the alphabet and speaking random words and sentences in English as the head reaper and his men "stood in vacant silence, with mouths wide open, grinning with evident delight."[3] The boss kept his promise and Yung returned to his mother that evening "loaded with joy and sheaves of golden rice . . . little dreaming that my smattering knowledge of English would serve me such a turn so early in my career."[4]

Yung continued to work various jobs in his village to help support his family with little hope of ever returning to school, until the day he received an unexpected visit from Dr. Benjamin Hobson, a missionary from Macao. Dr. Hobson had been searching for Yung Wing for some time, in an effort to honor a request from Yung's former teacher Mrs. Gutzlaff. The headmistress had already returned to the United States but before departing asked Dr. Hobson to see if he could locate one of her former students, a bright boy named Yung Wing. It was her hope that Hobson might convince the child to continue his education at the Morrison Society School. If Yung decided to honor her wishes and come to Macao, Hobson explained further, the boy could live at the family residence and work at the local hospital to help offset expenses—provided that his mother approved.[5]

For Yung Wing the welcome news "had more the sound of heaven in it."[6] With his mother's blessing the boy eagerly set out to resume his English studies at the Morrison Society School, where he would meet his mentor Reverend Samuel Robbins Brown—a long-time teacher at the school and a proud graduate of Yale University.

Reverend Brown was a popular teacher at the school and rarely tired of telling stories about his boyhood in far-distant America and his happy days at Yale—accounts that inspired many of the children to wish they could visit the place he so vividly described. Near the end of his tenure at the academy, as Brown was making arrangements to return to the United States, he surprised his class by announcing his intention to take a few students back to America with him, where they could continue their education. When Reverend Brown asked for interested students to stand up, Yung Wing was the first on his feet.

In the winter of 1847 Reverend Brown and three boys from the school—Yung Wing, Wong Shing, and Wong Foon (the Wong boys were brothers)—set sail for the United States on the *Huntress*. A number of generous patrons, including Andrew Shortrede, a Scottish proprietor and editor of the *Hong Kong China Mail,* and American merchants A. A. Ritchie and A. A. Campbell, provided funding for the boys' living expenses for a period of two years. The Olyphant brothers from New York, who were in the shipping business, offered the party free passage on the *Huntress*. "They treated us nobly," Yung recalled.[7]

Together with a large cargo of tea, Reverend Brown and the three boys departed from Whompoa on January 4, bound for New York and aided by a strong and stead north wind. "There was no accident of any kind," Yung wrote in his memoirs:

> . . . excepting a gale as we doubled the Cape of Good Hope. The tops of the masts and ends of the yards were tipped with balls of electricity. The strong wind was howling and whistling behind us like a host of invisible Furies . . . I realized no danger, although the ship pitched and groaned, but enjoyed the wild and weird scene hugely.[8]

On April 12 the *Huntress* safely docked in New York, already a bustling community of about 300,000 residents. From there, Reverend Brown and the boys traveled on to New Haven, Connecticut, for a brief tour of Yale and a meeting with Yale's president Jeremiah Day, then on to East Windsor, where Reverend Brown and his wife Elizabeth kept their residence.

The boys were boarded with Mrs. Phoebe Brown, the Reverend Brown's mother, whom Yung described as a remarkable New England woman of moral and religious character, in a small cottage a half mile from Monson Academy. With funds secured from their benefactors the boys paid for board and lodging, including fuel, light, and washing, which cost each of them, according to Yung's memoirs, about $1.25 a week. The boys had to attend to their own rooms and, in the winter, saw, split, and stack their own firewood.

In time, two of the three boys departed the United States for unrelated reasons. Wong Shing returned to China first, leaving behind his brother, who still hoped to attend college in America. As usual, funding was the problem. Both boys had been offered financing through American church societies, provided they agreed to use their education to become Christian missionaries. Neither felt a calling to missionary service however. Another offer was extended by the boys' previous benefactor Andrew Shortrede, on the condition they attend the University of Edinburgh to study medicine—Shortrede, a patriotic Scot, wanted Scotland to have the honor of training the first Chinese physicians. Wong Foon accepted the offer and graduated from the University of Edinburgh's medical school before returning to China, where he would gain a reputation as one of its most skilled surgeons and for many years he was in charge of the London Mission Hospital at Canton (Guangzhou). His brother Wong Shing, who had returned to China because of health reasons, ended up working with the London Missionary Society and assisted Dr. James Legge in his translations of Chinese classics.[9]

Yung Wing, now without his companions, finished the two-year commitment on his own with the hope of attending college at Yale. But once again, funds were nearly depleted. Yung appealed to friends and associates for help, among them Reverend Brown and Reverend Charles Hammond of the Monson Academy, but when rescue finally arrived, it was through the generosity of a Southern women's group called the Ladies Association of Savannah, Georgia, an organization in which Reverend Brown's sister was a long-standing member. Elated with their offer to sponsor his first college year, Yung departed immediately for New Haven to take his entrance examination. "How I got in, I do not know, as I had had only fifteen months of Latin and twelve months of Greek, and ten months of mathematics."[10] Nevertheless he was admitted, and Yung began his first year at Yale in the fall of 1850, the only Chinese in a class of ninety-eight freshmen.

At the end of his freshman year, dwindling funds were replenished by The Ladies' Association of Savannah and pooled with contributions from the Olyphant Brothers of New York, allowing Yung adequate resources to continue his studies. Yung also worked a variety of jobs on campus at Yale to make ends meet, including a term of service as an assistant librarian to the "Brothers in Unity," one of two college debating societies that owned libraries. In his senior year he was elected librarian, for which he received 30 dollars. He also entered English writing competitions that offered cash prizes and occasionally won, to the chagrin of his American classmates.[11] The combined sums were just enough to meet his bills even though his wants had to be "finely trimmed to suit the cloth."[12] With meager means and despite barely passing his calculus courses, Yung Wing graduated from Yale in 1854, making history as the first Chinese ever to earn a college degree in the United States.

It should be noted that while Yung Wing was the first person from China to have graduated from an American college, he was not the first Chinese ever to study in the United States. There is scant evidence of a few other Chinese students in the United States between 1817 and 1825 (although not at the college level) at a school established by the American Board of Commissioners for Foreign Missions in Cornwall, Connecticut. One student, Zeng Laishun, was perhaps the very first Chinese to attend an American college (in the 1840s) but he did not receive a degree, and returned to China in 1848.[13]

Nor were Chinese students the first foreigners to study in American colleges. By the mid-1800s when Yung Wing studied at Yale, students from other world regions had been enrolling in United States institutions for nearly a century. America's first foreign students came from Latin America, beginning in 1784 with Francisco de Miranda of Venezuela (America's first official foreign student), who studied at the University of Virginia.[14]

Between 1784 and the turn of the century, foreign enrollments in United States colleges and universities were relatively few—by most accounts well under two thousand in any given year.[15] The low numbers should not be surprising, however, given the obstacles that faced aspiring foreign students and scholars at the time. In the eighteenth and nineteenth centuries American colleges and universities were ill-equipped to teach or serve the few foreign students on campus and English-language training programs were nonexistent. International travel to and from the college or university could be time-consuming, costly, and even treacherous. Moreover, as late as the early twentieth century many college faculty members still rejected the notion that a multicultural classroom was beneficial. It was only after World War II that American educators fully embraced the idea of international education exchange and welcomed international students into their classrooms.

The escalation of foreign student enrollments after World War II prompted the development of all facets of international student services, but in Yung Wing's time there had been no foreign student services whatsoever. Aside from the help he received from his American friends or from kindly professors, Yung was essentially on his own in an alien environment, and his recollection of these challenges would someday become an important consideration in his vision for Sino-American education exchange.

YUNG WING'S VISION FOR CHINA

By 1854 Yung Wing had been in the United States for almost eight years. As he prepared to return to his homeland, paramount in his mind was the question of how to use American education to modernize China:

> All through my college course, especially in the closing year, the lamentable condition of China was before my mind constantly and weighed on my spirits. In my despondency, I often wished I had never been educated, as education had unmistakably enlarged my mental and moral horizon, and revealed to me responsibilities which the sealed eye of ignorance can never see, and sufferings and wrongs of humanity to which an uncultivated and callous nature can never be made sensitive.[16]

Yung Wing dreamed of an enlightened and modern new China rising from the acquisition of Western knowledge and training. He imagined future generations of Chinese youth who would enjoy the same educational advantages that he had experienced—and this objective became the guiding light of his ambition.

On November 13 Yung embarked on the *Eureka*, bound for Hong Kong, and accompanied by only one other passenger, Reverend William Allen Macy, who was on his way to assume a mission post. After a distance of 13,000 nautical miles and 154 days they docked at the port in Hong Kong and Yung traveled immediately on to Macao for a long-awaited reunion with his family. At last he could proudly tell his mother how he had succeeded in graduating from a prestigious American university with a degree of A.B.—an accomplishment comparable to earning the Chinese title of *Siu Tsai*, or "elegant talent."[17]

Yung took up residence in Guangzhou with the Reverend Voorman, a missionary under the American Board, and there began six months of Chinese studies in order to regain his writing and speaking skills, some of which he had forgotten during his eight-year absence. He worked for a time as an assistant to Doctor Peter Parker, who was serving in a temporary position as a United States commissioner; then went to Hong Kong to study law. When a career in law did not materialize, he moved to Shanghai and worked for a time in the Imperial Customs Translating Department, then later took a job as a clerk at a teahouse. To make ends meet after the teahouse suddenly went out of business Yung began translating on a freelance basis, a venture that would serve to put him into contact with a number of important people in Shanghai—officials who would later help him achieve his vision for education exchange.

At the time China was in the midst of a revolution—the Taiping Rebellion had been underway for several years and was gaining momentum.[18] The uprising had been championed by Hong Xiuquan, a village teacher and unsuccessful imperial examination candidate. A philosopher of sorts, Hong had formulated a new ideology based upon a permutation of Confucianism and Protestantism, and had succeeded in drawing thousands of disciples. In time many of those followers served to form a military organization whose purpose was to overthrow the Qing government—with the hope of fundamentally changing China.

Hong pronounced himself king of what he called the Heavenly Kingdom of Great Peace (*Taiping Tianguo*)[19] and under his influence the Taiping leadership began adopting revolutionary new policies. Many ancient Chinese practices—slavery, concubinage, arranged marriages, polygamy, prostitution, opium smoking, gambling, foot binding, judicial torture, and the worship of idols—were to be banished under the new regime. A policy of gender equality was also assumed under the new Taiping leadership and many women were appointed to positions of authority and leadership as officers or administrators in the army.

Changes imposed by the Taipings centered on a sort of socialism and included the prohibition of private ownership of land—an effort to allow the leadership to redistribute China's resources among the citizens "equally":

> All the fields throughout the empire, whether of abundant or deficient harvest, shall be taken as a whole: if this place is deficient, then the harvest of that abundant place must be removed to relieve it . . . thus, all the people in the empire may together enjoy the abundant happiness of the Heavenly Father, Supreme Lord and Great God. There being fields,

let all cultivate them; there being food, let all eat; there being clothes, let all be dressed. . . . All men and women, every individual of sixteen years and upwards, shall receive land.[20]

Many in China were ill-prepared for such radical reforms, however, and influential groups soon stood in opposition to the movement—in particular the Han Chinese scholar-gentry class viewed the changes as dangerous and they alienated themselves from the rebels and their reforms.

In the face of growing opposition, the Taiping army advanced as far north as Tianjinhad, and succeeded in capturing Nanjing (Nanking). By now, however, the outside resistance to the group's causes had led to internal feuds and corruption within the leadership, rendering the region and the regime unstable. The British and French, judging from afar that it was easier to deal with a weakened Qing empire than a tottering Taiping regime, came to the defense of the imperial army. Under the command of General Charles "Chinese" Gordon,[21] the Western military, combined with imperial forces led by Zeng Guofan (Tsang Kwoh Fan) and Li Hongzhang (Li Hung Chang), ultimately crushed the rebellion but only after fourteen years of conflict and an estimated 30 million deaths.[22] Years later both Zeng and Li would become dynamic supporters of education exchange with the United States, in part due to their association with Yung Wing but also because of their exposure to Western weaponry during the Taiping Rebellion.

Yung Wing was at first sympathetic to the Taipings and felt they had grounds to justify their attempted overthrow of the Manchu (Qing) regime. He even briefly entertained the idea of joining the rebels, although upon further consideration concluded that his original plan of recovering his Chinese language skills was a better course of action for accomplishing his long-range educational goals for China.

The only extended contact Yung actually had with the Taiping leadership was in the fall of 1859 when a small party of missionaries planned a trip to visit the rebels in Nanjing. Yung Wing accepted an invitation to join them, viewing it as an opportunity to observe the Taiping officials and their new regime firsthand. During that trip Yung was invited to call upon Kan Wong, nephew of the rebel chief, who asked Yung to pledge his allegiance to the Taipings.[23] Yung declined, offering instead his assistance in any administrative duties the new government might require—an offer that was never accepted as the rebellion came to a close soon afterward.

MANAGING BARBARIANS

The year 1860, near the end of the Taiping Rebellion, was a turning point for China.[24] The Imperial Palace had been burned to the ground and the beautiful *Yuanming Yuan*, the Garden of Perfect Brightness, had also been devastated. Aid from better-equipped Western troops had helped the imperial leadership bring the rebellion to an end but the years of fighting and the leveling of the formerly sacrosanct palace had seriously weakened China—not just militarily and economically, but also emotionally. Chinese officials could no longer disavow the superiority of Western forces. In an 1864 letter sent to the Central Foreign Office, Li Hongzhang, then governor of Jiangsu Province, wrote:

> Chinese gentry scholars are obsessed with diction and syntax only, while the military officers are recklessly uncouth . . . In time of peace they mock at foreign machines as a display of wicked craft, while in time of war they demonize the western firearms, which they believe to be beyond their power to learn.[25]

Growing numbers of government leaders conceded that China must acquire new and modern technology from the West in order to survive. "The wound to China from these events was too deep to be ignored," Y. C. Wang would later write, "and the way was prepared for reform."[26]

Acknowledging that China needed anything from outside its borders was a problematic admission for any official of the Qing court. For two thousand years, even before the Han dynasty established power in 202 BCE, China believed itself to be the "center of the world."[27] The Central (or Celestial) Kingdom, *Khongguo*, rejected all outside influence as inferior and was conventionally unsupportive of any education beyond the Confucian classics. Envoys who visited China from other nations were considered no more than representatives of barbarians, expected to kowtow to the emperor to signify their submission.

For centuries the occasional receiving of *liuxuesheng* (foreign scholars) from nearby countries such as Japan and Korea had been the extent of China's educational reach.[28] Some Chinese had traveled to other regions of Asia for various types of learning, but not until the nineteenth century did China actively seek any knowledge from the West. The military defeats of the Opium Wars and the rebellions that followed (the Taiping Rebellion in the south; the Nian Rebellion in the northeast; and the Muslim revolts in the northwest) had finally and forever severed the ancient belief that the Son of Heaven (the emperor) governed the world from the Chinese epicenter of knowledge and power.

China's war-weakened condition degenerated further still with the enforcement of several treaties, including the Treaty of Nanjing that ended the first Opium War in 1845 and the Treaty of Tientsin in 1858 that ended the second Opium War. Among other things, the treaties demanded huge reparations by the Qing government, had rendered China virtually helpless in prohibiting the entrance of Protestant missionaries, and even limited the government's right to try Westerners accused of committing crimes in China.[29] Furthermore, treaty terms recognized Western authority over trade in various regions of China, forced the opening of multiple ports along its southern coast for further trading and ceded Kowloon and Hong Kong to the British. Britain, France, and America each demanded extraterritoriality, further undermining Chinese sovereign rule. China was quickly losing its grip of authority over its own affairs and it was now imperative, officials agreed, to deliberate alternate methods of "managing barbarians," and among those options was the possibility of importing Western technology.[30]

A number of approaches for acquiring Western knowledge were considered. One idea was to establish modern schools in China and bring in foreign experts to teach Western technology and languages. Another suggestion was to send periodic delegations from China to the West to observe technology in action, witness the secrets of Western wealth and power, and then bring back armaments to study.[31]

Around 1863 the Qing court, even in the midst of opposition from conservatives, was leaning toward a third option—sending students west to earn college degrees in science and technology. Returning students could then apply their expertise to China's modernization. Some objected to the new plan's focus on technology rather than on the traditional values of "right behavior" as a means of securing the national interests. Further concerns were raised over the time and expense that would be required in sending students abroad. And some worried that China might "lose face" in the eyes of the world by admitting its need for outside help.

It was pointed out, however, that the time involved in sending students to study in the West was similar to the time required for learning the Confucian classics in preparation for the traditional imperial examinations—a venture that for centuries had prepared students for lifelong bureaucratic service. With a similar allotment of time, it was argued, Chinese students might acquire far more usable knowledge from the West than if they studied the classics.

In spite of widespread resistance, Viceroys Zeng Guofan and Li Hongzhang (the Taiping rebellion war heroes had since been elevated to positions of government leadership) had in fact already taken a number of important organizational steps designed to lend support to the study-abroad viewpoint. The Bureau of Foreign Affairs, for example, was put into operation in 1861 to aid collaboration with other nations; the College of Foreign Languages (including English) opened in 1862; then the following year the School of Western Language and Science was established. Circumstances would soon put Viceroys Zeng and Li in contact with Yung Wing, an association that would lead them to choose the United States as China's primary study-abroad destination.

MEN AND MACHINES

In the postrebellion years Yung reinstated his search for gainful employment, first attempting an enterprise with Taiping tea, then working as an agent for a tea-packing company in the port of Kew Keang. Later he started a commission business that he continued for almost three years, and it was during this time that Yung Wing "caught the first ray of hope of materializing the educational scheme I had been weaving during the last year of my college life."[32]

That ray of hope came in 1863 in the form of a letter from an old friend named Chang Shi Kwei, who lived in the city of Ngan Khing, the capital of An Whui Province. Yung had made his acquaintance in Shanghai in 1857, and since then Chang had risen in official rank to become an assistant to Viceroy Zeng Guofan. The message in the letter was to the point—the viceroy had heard of Yung Wing and wanted to meet him.

Yung Wing was puzzled by the invitation. Viceroy Zeng had been invested with almost regal power by the Qing government in order to deal with the Taipings, and at the time Yung was summoned, Zeng was essentially the most powerful man in China. Yung was at first fearful that the invitation might have something to do with his near-allegiance with the now-defeated Taiping rebels. Faced with the possibility of encountering an angry viceroy, Yung declined the invitation, explaining that the tea season had set in and it would be impossible for him to come and pay his respects to His Excellency until the work was completed.

Two months had passed when Yung received a second letter, this time from Li Sien Lan, a distinguished Chinese mathematician Yung had met in Shanghai. Li Sien Lan explained that he had told Viceroy Zeng of Yung's unique "completely Western" education, and of Yung's great desire to help China prosper through education abroad. It was this information that had piqued Zeng's interest and prompted His Excellency to seek an introduction. Li further explained that the viceroy was planning to ask Yung to give up his mercantile business and instead go to work in the service of the state government in Ngan Khing, to help with a special project.[33]

With this new information Yung's fears were eased and he immediately planned his trip to Ngan Khing to meet Viceroy Zeng:

> In view of this unexpected offer, which demanded prompt and explicit decision, I was not slow to see what possibility there was of carrying out my educational scheme, having such a powerful man as Tsang Kwoh Fan (Zeng Guofan) to back it . . . Thus ended the correspondence which was really the initiatory step of my official career.[34]

Yung liked Zeng Guofan immediately, describing him as a perfect gentleman and a nobleman of the highest type.

Viceroy Zeng's experiments in building China's first steam vessels at the arsenals in Shanghai had provided him with some understanding of the intricate network of technical skills used by the modern armies and navies of the West. His plan now was to strengthen China's armed forces by introducing those same technical skills into China as rapidly as possible, by means of training schools at the sites of the arsenals.[35] The viceroy's vision, and the reason Yung and others had been summoned, had to do with the development of a machine shop in Kow Chang Meu, about four miles northwest of Shanghai.

By the close of the discussions, the Viceroy had put Yung Wing in charge of finding and purchasing the world's best machines and machine parts to serve as a foundation for the project, and Yung was permitted to decide from which country the machines would be purchased—England, France, or the United States. Yung lost no time in selecting the United States and immediately made plans to begin his journey.

After a month's layover in England, Yung crossed the Atlantic in one of the Cunard steamers and landed in New York in the spring of 1864, ten years after his graduation from Yale and just in time to attend the decennial reunion of his class. The American Civil War was still going on, which meant that nearly all of the machine shops in the country, particularly those in New England, were busy filling government orders. After an extensive search, the Putnam Machine Company in Fitchburg, Massachusetts, agreed to fill Yung Wing's order for machines, which they said would take about six months to produce.

Yung took advantage of the waiting period to attend his class reunion in New Haven and then made a side trip to Washington to offer his service as a volunteer courier for the armed services for the six-month duration.[36] As an American citizen (he had become a naturalized citizen in 1854, the year he graduated from Yale) Yung believed it was nothing less than his duty to show his patriotism and loyalty for his adopted country by offering service during a time of war. As a precaution Yung had left instructions for a colleague to take over his work as commissioner for the machine shop project if he should not return.

Brigadier General Barnes of Springfield, Massachusetts, a man Yung had met as a student at Yale, happened to be the man in charge of the Volunteer Department in Washington. Learning of Yung's commission to obtain machinery for China, Barnes rejected his offer of military service, suggesting that Yung's time would be best spent attending to those duties. Other historical references claim that Yung was told he could not join the armed forces because he was "not really an American." In either case the army's rejection assured that Yung would avoid the battlefield, return to China upon completion of his machine mission, and resume his goal of establishing a program of Sino-American education exchange.

ANSON BURLINGAME

Emerging from the Western front at about the same time was another dynamic individual who shared Yung's passion for building stronger ties between China and America—a man whose influence would directly impact Yung's success in directing China's education trade toward the United States. Anson Burlingame, the first of eight children, was born in New Berlin, New York, on November 14, 1822.[37] Burlingame's ancestors had come to America during Puritan times, first settling in Rhode Island and then relocating to New Berlin, where Anson's father and grandfather were both Methodist ministers. The family later moved to Ohio, then on to Michigan. The young Anson graduated from the University of Michigan and later attended Harvard's law school, graduating in 1846, a year before Yung Wing's arrival in New Haven.

Burlingame practiced law for a time in Boston, and there developed an interest in politics, associating himself with the Free Soil party. Proving to be an effective orator for the Van Buren–Adams national ticket in 1848 and in 1852, he became a popular figure in the region and was elected to the state senate. Two years later he was elected to the United States House of Representatives on the American Party ballot. In 1855 Burlingame changed his political affiliation to help establish the new Republican Party in Massachusetts, after which he served in Congress for three terms, until 1861.

That same year President Abraham Lincoln selected Burlingame to be the United States minister to Austria. But the Austrian imperial government, which had strongly objected to Burlingame's outspoken support of Sardinian and Hungarian independence, promptly rejected his appointment. So in a fateful twist of events, Burlingame was reassigned to China.

Anson Burlingame's relationship with China would be an extraordinary one. He grew to love the Chinese people and increasingly channeled his diplomatic efforts toward improving Sino-American relations. Burlingame recognized a window of diplomatic opportunity following the Second Opium War and took steps to initiate a genuine reconciliation between the two countries. In Burlingame's view America's "posture of arrogance and threat" toward China had served only to lend support for those in the Qing court opposed to anything that would lead to greater contact with the West.[38] In an 1862 letter to Secretary of State William Seward, Burlingame wrote that "If the treaty powers could agree among themselves to the neutrality of China, and together secure order in the treaty ports, and give their moral support to that party in China in favor of order, the interest of humanity would be sub-served."[39] Burlingame's ideas rallied support from important officials, among them China's Ministry of Foreign Affairs, British Consul Robert Hart, and British minister to China, Rutherford Alcock.

Another passionate spokesman for Sino-American reconciliation was Xu Jiyu, a member of China's Ministry of Foreign Affairs. After witnessing the victory of the British fleet during the Opium War, Xu had been inspired to study Western history and in the process became an ardent admirer of "kingless America" and George Washington. As a gesture of gratitude for Xu's support, his friend Anson Burlingame presented him with a copy of one of Gilbert Stuart's portraits of Washington, and in a tribute Xu wrote:

> He (Washington) was the successor to the sages of Three Dynasties: in a country the best governs, the people are the most important, and the warrior spirit is not worshipped. I have seen his portrait: it shows his unequaled fortitude. . . . The United States of America has a territory of ten thousand *li,* but it does not have princes and dukes and inherited nobilities; public affairs are placed before the public for debates and discussions, a truly unprecedented system. What a wonder![40]

A selection from Xu's inspiring words would later be inscribed on a granite block and placed on the Washington Monument at the 300-foot level.

From his new diplomatic position in China and now befriended by important officials such as Xu, Anson Burlingame's influence and respect reached a high level. When he stepped down from his American post, the Chinese government invited him to assume a new position, this time representing the Chinese government as China's ambassador-at-large. It was an unprecedented action—never before in its long history had the Celestial Kingdom offered its representation to any non-Chinese. The extraordinary decision was a demonstration of China's sincere desire to improve long-strained Sino-American relations with the help of a unique individual who loved and understood both countries.

Prince Gong Qinwang, who headed up the board of governors of Zongli Yamen (Ministry of Foreign Affairs), was the one to first seek Emperor Tongzhi's approval for Burlingame's appointment as China's envoy:

> The American minister Anson Burlingame . . . is a man of peace . . . Last year he even helped China resolve difficulties and settle disputes [with foreign countries] when he was away in America. In the recent farewell dinner . . . he said in the future he will work with all his effort to help settle disputes that are unfair to *China.* . . . [41]

It was not essential, Prince Gong argued, for a country to use its own countrymen exclusively for its representation. He was confident Burlingame would serve China well and the emperor was convinced.

In a later statement to Secretary of State Seward, a humble and grateful Burlingame said that "when the oldest nation in the world, containing one-third of the human race, seeks, for the first time, to come into relations with the West, and requests the youngest nation, through its representative, to act as the medium of such change, the mission is not one to be solicited or rejected."[42] Prince Gong presented Burlingame with the imperial decree, written on heavy yellow parchment and wrapped in yellow satin brocade (yellow was the imperial color) and encased in a yellow box. "It is the greatest complement ever to any man," Sir Rutherford Alcock affirmed.

In 1868 Burlingame, accompanied by a mission from China, traveled to the United States to negotiate what was essentially a revision of the 1858 Treaty of Tientsin, stressing equal treatment of the Chinese. Signed

36 *A History of Higher Education Exchange*

Figure 2.1 Anson Burlingame and the Chinese Embassy, circa 1868.

in Washington, DC, on July 28 and drafted by Secretary of State Seward, it would become known thereafter as the Burlingame Treaty, or the Burlingame-Seward Treaty.[43] Under its terms the United States and China were to recognize "the inherent and inalienable right of man to change his home and allegiance, and also the mutual advantage of the free migration and emigration of their citizens and subjects, respectively for purposes of curiosity, of trade, or as permanent residents."[44]

Included in its terms was an agreement for both nations to respect the territorial sovereignty of the other. At the insistence of the United States was the inclusion of the free-immigration provision, designed to counter the Chinese government's prohibition of its subjects emigrating. Article VII stated that Chinese subjects should be allowed to enjoy all the privileges of the public educational institutions under the control of the government in the United States.[45] Reciprocal privileges were provided for Americans, making the treaty an important influence in the establishment of the first Sino-American education exchanges.

YUNG RETURNS TO CHINA

Meanwhile in New England, Yung Wing's order had been completed, and in the spring of 1865 the machines were loaded onto a ship in New York harbor, bound for Shanghai. Yung decided to take passage in the opposite direction, by way of San Francisco, in order to accomplish his goal of circumnavigating the world at least once in his life.[46]

When Yung finally reached Shanghai, he discovered that the machinery had arrived almost a month before. Viceroy Zeng Guofan, he also learned, had gone to Chu Chow in the northern part of Kiangsu Province to establish his headquarters, and Yung was to go there to report on the machinery purchase. Soon thereafter the viceroy toured the Kiang Nan Arsenal and Yung Wing showed him what had been brought from America. "He went through the arsenal with undisguised interest. I pointed out to him the machinery which I bought for him in America. He stood and watched its automatic movement with unabated delight, for this was the first time he had seen machinery, and how it worked."[47]

Zeng's tour of the arsenal provided Yung with the opportunity to once again initiate a conversation with the viceroy about China's educational future. Through these new discussions Yung convinced Zeng to annex a school next to the arsenal where Chinese students might be taught mechanical engineering, thus enabling China to eliminate, in time, the employment of foreign mechanical engineers and machinists. A translating department was established for the school under the direction of John Fryer, who took on the task of transcribing many of the basic works of the various branches of science into Chinese.[48] These victories were significant to Yung Wing, as the school at Kiang Nan Arsenal represented his first success in securing any sort of education-based solution for China.

With the success of the machine mission, Zeng sent an official document to the Qing court asking that Yung be awarded the fifth civil rank (there were nine) within the bureaucratic hierarchy, in appreciation for his service. In this capacity, for full-dress occasions Yung was awarded the privilege of wearing an elegant robe embroidered with silver pheasants, accompanied by a hat adorned with a peacock feather—a sign of great honor. His reception and acceptance in the imperial court, especially among the more conservative members (who had regarded him more as a foreigner than as a Chinese because of his years in America), was now decidedly elevated.

YUNG'S QUEST FOR IMPERIAL SUPPORT

Yung Wing hoped his new status would assure Zeng Guofan's support as he pressed for a program of Sino-American education exchange. Another of Yung's old friends, Ting Yih Chang, was already an important ally. Known for his openness to progressive ideas, Ting had been appointed governor of Kiangsu Province and characteristically, when Yung Wing shared his dream of an educational mission to the United States, the governor showed genuine interest. Ting suggested Yung put his ideas and proposals in writing so that they could be formally presented to Prime Minister Wen Seang. This unexpected vote of confidence, Yung later wrote, "came like a clap of thunder and fairly lifted me off my feet."[49] Yung immediately left for Shanghai and, with the help of a friend, carefully drew up four proposals.

The first proposal was for the development of a steam company that would operate on a joint stock basis. No foreigner would be allowed to be a stockholder, and it would be managed and worked by Chinese exclusively. An annual government subsidy was to be contributed based on a percentage of the "tribute rice" carried to Peking (Beijing) from Shanghai and other places where tribute rice was paid to the government instead of monetary taxes. The rice had traditionally been taken to Peking via the Grand Canal in thousands of flat-bottom boats built expressly for that purpose, an enterprise that for centuries had supported a large population living along that route. The transports had been plagued by difficulties, however. In the extended length of time it took to move the rice to Peking by this method, a fair percentage of it was inevitably lost from theft and also from fermentation, which rendered the rice inedible. To help alleviate these problems, part of the rice was shipped by sea in Ningpo junks to Tientsin and from there on flat-bottom boats to Peking. However, this more expedient method still resulted in time and product losses. Yung Wing suggested using steam vessels instead, to do the work quickly and more efficiently, supplanting both junks and flat-bottom boats.

Secondly, Yung proposed that the Chinese government select youths to be educated in the West in preparation for public service in China. One hundred and twenty students could be sent in increments of thirty students per year, Yung suggested, over a period of four years. The average age of the selected boys should be around twelve to fourteen years,[50] and they would have fifteen years to complete their studies. If the initial dispatches were successful, the venture could be continued indefinitely. Yung proposed that Chinese teachers be provided to maintain the boys' knowledge of China while in the United States, a provision prompted by his own loss of language skills after his extended stay at Yale. Two commissioners should be appointed to manage the enterprise, and a government appropriation of a percentage of revenue from Shanghai customs could finance the mission.

The third proposal encouraged the Chinese government to open the mineral resources of the country, which would lead indirectly to the introduction of railroads to transport mineral products from the interior to the seaports. Yung believed this proposition was the least likely to be adopted because of China's lack of qualified mining engineers, and also because of the superstitions of Fung Shui. Many Chinese held to an ancient doctrine that structures such as railroads could anger the spirits or *genii* that ruled over winds and waters, causing them to reciprocate with floods and typhoons.

In the fourth and final proposal Yung suggested the Chinese government prohibit missionaries of any religious sect or denomination from exercising any sort of jurisdiction over their converts, in either civil or criminal cases. The four proposals carefully drawn up, Yung presented them to Governor Ting for transmission to Prime Minister Wen Seang in Peking. On the sage advice of a friend, Yung had placed the four proposals in their particular sequence for a reason:

> "Of the four proposals, the first, third and fourth were put it to chaperone the second, in which my whole heart was enlisted, and which above all others was the one I wanted to be taken up; but not to give it too prominent a place, at the suggestion of my Chinese teacher, it was assigned a second place in the order of the arrangement."[51]

An official review of Yung's proposals would have to wait, however, because about the same time the document arrived in Peking, Wen Seang's mother passed away. In keeping with Chinese tradition, her death obliged Wen to go into mourning for a period of twenty-seven months and his attention to all public affairs was put on hold—including any review of Yung's proposals. Unfortunately, Wen Seang never returned to his duties as prime minister, because only three months after the passing of his mother, Wen also died. Therefore the carefully crafted proposals did not get an official reading and Yung's dream of sending Chinese students to America for China's modernization was once again on hold.

Undeterred, Yung Wing persisted in contacting Governor Ting with further details of his plan. It would not be until the Tientsin Massacre however, in early 1870, that another opportunity for Yung to offer his proposals to the Chinese government would finally present itself.

The Tientsin Massacre had been sparked by the superstitions of the Tientsin populace, who had come to regard the work of the Catholic nuns and the Sisters of Charity with growing suspicion.[52] As part of their regular charity work, the sisters had been in the practice of taking in and caring for foundlings and castaway orphans. The children were brought to hospitals, where they were raised and educated for service in the Roman Catholic Church. This work, seen as good and worthwhile by the sisters and by the church, was misunderstood by many of the local citizens who had come to believe rumors of diabolical acts being inflicted on the innocent children. Word spread of the alleged atrocities until angers flared and at one point an infuriated mob of Chinese citizens burned down a Protestant church, destroyed a Roman Catholic hospital, and killed several of the Sisters of Charity in the process.

High-ranking imperial officials were immediately dispatched to the region to help squelch the conflict, among them Ting Yih Chang. Yung took advantage of his unexpected accessibility and asked to be allowed to present the four proposals once again, this time to the Board of Commissioners (a board over which Zeng Guofan presided). Governor Ting agreed and took up the matter in earnest, holding several private interviews with members of the commission.

It was very late one night when Governor Ting sent orders that Yung Wing should be awakened for an important message—that Viceroy Zeng and the other commissioners had unanimously agreed to sign their names in support of all four of Yung's proposals. The news disallowed any further sleep and Yung spent the rest of the night lying on his bed " . . . wakeful as an owl, I felt as though I were treading on clouds and walking on air."[53] Two days later the signed document was on its way to Peking by pony express.[54]

A number of factors had predisposed Viceroy Zeng's decision to accept Yung's proposal and send students to the United States rather than Great Britain, France, or Germany. The Japanese, when confronted with the same decision, had chosen Germany because it was Japan's view that Germany's victory in the Franco-German conflict had established their military superiority over other Western nations. In addition, the political organization of Germany was deemed more suitable to Japan's aristocratic society than the democratic parliamentary systems of Great Britain and France. However, in China's case the final choice was heavily influenced by the fact that Yung Wing had the advantage of personal experience with the American system and therefore a firsthand understanding of the problems that Chinese students would confront.

Another important consideration influencing China's educational destination was the aforementioned Burlingame Treaty. By choosing America as the country to which it would send its students, China was showing respect for Anson Burlingame's extraordinary efforts toward the promotion of peaceful collaboration and cooperation between the two countries.[55]

A decision to initiate Sino-American education exchange would not be without controversy, however, and many respected conservatives questioned the wisdom of exposing Chinese youths to Western culture for long periods of time. In a calculated effort to balance old and new perspectives, Viceroy Zeng directed Governor Ting to recommend a man known to uphold conservative ideals, Chin Lan Pin, to serve as Yung's co-administrator in the operations of the newly authorized mission. Chin, who had been a clerk in the Board of Punishment, was chosen partly because he was a member of the Hanlin college and therefore had been educated in the "regular" Chinese way, with a focus on Confucian classics. His inclusion was intended to deflect opposition from conservatives who might object to a government mission being handled solely by the "Americanized" Yung Wing.

"The wisdom and the shrewd policy of such a move appealed to me at once, and I accepted the suggestion with pleasure and alacrity," Yung declared.[56] Chin Lan Pin was called immediately to Tientsin to meet Yung Wing and begin work on the project. Evidently he was pleased to quit Peking, where he had been doing the same job for nearly twenty years. In fact, he had never filled a government position in any other capacity, nor did he exhibit any practical experience in the world of business or education. Nevertheless, Yung Wing and Chin Lan Pin were officially assigned as co-commissioners of the new Chinese Educational Mission (CEM). It was the winter of 1870 when Yung Wing's proposal to send Chinese youth to study in America, a plan he first envisioned at Yale in the 1850s, was at long last officially sanctioned by the imperial government.

THE FIRST DISPATCH OF STUDENTS

The responsibilities for overseeing the new Chinese Educational Mission were divided between the two commissioners. It was agreed that Yung Wing would handle everything involving the students' American education, including finding appropriate housing situations for each of them. Chin Lan Pin was assigned the responsibility of assuring that the boys kept up with their knowledge of China and the Chinese language throughout their stay. Financial issues were to be handled jointly by both commissioners. Two teachers, Yeh Shu Tung and Yung Yune Foo, were assigned to provide Chinese studies for the boys and an interpreter, Zeng Laishun, was also assigned to the project.[57]

Yung Wing's plan was to be carried out much as he had originally proposed. The boys would be recruited from the various provinces and then sent to the United States in four separate dispatches of thirty students each, for a total of 120. The boys, who would range in age from ten to fifteen, were to be of respectable parentage (or to have respectable guardians) and a medical examination to assure their good health was required. Candidates were tested to measure their knowledge of Chinese reading and writing and everyone had to pass an English examination as well. After successfully passing the preliminary requirements, candidates were then obliged to attend the preparatory school in Shanghai for at least six months before they would at last be ready for the long voyage to their new home in America.

Once in the United States the students would be expected to undergo quarterly and annual examinations to gauge their progress in Chinese studies, and at specific intervals commissioners were to summon the students together to read from the *Sacred Book of Imperial Edicts*.[58] It was mandated that in the eighth month of each year Chinese calendar books containing information about China's customary rituals were to be issued by the customs service and sent to the students—the expectation being that the traditions would be adhered to during their stay, a practice that would "preserve and develop their sense of propriety and reverence."[59]

Before committing to this demanding program, students were asked to secure a signed letter from their parents (or guardians) granting permission for their son to be sent abroad for a period of fifteen years—with the understanding that they could not hold the Chinese government responsible for illness, injury, or death. An initial budget of 1,200,000 taels was allotted by the government to finance the students' stay abroad; however, the figure soon had to be raised to 1,489,800 due to unanticipated expenses—a truly enormous sum for agricultural China to spend on such a venture.[60] The funds were to be set aside from the receipts of the Imperial Maritime Customs at Shanghai.

Upon completion of their studies in America, the plan would then allow graduates a period of two years for travel before they were obliged to return to China and report to the Chinese Foreign Office. Then, awards of official rank and appointments to government service would be issued based on the student evaluations submitted by the CEM commissioners. Because the students were dependents of the government, they would not have the option of withdrawing from their studies before completion, nor could they seek naturalization abroad or secure their own employment.[61]

With policies basically in place, a preparatory school to accommodate the first thirty boys was begun in Shanghai. Liu Kai Sing, who had served for many years as the viceroy's first secretary in the Department of Memorials, was appointed superintendent upon its completion and though his efforts all four installments of students would be prepared for their trip to America.

Recruitment activities were well underway for the first installment but despite its close proximity to the preparatory school few students presented themselves from the Shanghai area. It was difficult to notify people of the opportunity in many of China's regions, such as the northern regions and the Yangtze Valley, because of the limited distribution of any sort of news in those areas at the time. A few families had seen the invitation sent out by the local magistrates, but many were dubious—China was a land where rewards were known to come only from hard labor, and an offer from the government to educate their sons and also to pay them a modest stipend was viewed with suspicion.⁶²

Dresses worn by students before departure for the States.

Liang Yu Ho (M. T. Liang)   *Tong Shao Yi*

Figure 2.2 Chinese Educational Mission students before leaving for America, 1872; Thomas LaFargue Papers, Manuscripts, Archives and Special Collections, Washington State University Libraries.

In order to secure enough qualified students for the first dispatch, Yung Wing found it necessary to travel south to the region around his home, where he could recruit students from families who had more exposure to Westerners and Western ideas. Of course those parents were also hesitant to send their sons to a strange country for fifteen years. Some wondered if there could be truth to the rumors—among the most egregious was that the Americans were planning to skin the boys alive, cover them with dog hides, and display them for profit as strange animals. Persistence, and parents' recognition of a unique opportunity, finally produced enough candidates, many from Canton's district of Heang Shan. In the final count the vast majority of the 120 Chinese Educational Mission students were recruited from the south—a circumstance that would receive some criticism.[63]

After several months of study in the preparatory school in Shanghai, the first thirty boys were finally ready to make the long voyage to America. Unfortunately their mentor Zeng Guofan's untimely death in 1871 prevented his witnessing their historic departure. Zeng's long-time colleague Li Hongzhang was appointed to assume Zeng's mentorship and to oversee the new Chinese Educational Mission. Li was a man Yung Wing described as being altogether different from his predecessor. According to Yung's autobiography, Li was a man with a nervous temperament who enjoyed flattery and praise, or as the Chinese put it he was "fond of wearing tall hats."[64] It was under Li's official command that the CEM was launched forth.

In February of 1872 Yung penned a letter to Yale's president Noah Porter, describing the Chinese government's intention to send its first dispatch of students to the United States, earnestly requesting his guidance. Porter immediately agreed to help, and it was with his direction that housing and other accommodations were investigated in preparation for the boys' arrival.[65] Arrangements more or less in place, the first dispatch of thirty elegantly dressed Chinese boys, fresh from preparatory school and with baggage in tow, bade farewell to their families and friends and passed through China's once-barred borders to board a ship bound for *meiguo*, the beautiful country.

3 The Chinese Educational Mission

The recent arrival of Chinese youths in New England was the subject of an August 18, 1873 article in the *New York Times*. The children had been hand-selected by the imperial leaders, it said, entrusted with the awesome assignment of initiating an extended program of education exchange with the United States of America—a project that if successful would help modernize China:

> In the year 1871, Tsang Kwoh Fan (Zeng Guofan), a statesman of the highest order, a man of great energy and most rigid integrity, one who struck a death-blow upon the rebels in the city of Nanking . . . who subsequently became the Viceroy of the Kiang Nan . . . memorialized the emperor to select 120 clever youths, irrespective of birth and position, to be sent to the United States to receive a collegiate as well as a professional education.[1]

The Chinese Educational Mission (CEM) would turn out to be a transformative undertaking. In addition to initiating a collaboration of academic exchange that would continue for the next century and a half, it opened new channels for diplomatic relations between the two countries. Championed by Yung Wing, advanced by Anson Burlingame, and mentored by Zeng Guofan, the CEM was one of the first initiatives undertaken in the Qing government's Self-Strengthening Movement. Of the four study programs launched as part of that movement, the CEM was by far the most ambitious—the other three programs had sent a combined total of thirty-eight naval and military cadets to Europe.

The project had met an extraordinary reception in the United States, a warm response that was reflective of the country's mood in the decade that followed the ending of the Civil War. Legislation had brought healing between the North and South as a new tolerance toward minorities was upheld—a brief postwar period of charity and acceptance. For the CEM students, it was an opportune time to come to America.

Satchels and supplies in tow, in the fall of 1872 thirty finely appointed boys and their families gathered at the port city of Shanghai. The imperial government had outfitted all of the students with the long gowns customarily worn by Chinese scholars. Shoes, coats, caps, and other provisions were provided as well, to accommodate their immediate needs but also to assure that the students would present a dignified and unified appearance when they arrived in America. What lay ahead must have been almost impossible to imagine—fifteen years apart from all that was familiar, in an inconceivable place, as distant as the moon. It was the last time the mothers and fathers would be able to embrace their children, because if the Chinese Educational Mission progressed as planned, the boys would return as young men.

It was customary, a matter of protocol, for the students and accompanying teachers to pay respects to the *Daotai* (*Taotai*), the chief magistrate of Shanghai, before their departure.[2] As a gesture of mutual cooperation and friendship in the spirit of the Burlingame Treaty, the group also called upon the American consul in Shanghai, George F. Seward, the nephew of Abraham Lincoln's secretary of State. Then on September 30, with "heavy hearts and vague feelings of the future,"[3] the students and the CEM staff boarded a ship bound for America.

From Shanghai there were stops at Nagasaki and Kobe, so it took a full week just to reach the port in Yokohama. It was during one of these extended intermediate stops that the boys first witnessed an "iron horse" or steam engine train, the sort that China would not build for another ten years.

The long trip from China to America must have seemed tedious but in fact travel had improved considerably since the days when Yung Wing first made the journey. Sailing ships had given way to steamships and the establishment of coaling stations in Japan had made possible a more direct, and considerably faster, passage across the Pacific Ocean. From Yokohama the party took the paddle-wheel steamer *Great Republic* on to San Francisco, crossing the Pacific in three weeks.[4] The ship was outfitted with one hundred first-class cabins, nearly a third of them occupied by the CEM students and their escorts. To pass the time the boys were required to study and they also wrote to their families, letters that were exchanged mid-ocean with a ship going in the opposite direction. Also on board, but relegated to steerage, were about one thousand less fortunate passengers comprised mostly of Cantonese laborers going to America to look for work or to seek their fortunes.

The CEM group was in San Francisco for three days, residing at the Occidental Hotel, an elegant facility that sported an elevator and running water (both hot and cold), wonders the boys would later document in their memoirs. Group and individual portraits were taken at the nearby photography studio of Thomas Houseworth and Company, and the boys were introduced to a number of prominent residents. Even though their arrival coincided with a time of increasing resentment of the local Chinese "coolies" in California, by all accounts the CEM party was warmly welcomed and treated with great courtesy.

Figure 3.1 Chinese Educational Mission students arrive in San Francisco, 1872.

The trip from Oakland, California, to Springfield, Massachusetts, involved a week-long journey on a railway that had been constructed just a few years earlier, chiefly with the labor of hundreds of Chinese "coolies." The Central Pacific transported the CEM party first to Ogden, Utah, and from there they rode the Union Pacific to Omaha, Nebraska. The Chicago and Rock Island took them from Omaha to Chicago, the Lake Shore and Michigan Southern on to Buffalo, New York, and then the New York Central on to Albany. Finally, the Boston and Albany delivered them safely to the station in Springfield. Every stop required the transfer of everyone's luggage and supplies. Along the way, because there were few dining facilities on trains at the time, passengers were obliged to find meals for themselves during their brief twenty-five-minute station stops at the various towns en route.

The overland journey by rail was long and tiresome, but it provided some remarkable experiences for the young passengers. The boys witnessed the extraordinary landscape of America's western frontier and even sightings of "genuine red Indians with eagle feathers projecting from their black hair, their faces painted in different colours . . . armed with bows and arrows."[5] When the group at last reached Hartford, they were met at the station by an elated Yung Wing, who had arrived in Connecticut in advance to arrange for the boys' preparatory schooling and living quarters.

ROOM AND BOARD

From the outset there had been disharmony between Yung Wing and his co-commissioner Chin Lan Pin over living quarters and a litany of other issues. Altercations had arisen over many of the initial arrangements—budgets, sources of funding, the types of costumes that would be provided, and whether the students should be allowed to attend extracurricular sports activities or church. "He [Chin] had never been out of China in his life . . . " Yung lamented in his memoirs. "The only standard by which he measured things and men was purely Chinese."[6] The discord between the two men was destined to persist.

One of the persons Yung had called upon for advice regarding the boys' housing arrangements was Professor James Hadley, a man he had known at Yale. Hadley was delighted to learn that his old friend had returned with "such a mission in (his) hands"[7] and recommended he get in touch with B. G. "Birdsey" Northrop, the commissioner of education for Connecticut. It was Northrop's suggestion that the students be housed with New England families, by twos or fours, where they could be cared for and learn firsthand about the American lifestyle. Here they could also receive preliminary instruction in conversational English and other topics to help prepare them for enrollment in the area schools.

President Noah Porter of Yale, who had been consulted early on, agreed with Northrop's plan wholeheartedly. Since most of the boys spoke very little English, he reasoned, they would likely learn it faster and with more utility while living in a completely English-speaking environment. Porter advised too that they should be housed in a number of villages scattered around the Connecticut Valley rather than in one central place. Separating the boys might encourage them to adapt even more quickly to the American lifestyle and their presence would likewise provide unique cultural opportunities for the citizens of various towns.

With further help from Birdsey Northrop, an estimated 120 New England families came forward to volunteer their homes, so that by the time the boys arrived in Connecticut there were ample beds to meet their needs. The arrangement was not strictly voluntary. Host families were paid a modest fee for their services from CEM funds, but by all accounts the vast majority of citizens who signed up demonstrated a genuine desire to care for the young boys and to support the educational mission.

From the outset there were cultural lessons to be learned. One of the American ladies, for example, in her eagerness to greet the young lad assigned to her family's keeping, instinctively embraced him with a kiss. The surprised student maintained his dignified composure at this unexpected show of motherly affection, but not without some difficulty—in the fashion of some Chinese families at the time he had not been kissed since he was a baby.[8]

The journals and memoirs of the CEM students abound with colorful stories of the host families and adjustment to America. One recalled that shortly after he and another student moved into their accommodations, the lady of the house announced they would all be attending Sunday school the following morning, but with a limited understanding of English the boys only recognized the word "school." Bright and early the next day both students arose, donned proper classroom attire, and gathered their books in anticipation of what they thought was going to be their first day of American education. Instead they were led to the front door of a local church. Forewarned that Americans would try devious ways to trick them into becoming Christians, the terrified boys turned and ran back to the relative safety of their room.

In time, most of the CEM boys participated in church functions with their American families, as religion was a significant component of nineteenth-century New England society and such activities were almost unavoidable. Almost all of the host families were members of the Congregationalist Church, the predominant denomination in Connecticut and Massachusetts at that time. For many of the CEM students the church became an integral part of their American experience and some converted to Christianity. But for the most part the boys enjoyed the religious and social activities sponsored by the churches while continuing to adhere to their traditional beliefs, in spite of steady pressure from some of the American hosts.

Not all of the hosts comprised traditional families. Of the first thirty-seven host "families" who volunteered, about sixteen were single women, including widows, those yet to be married or older unmarried "spinsters." Each of the American host families, called *shi* (teachers), was provided a set of instructions detailing their responsibilities. Together with the boys' day-to-day needs the host families were expected to provide education in English and other subjects. For their services they were paid 16 dollars each week for two boys sharing one room to cover board, washing, fuel, lights, and instruction. At one point the regulations were revised to require the families to give the boys 1 dollar a month for pocket money. To receive their reimbursement, hosts had to submit accounts of expenditures to the headquarters in Hartford, along with progress reports on each student.

Early on, the CEM boys established friendly relations with their American neighbors and classmates, and Connecticut folklore is rich with stories of the Chinese students' antics and escapades—like the day the boys spent chasing wild pigs through the village and down to the "Flats," creating plenty of chaos and apparently a good deal of community fun.[9] Sometimes the boys found opportunities to develop interests and learn new things outside the classroom through the generosity of American friends. For example, one of the boys was fascinated with American chickens, so neighborly Deacon Hyde allowed him to raise a flock of Plymouth Rock in his yard. Upon returning to China the student was granted special permission to transport a crate of his prized birds with him.

Living with local host families introduced the boys to American life in the style of the strictly disciplined New England household. One of the CEM students, Y. T. Woo, recalled that his host Mrs. Bartlett was quick to admonish the boys if they held their knife and fork incorrectly at the dinner table, or if she heard talking in the boys' attic rooms after nine or ten o'clock. She would call from below, "Boys, stop talking, it is time to sleep."[10] Woo added that "Old Mr. Bartlett" used to have prayer meetings each day, one morning and one evening, that the boys were expected to faithfully attend.

In these settings the boys became Americanized with amazing rapidity, quickly learning how to communicate in the schoolroom, the church yard, and on the playground. Almost immediately the Chinese boys wanted to wear Western style clothes like the other children instead of their assigned gowns. Chiding from their American classmates, who thought the robes and long braids made them look like girls, had resulted in hurt feelings and reportedly a few black eyes. Soon they would shed their long silk gowns and with them, according to a few accounts, some of their dignified Chinese manners. Yung Wing, who had experienced the same sort of teasing when he first came to America, instantly sympathized with their plight and supported a change of dress policy—a suggestion quickly rejected by co-commissioner Chin Lan Pin.

The boys gradually adopted American clothing anyway, in spite of Chin's objections; however, they were ordered to maintain their queues, the long braids worn to symbolize obedience and loyalty to the Manchu regime. A student found guilty of cutting off his braid during the early CEM years was subject to being promptly returned to China, a fate that befell two of the CEM boys. One was Zeng Pu, who insisted that rowdy classmates had forcibly cut off his queue (some speculate he may have done it himself) and the other offender was Zhong Juncheng. In light of the penalty, most opted to tuck the long braids into their jackets or wrap them neatly around their heads to better hide them under hats.[11] They were allowed to discontinue shaving their foreheads, however, a practice all of the boys were quite willing to eliminate from their grooming regimen.

SIDE TRIPS AND THE COOLIE ISSUE

It was becoming commonplace for Yung Wing to play the role of mediator between the conservative ideals of Chin Lan Pin and the desires of the increasingly Americanized boys over head-shaving, queues, clothing, public behavior, dating, and a long list of other issues. Yung's voice of support would temporarily fall silent, however, when he was summoned back to China for a period of several months, leaving the boys temporarily at the mercy of co-commissioner Chin.

Yung's return to China in 1872 was a consequence of a previous commitment to introduce Chinese officials to the newly developed Gatling gun. The presentation of the product to China's government had been entrusted to Yung by the inventor and president of the company himself, Dr. Gatling.[12] Impressed with his demonstration of the weapon's capabilities, the imperial court authorized Yung to purchase fifty guns at a cost of about $100,000, a sizable purchase in 1872 and only the first of several orders.

Yung's participation in the demonstration and purchase of weapons for China diverted him from his CEM duties, but in fact the side trip was in keeping with his overarching objective. Yung wanted China to import American technology through academic exchange, but from the beginning his intention was also to amass machines and weaponry to go with it. In this context Sino-American higher education exchange has always coexisted with China's efforts rebuild its economy and military security.

As Yung completed his duties relating to the weapons purchase, his return to America was delayed. Viceroy Li was enlisting Yung's immediate assistance with another matter—the controversial coolie issue. The Peruvian commissioner was on his way to Beijing to meet with Li, and to present his case for releasing greater numbers of coolies to support Peru's growing industries.

The emigration of Chinese coolies was a sensitive issue that was attracting world attention. The controversy would help to drive America's first immigration policies—regulations that would not just affect coolies but also Chinese students' ability to enter the United States. Two acts of Congress, one in 1862 and another in 1864, had already been leveled at the trading and transferring of coolies to the United States by American vessels, as governments such as Peru and Cuba were actively promoting increased levels of coolie emigration for their labor needs. During the 1860s an estimated 30,000 Chinese coolies were being sent to Cuba and Peru annually, according to an 1867 report in *Harper's Weekly*.[13] That year there were at least 2,000 whose eight-year contracts had just expired and these coolies were slated to be brought to the United States, mostly to Louisiana. Americans were voicing concern.

Yung sat in on the meeting as Li had requested, and recognized immediately that the Peruvian commissioner's review did not represent the truth of the situation:

> In his [the commissioner's] conversation he pictured to me in rosy colors how well the Chinese were treated in Peru; how they were prospering and doing well there; and said that the Chinese government ought

to conclude a treaty with Peru to encourage the poorer class of Chinese to emigrate to that country . . . [14]

Yung knew this to be untrue, as he had himself witnessed the reality of the coolie situation. In 1855, when Yung returned to China after graduating from Yale, he happened to walk past a large crowd of coolies in Macao who were tied together by their queues, herded like slaves toward a waiting ship. Disturbed by what he saw, Yung did some investigating and learned that most of these hapless "coolies" had either been misled or forced, through one coercive means or another, to sign labor contracts that in practical terms would keep them in servitude for life. Appalled by what he learned, Yung attempted to activate the local officials by speaking out publicly against the cruel process. His efforts had resulted in the arrest of two or three of the "kidnappers" in Canton, and as punishment they were forced to wear forty-pound wooden collars, night and day, for a period of about two months.

Yung privately recounted this story to Li Hongzhang and expressed earnest misgivings about sending any more of China's peasants to what in effect were Peruvian labor camps. Unsure what to do, Li ordered Yung to travel to Peru and personally investigate the alleged abuses and return with a full report.

Yung traveled first back to Connecticut to check on CEM activities, and then on to Peru, now accompanied by the Reverend J. H. Twichell and the Dr. E. W. Kellogg, his future brother-in-law. The extended trip would keep Yung away from his preferred duties for another three months but during that time he was able to observe and record horrific tales of abuse in Peru. With photographs and witnesses attesting to the severity of the situation, the viceroy refused to sign the coolie treaty.[15]

The Chinese government had similarly enlisted CEM co-commissioner Chin's help in investigating and averting the Chinese coolie trade in Cuba, and based on the strength of both inspections the routine of exporting Chinese coolies for labor had received its death blow.[16] Although thousands of already-indentured coolies would still have to serve out their terms, any arrangement for furthering the practice with either Peru or Cuba was averted. Then both of the commissioners were finally allowed to return to Hartford and get on with the day-to-day work of the Chinese Educational Mission.

DANCING WITH MARK TWAIN'S DAUGHTERS

With rare exception the boys of the Chinese Educational Mission progressed through their respective American high schools and academies successfully. The students then began enrolling at Yale, and other prominent institutions of higher education, where they continued to excel both in and out of the classroom. Most adapted easily to the academic and social culture of the American college campus and many took on some sort of "American" nickname, either cast upon them in a spirit of friendship by their American classmates—or sometimes they were self-imposed: "Flounder," "Breezy Jack," "Charlie Cold Fish," "Ajax," "Fighting Chinee," "Alligator," and "Big Nose," to name just a few. Many of the amicable young men were enthusiastic participants in popular campus activities and many victories were won by the "Orientals", CEM's baseball team at Yale. [17]

William Lyon Phelps, a classmate of several of the CEM students who attended Yale, wrote many years later (1939) of his recollections:

> The boys were dressed like us, except they wore long queues. When they played football, they tucked those queues inside their shirts and sometimes tied them around their heads; for if the queue got loose, it afforded too strong a temptation for opponents . . . they became excellent at baseball, football, hockey on the ice . . . and in fancy skating they were supreme. When the bicycle was invented, the first boy to have one at school was Tsang; and I can see him now riding the strange high machine up Asylum Avenue.[18]

The CEM students enriched other time-honored bastions of campus culture, such as Yale's prestigious rowing team. In both 1880 and 1881 the coxswain for the Yale varsity rowing crew was CEM student Chung Mun-Yew, a popular figure around campus whose antics still live on in Yale folklore. One account appeared in a 1912 issue of the *Hartford Courant*, describing Chung as the "little coxswain" who never lost his composure—except once. As the story goes, during a race with Harvard in 1880 and as both crews were nearing the finish line in an uncommonly close competition, at the last possible moment Chung suddenly broke out with a thundering "Damn it boys, pull!"[19] The stunned rowers responded with regenerated zeal to the unexpected command and Yale handily won the race.

Just as the CEM students were putting their stamp on American campus culture, current events were likewise making lasting impressions on the boys. The years the CEM students were in America could scarcely have occurred at a more exciting time in the nation's history. For example, in 1876 they were able to attend the hundredth anniversary of the United States—the Centennial Exhibition. Held in Philadelphia, the exhibit hosted thirty-seven countries, among them China's Qing Empire.

Li Gui, a customs official who had come to view the exhibition as part of a delegation sent by the Qing government, met with the CEM boys during the tour. Amazed by the exhibits of machinery, Li described the experience in his book, *New Records of Travels around the World*. "Since ancient times in China machine-making techniques were libeled as diabolical tricks, which would only lead to wily scheming," said Li, "but now wily would it be if the scheming were applied to benefiting the country and the people?" At the exhibition Li (along with the CEM students) witnessed the Corliss

Centennial Steam Engine, water pumps, dredgers, sewing machines, looms, typewriters, fountain pens, slide projectors, and machine-manufactured paper. Displays had been set up to demonstrate Thomas Edison's newly invented electric light, and Alexander Graham Bell's telephone.

As part of the Centennial Exhibition, the CEM students had a unique opportunity—a chance to publicly display their own work. The Connecticut Educational Commission set up the exhibit, and in it they included a number of English essays written by the CEM boys, a display visited by none other than President Ulysses Grant. Learning that the Chinese Educational Mission students were there in Philadelphia, he asked to meet them. A welcoming ceremony was arranged and the president shook hands with each of them, a great honor for the students.[20]

The students' reception in Connecticut social circles had been equally hospitable throughout their stay. They were received by many of the important families of the day. Classmate Phelps recalled with envy that when the Chinese boys entered the social arena "none of us had any chance. Their manner to the girls had a deferential elegance far beyond our possibilities . . . at dances and receptions, the fairest and most sought-after belles invariably gave the swains from the Orient their preference."[21]

Some of Connecticut's local residents, among them Samuel Clemens (Mark Twain) and his friend the Reverend Joseph Hopkins Twichell, took special interest in the boys, leading them on long hikes through the beautiful Connecticut countryside and feeding them bear meat and venison, in the manner of American trappers and hunters. The Clemens family sometimes hosted events for the CEM boys in their home. Decades later Yung Wing's granddaughter Elsie told the story of an ex-mission student who, when he was much older, had boasted to his Chinese friends that he used to "dance with Mark Twain's daughters."[22]

HELL HOUSE

The CEM headquarters was set up in a facility in Hartford, Connecticut. Yung Wing had intended to locate the headquarters in Springfield, Massachusetts, partly because it was the home of Dr. A. S. McClean and his wife, a couple Yung had befriended in his college days. But on the advice of Birdsey Northrop and others, he established the headquarters in Hartford on Summer Street, and instead used Springfield as a distribution center for incoming students.[23] Yung had hoped for a larger and more impressive facility, but this would do for now.

The headquarters, known in Chinese as the *Zhuyang ju* or Staying Abroad Office, was the home of the administrative component of the CEM, referred to as the Chinese Educational Commission (CEC). First housed in a cramped rental space, the CEC staff was later able to move into a spacious building; then in 1877 the headquarters relocated a final time to what would be their permanent headquarters at 400 Collins Street, near the prestigious Nook neighborhood. This large three-story house was spacious enough to accommodate all of the CEM leaders and students at the same time with its large meeting hall, sleeping quarters, kitchen facilities, and several classrooms. It had been constructed under the supervision of Springfield architect Eugene C. Gardner, at the cost of about $55,000.

The original CEC staff consisted of the chief commissioner, an associate commissioner, a translator, and two Chinese instructors, who were paid salaries ranging from 160 to 250 taels or about 240 to 675 dollars per month—wages considerably higher than Americans occupying similar positions at the time. The headquarters served to administer the CEM, but it also served as China's de facto diplomatic representative in the United States until a permanent legation was set up in Washington in 1878. Thus, in lieu of official representatives, Yung Wing and Chen Lan Pin in effect served in that capacity. It was for this reason that they were sometimes called upon by the Chinese government for "side trips" relating to other concerns (such as the coolie issue) while they were also managing the affairs of the CEM.

Hartford turned out to be an ideal choice for the CEM headquarters. Congress had ratified the Fifteenth Amendment in 1870, giving qualified citizens the right to vote regardless of race. Two years later Congress passed the Amnesty Act, which restored civil rights to citizens of the South, and then the Civil Rights Act in 1875 gave equal rights to African Americans in public accommodations and juror duty. In this spirit of progress and acceptance, postwar Hartford had emerged as a center of trade and manufacturing and a repository of substantial wealth. Its residents included some of America's most promising artists and writers, including Harriet Beecher Stowe, who had written *Uncle Tom's Cabin* in 1851, and Mark Twain, author of *Huckleberry Finn* and other books destined to become American classics. The Hartford community was receptive to the idea of hosting the Chinese Educational Mission and the citizens welcomed the headquarters and the CEM staff to their city.

The CEC staff was grateful for the reception and worked to build good public relations with their American neighbors. They actively cultivated and entertained Hartford's elite and many of the town's most influential citizens could be found at the annual reception during the Lunar New Year. On at least one occasion Connecticut's governor Charles B. Andrew was a guest.

The CEM headquarters was a social venue but also a center of learning. Classes taught there included Chinese classical literature, poetry, calligraphy, and composition and for the CEM students, attendance was mandatory. In addition to classes, students were expected to gather periodically to hear instructions from their teachers and also from the imperial court, which expected them to observe all Chinese holidays and nationally recognized occasions. It was not long before the youths grew tired of what many of them considered a tedious routine, one which crowded their schedules and seemed to have little relevance to their new Americanized lifestyle. Some of the students began referring to the facility as "Hell House," a comment that would not go unnoticed by Chinese officials.[24]

THE FINAL DISPATCHES

The second installment of thirty students was dispatched from China in 1873, the third the following year, and the final dispatch reached America in 1875, not long after the Hartford facility was completed. The last dispatch had in their company a new commissioner, Ou Ngoh Liang, along with two new teachers and a new interpreter, Kwant Kee Chen—all appointed by Li Hongzheng. The new commissioner had been sent to replace Chin Lan Pin, who was returning to China with the teacher Yeh Shu Tung for an extended leave of absence. One of the interpreters, Tsang Lai Sun, had also resigned and required a replacement. The change in personnel would have a watershed effect on the Chinese Educational Mission.

Along with the changes in personnel had come an official notification—that both Chin and Yung were to be appointed as Chinese commissioners to Washington, DC. The appointment was intended as an honor, but Yung's thoughts were about the fate of the CEM. He was being sent away from Hartford at a time of upheaval in the mission's operations and when, in his estimation, the CEM needed his guidance the most—he likened it to a father leaving his children. Yung sent a letter of appeal to Viceroy Li, hoping for a reversal of the decision:

> . . . while I appreciated fully its significance, the obligations and responsibilities inseparably connected with the position filled me with anxious solicitude that my abilities and qualifications might not be equal to their satisfactory fulfillment. In view of such a state of mind, I much preferred . . . to remain in my present position as a commissioner of the Chinese mission in Hartford . . . [until] the Chinese students should have finished their education and were ready to return to China. . . . In that event I should have discharged a duty to "Tsang the Upright. . . . "[25]

Four months later Yung received word from China that a compromise had been reached. Yung was to honor his Washington appointment, but only as an assistant, a change that would allow him to continue his supervision of the CEM alongside Ou Ngoh Liang, the newly appointed commissioner.

Ou Ngoh Liang was much younger than his predecessor Chin Lan Pin. Yung described him as a man of quiet disposition, showing no inclination to "meddle with settled conditions or to create trouble . . . he had the good sense to let well enough alone."[26] However, to Yung's disappointment, Ou soon left the position (1876) and was quickly replaced by Woo Tsze Tung, a man Chin Lan Pin had personally recommended to Viceroy

Li. The appointment of Woo as co-commissioner would effectively initiate the demise of the Chinese Educational Mission.

According to Yung Wing's memoirs, Woo Tsze Tung was "regarded by all his friends as a crank," who lacked competence. He also seemed solidly adverse to the goals of the CEM. "From this time forth the educational mission found an enemy who was determined to undermine the work of Zeng Guofan and Ting Yih Cheong, to both of whom Woo Tsze Tung was more or less hostile."[27] Woo was a conservative who, even before his arrival in New England, had regarded the CEM as subversive to the principles of Chinese culture. It was Yung's belief that by recommending Woo, Chin Pan Lin had revealed his own heart—that of an uncompromising Confucian that "gnashes its teeth against all and every attempt put forth to reform the government or to improve the general condition of things in China."[28]

Woo Tsze Tung officially assumed his duties as the new CEM commissioner in the fall of 1876 and immediately found fault with nearly everything involving the mission. In his view the students had been mismanaged and overindulged. They were allowed to participate in too many noneducational activities, had shed their traditional garments, and some had cut their hair in defiance of the Qing government's wishes. Several had become Christians and some dated American girls. From Woo's perspective the young men had adopted the rebellious and undignified manner of American youth, rejecting their noble Chinese heritage.

Rather than sharing his many concerns with his co-commissioner Yung Wing, Woo bypassed his authority completely, and instead sent long lists of grievances not just to his friends in China but also to Viceroy Li. "They [the students] played more than they studied," said Woo, and had "formed themselves into secret societies, both religious and political."[29] Woo alleged that if the young men were allowed to continue this behavior they would not only lose their love of China, but upon their return they would be good for nothing. In his judgment the mission should be broken up and the students recalled to China, the sooner the better.

It was Viceroy Li himself who finally alerted Yung to the messages Woo had been sending to China. Yung was outraged. He considered Woo's actions to be nothing less than a betrayal of the project, and came immediately to the defense of the CEM students and the mission, assuring Li that the stories had been no more than malicious misrepresentations of the truth. He flatly accused Woo of jeopardizing educational goals that had been so important to the late Zeng Guofan, adding that "Woo should have been relegated to a cell in an insane asylum or to an institution for imbeciles."[30] Yung accused Chin Lan Pin of similar levels of incompetence, both in his performance as CEM commissioner and in his current Washington post.

In spite of the exchange of accusations, the CEM continued on for a time. The final downturn began when Yung Wing submitted several applications to the State Department to seek admission for CEM students to the Military Academy at West Point and to the Naval Academy at Annapolis.

It was understood from the beginning, at least from the Chinese perspective, that when the students were eligible some would enroll in the military academies to learn America's secrets of military strategy and weaponry. The United States must have remembered things a bit differently, because the response Yung received from both institutions was the same—there was "no room provided for Chinese students."[31]

"THE CHINESE MUST GO!"

Yung received the rejections from the military academies at a time in America's history when prejudice against the Chinese was reaching an all-time high—the postwar period of acceptance toward immigrants had apparently run its course with the influx of coolies and other so-called undesirables. Intolerance had spread across the nation and the Burlingame Treaty, enacted only a decade before in a spirit of friendship was now in Yung's estimation "trampled underfoot unceremoniously and wantonly, and set aside as though no such treaty had ever existed . . . "[32]

It was Yung Wing's letter to Li Hongzhang informing the viceroy of the rebuff that sealed the mission's fate. Viceroy Li regarded the rejection as nothing less than a betrayal—an egregious violation of the Burlingame Treaty. He was not alone in his indignation. An article in an 1879 issue of *Harper's Weekly*, "A Breach of National Faith," voiced the opinion of many Americans :

> Congress has announced to the world that the United States intends to break treaties at their pleasure. The preemptory abrogation of the Chinese treaty is a beach of public faith which sullies the good name of the country, and puts every other nation on guard in undertaking any dealings with us which depend on our honor.[33]

The afterglow of cooperation in the years immediately following the signing of Anson Burlingame's treaty in 1868 had faded with the rising numbers of poor and uneducated Chinese who had settled in the United States after failing to find their fortunes. Initially the Chinese had been welcomed for their contribution to the workforce, but those failing to strike it rich, the vast majority, had stayed on in America to became laborers, launderers, shopkeepers, or servants, taking on whatever jobs were available in order to survive and congregating for security and protection from belligerent Americans in areas that would become "Chinatowns." Few had a means of purchasing a ticket back to China and thousands were essentially stuck in a land that was growing increasingly hostile. Citizens openly accused the Chinese of taking American jobs and of being an unwelcome burden on American society, and it some areas there were episodes of mob violence.

Unflattering cartoons with cruel captions stating that the Chinese "worked cheap and smelled bad," among other unfavorable accusations, fueled the propaganda.[34] In California, the slogan of the Workingman's Party was "The Chinese Must Go!" and America's growing disdain for the Chinese grew increasingly open and unabashed, demonstrated in a *Harper's Weekly* article written by John Draper. "He's too filthy, the moon eyed leper. He lives in one room of a tenement shanty, with 20 others as nasty as himself . . . as to morality, he makes himself tipsy with opium. . . . "[35]

Beneath the editorial slurs, the real offense of the Chinese was that he cheapened labor. Political leaders across America felt the pressure of a public outcry against the "yellow peril"[36] and most were unwilling to incur the wrath of the voting public by treating the Chinese equally—as they had agreed to do with the enactment of the Burlingame Treaty. The supremacy of "states' rights" was typically cited as the reason for failure to interfere with local anti-Chinese policies.

The growing atmosphere of hostility between the United States and China provided a convenient opportunity for those who opposed the continuation of the CEM.[37] Taking full advantage of the viceroy's disappointment over the alleged violations of the Burlingame Treaty, commissioner Woo redoubled his efforts to break up the mission—this time with the aid of ex-commissioner Chin Lan Pin. Now, even longer lists of grievances were sent to Viceroy Li. Further goaded by those in the ranks of the reactionary party who were also pressing for the recall of the CEM, the viceroy finally yielded, agreeing to end the project.

To his great dismay, Yung Wing had not been consulted on the decision because his conspirators had alleged he was incapable of providing an impartial opinion on the subject. As Chin and Woo rejoiced in their victory, the CEM students were given the official mandate—to cease their studies and return to China immediately.

The friendly relationship between the United States and China that ignited from the Burlingame Treaty had now cooled to the point of animosity. It was 1881 and the students were returning home just months before America would pass the Chinese Exclusion Act, legislation that would take effect in 1882, marking the first time in United States history that the government would enforce immigration limits on any designated nationality.

PROTESTS AND PLEAS

A number of influential Americans stepped forward to enlist their support for the continuation of the CEM, among them the Reverend J. H. Twichell, the Reverend John W. Lane, Yale president Noah Porter, University of Michigan president James B. Angell, Amherst president Julius Seelye, Samuel Clemens (Mark Twain), T. F. Frelinghuysen, and John Russell Young.[38] Each appealed to local and national government officials, voicing the conviction that the mission was a genuinely worthwhile endeavor, soliciting help in finding a way to overturn the mandate. Yale president Noah Porter became the chief architect of a letter to Tsung Li Yamun at the Office for Foreign Affairs, one that passionately petitioned the Chinese government to reconsider their decision:

> The undersigned, who have been instructors, guardians and friends of the students . . . exceedingly regret that these young men have been withdrawn from the country, and that the Education Commission has been dissolved . . . [they] have generally made a faithful use of their opportunities, and have made good progress in the studies assigned to them. . . . With scarcely a single exception, their morals have been good; their manners have been singularly polite and decorous, and their behavior has been such as to make friends for themselves and their country. . . . In these ways they have proved themselves eminently worthy of the confidence which has been reposed in them to represent their families and the great Chinese Empire in a land of strangers . . . we would respectfully urge that the reasons for this sudden decision should be reconsidered. . . .[39]

The letter went on to suggest that a committee be appointed, comprised of eminent Chinese citizens, to further examine the truths of the accusations against the boys and the mission. Their pleas were unheeded.

The local community was saddened to see the Chinese Educational Mission come to a close. A collective fondness for the boys had developed in the towns and villages where the students had lived and studied and the feeling of loss was made clear in an article in the *Hartford Daily Courant*:

> The bright-faced, gentle-mannered lads, who, since their arrival in Hartford, have unconsciously done so much toward dissipating the popular prejudices that formerly clustered about the name of Chinamen, are really leaving us. Some of them started on their long journey yesterday . . . Hartford is unfeignedly sorry to see the boys go, and her best wishes accompany them.[40]

Six weeks later the paper printed a final farewell. "Yesterday afternoon the last delegation of Chinese students left the city," it said, "Their departure . . . was witnessed by a large crowd of spectators and friends."[41]

The recall had happened at an especially inopportune time for the CEM students. More than sixty were studying in preparatory and technical schools, but most had just begun their training. Only two students had graduated from Yale—twenty others were still enrolled. Four were attending Columbia, seven were enrolled at the Massachusetts Institute of Technology, and five at Rensselaer Polytechnic Institute.[42] Just a few more years would have enabled most of them to qualify for high positions in engineering, mining, shipbuilding, communications, and other technical fields in China. Now in question was their ability to effectively use their limited training toward the modernization of China, a concern that would significantly lower their once-elevated status among their countrymen.

As the students said good-bye to their American families, schoolmates, and friends, they were mercifully unaware of the unhappy reception that awaited them in their homeland—a sad and unexpected turn of events that Yung Wing believed "could not fail to make an impression upon their innermost convictions of the superiority of Occidental civilization over that of China."[43]

Not every boy returned to China. Three had lost their lives while in the United States, among them Paun Min Chung from Guangdong Province, who died of consumption in Troy, New York—a disorder he had contracted while camping at the seashore, according to *The Troy Times*. Paun had been converted to Christianity by the Reverend Clark and the fifteen-year-old allegedly died professing the Christian faith—his last words being those of the Lord's Prayer, with "Amen" at his final breath. He was buried at Groe Cemetery in Hartford. In its December 1, 1879, issue the *New York Times* had printed a verse the young man penned only days before his passing:

Dr. Clark has saved my heart
Where I lie there let me die,
Where'er I be, there bury me.[44]

Tan Yew Fun and Tsao Ka Chuck also lost their lives while in America. A few other students simply refused to leave and went into hiding.

THE BOYS RETURN HOME

In July of 1881 the first group of CEM returnees left New England en route to San Francisco. There they would remain for several days, with little to do but dwell upon their unhappy fate, as they awaited the arrival of the next China-bound steamer. To help the young men pass the time, members of the Oakland baseball team invited them to play in a friendly match. Unaware that several of the CEM students had played skillfully with the "Orientals" team at Yale, the Oakland players assumed it would be an easy win, but to their embarrassment the CEM boys "walloped them, to the great rejoicing of their comrades . . . "[45] The pitcher for that impromptu game happened to be southpaw Liang Dunyan (Liang Tun Yen), who would someday become minister of communications for China's first republican government.

On August 21, 1881, the evening before the second group would begin their trip back to China, twenty-seven of the forty-nine returnees met at the home of Fanny Bartlett in Hartford to sing hymns and have a last friendly gathering. Several who had lived with the Bartletts—Cai Shaoji,

Huang Kaijia, Liang Dunyan, and Wu Yangzeng—were present along with community friends such as the Reverend Joseph Twichell, pastor of the Asylum Hill Church, where many of the boys had attended services with their host families.

The following day the students again gathered together, this time at Hartford's Asylum Street depot, with "baggage, consisting of about forty trunks and boxes" in a massive pile on the platform.[46] These young men looked very different from the boys who had arrived several years before. With the exception of their queues they looked and dressed much the same as the American passengers. They were "a smart-looking lot of boys, and acted just like a party of American students," reported the *Springfield Republican*. "Some of them wore gold-trimmed eye-glasses, nicely balanced before their almond eyes, and gazed with the air of connoisseurs upon such specimens of female beauty as flitted by."[47]

By all accounts the warm farewells given the students were genuine and heartfelt. As the returnees waited in San Francisco to board the ship to China, a large number of local citizens—the staff of the Chinese consulate among them—came to the wharf to wave good-bye, singing popular hymns such as "In the Sweet By and By" and "Old Hundred." Zhu Baokui later wrote that it was only then, as they sang together on the dock, that he fully realized he was forever "leaving the land of freedom" and the many friends he had made there.[48] The last group of CEM returnees left Hartford in late September of 1881, just after the death of President James A. Garfield. Each of the boys wore a silk ribbon to symbolize their respect.

The CEM students' arrival in China was bittersweet. "We were treated coolly by the officials in Shanghai," Huang Kaijai recounted, remembering that they were "thrilled . . . thinking what a joyous welcome was waiting for us, and what a sea of familiar faces. . . ."[49] Indeed, no such reception awaited them. The students were taken on to the harbormaster's office not on sedan chairs or even rickshaws, but on large, open, and uncomfortable wooden wheelbarrows typically used for the lower classes. Wong Kai-kah relayed the events of the first few days in a letter to Fannie Bartlett (the complete transcript is included in the appendix):

> We came to the Harbour Master's house, and after a roll-call and a substantial supper, not elaborately prepared, we were dispatched with a detachment of Chinese marines acting as a guard over us to prevent our escaping . . . to the "Knowledge Wishing Institution" inside the city behind the court of the Shanghai Taotai. Your Western imagination is too sublime to conceive a place so vile as this so-called institution; you may have read about Turkish prisons or Andersonville Horrors, but compared to this they must have been enviable places.[50]

Four days of mostly unnecessary delays dragged on, with family members outside, anxiously awaiting the first sight of their long-absent sons. The students were eventually released but only after each of them offered their obligatory kowtows to the Shanghai *Daotai*.

For a brief time some still held hope that Yung Wing's continuing efforts could change the government's mind—that they would be permitted to return to America to finish their degrees. But it was not to be. Yung finally departed the United States after all the boys had gone and the CEM building closed, in late 1881—Chin Lan Pin had retreated a year earlier.

Upon his return to China, Yung Wing's first order of business was to stop in Peking (Beijing) to report to the government—a customary step for diplomatic officers at the close of their terms. On his way he stopped in Tientsin, where he called upon Viceroy Li Hongzhang. Li questioned why he had allowed the students to return to China. Bewildered, Yung simply said that he thought he was carrying out an imperial decree as ordered. Li went on to explain that in his heart, he had actually wanted the students to remain in America to complete their studies, and was hoping Yung Wing would find a way to justify the continuation of the CEM. Yung was stunned. It had not occurred to him that Li had any second thoughts about the recall. "How could I have been supposed to read [the viceroy's] heart at a distance of 45,000 *lis* . . . ?"[51]

"Well," said Li, "I know the author of this great mischief" (meaning the new commissioner Woo Tsze Tung.)[52] Commissioner Woo, who was also in Tientsin at the time, was from that point effectively disenfranchised from Li's favor, and to his great dismay was repeatedly refused an audience with the viceroy.

A disheartened Yung Wing, his official duties now complete, would soon be called back to the United States because of his wife Mary's declining health. Yung was convinced that her physical maladies had been worsened by rumors that he might literally lose his head if he remained in China. Mary Kellogg Yung did regain some strength under her husband's care, but in the winter of 1885 her condition deteriorated and she died shortly thereafter of what was diagnosed as Bright's disease. She was survived by a devastated Yung and their two sons, Morrison Brown Yung and Bartlett Golden Yung, aged nine and seven. "Her death made a great void in my after-life, which was irreparable . . . "[53]

WHAT BECAME OF THE CEM BOYS?

In a 1910 issue of the *New York Times* there appeared an article by Gilbert Reid, titled "Graduates of Our Colleges in High Posts in China." In it were accounts of several of the CEM students—a progress report of sorts, some thirty years after the mission's recall. "What became of those young men who were received into the homes of our best people in Hartford, in Springfield, in Andover, at Exeter, in New Haven, in New York . . . ?" Reid asked in an opening paragraph. "Was the commission a failure? Have the students gained renown for themselves and for their country? Have they given credit to the instruction which they received at the hands of our own great scholars?"[54]

Three decades earlier, when the CEM students were recalled to China, most of the young men were assigned to work in one of the new Self-Strengthening projects that were just getting underway. By this means many of the CEM students became instrumental in the operations of new enterprises such as the Telegraph Administration, the Kaiping Mines, the Tianjin Naval Academy, and the Tianjin Medical School, in addition to the Zongli Yamen and the newly established diplomatic corps. CEM students were distributed by the government to the various technical colleges and institutions that had been established by Li Hongzhang in Tientsin.[55]

It would take years, however, for the former students themselves to have any real impact. The circumscribed tasks the students had been given upon their return were simply what the imperial government expected of them. Only after the Confucian order was shaken at the end of the century did the students find the opportunity to play a transformative role.

A look at the occupational progression of those assigned to the navy will provide an illustration of how former CEM students gradually rose in status. Most of those destined for naval careers had been initially assigned to the Naval College and Torpedo School at Fuzhou (Foochow), or to the Northern squadron at Tientsin, all charged with the task of improving China's lackluster navy, incomplete educations aside. The imperial government had made some lackluster attempts to modernize the navy twenty years earlier (1863) but to little avail. The efforts had been grossly underfunded and some blamed the Empress Dowager Cixi, who was suspected of having diverted a sizable portion of the money for the building of a new Summer Palace.[56] The result was a fleet of inferior ships stocked with arms and ammunitions of questionable quality. Soon the CEM returnees who had been assigned to the Foochow facility would witness this "modernized" navy engage in an actual conflict.

Ships of the French fleet, which had been docked peacefully in Pagoda Anchorage of Fuzhou for months, reportedly without warning opened fire upon a nearby Chinese squadron. The French fleet, which included eight heavily armored cruisers, easily devastated most of China's vessels, which consisted of only two armored ships and nine converted wooden junks. Apparently unsatisfied with the leveling of the ships, the French proceeded to bombard the Fuzhou Arsenal, rendering its docks and workshops to ruins.

By all accounts the former CEM students fought valiantly, but four lost their lives during the clash—Kwong Wing-chung, Sit Yau-fu, Yang Sew-nan, and Wong Kwie-liang. A fifth CEM returnee, Yung Leang, narrowly escaped death when his ship sunk and he had to swim to shore.[57] (Three more of the CEM group—Chin Kin-kwai, Shen Shao-chang, and Wong Chu-lin—would later lose their lives in similar fashion while commanding naval ships in the upcoming war between Japan and China.)

The American minister to China saw the Pagoda Anchorage disaster as an opportunity to bring attention to America's rekindled desire to resume education exchange with China. He publicly praised the valor and bravery of the former CEM students during the siege, emphasizing that they had done China a great service, and that "their education in the United States had not proved fruitless."[58] The status of the American-educated officers began to elevate as a result of this and other acclaim, and a few began ascending to high ranks in China's navy.

To that point, with rare exception, the former CEM students had been treated like "yamen clerks and coolie mechanics" in their job assignments and most had not been able to progress above the lower ranks.[59] However, by the ending years of Manchu reign, two former CEM students had risen to the rank of admiral (Tsai "Fighting Chinee" Ting-kan and Woo Ying-fu), and another had been appointed vice-minister of the Chinese Navy.

The period that followed China's overwhelming defeat at the hands of Japan (1895) further bolstered the status of the American-educated officials. The shock of defeat by the *woren* or "people of diminutive stature," as the Japanese were mockingly called, brought forth new and urgent pleas for a revitalized program of modernization, using education and technology from the West—as Japan had successfully done.[60] Several more years would pass, however, before the Chinese government would again officially endorse training in the United States.

After 1895 there was new and widespread support for the rapid expansion of China's railroads and telegraph systems, and the development of its mining industry. As new projects for improvements were put into place, the American-trained Chinese were called upon to administer them, allowing many of the former CEM students to rise to high posts within these industries and also in the government. Despite their incomplete American educations and the inhospitable conditions of their return, many of the CEM students had become instrumental in laying the foundations for China's modernization. It was under their leadership that China developed its telegraph systems, railroads, mining industries, and military facilities, efforts that would slowly push the Celestial Kingdom into the Industrial Age.

A long list of former CEM students contributed to China's modernization and quite a few now occupy places of honor in Chinese history. The following sections provide brief biographical accounts of several of those most notable and well-known, among them Jeme Tien Yau, Liang Dunyan, Y. T. Woo, Luk Wing Chuan, Ouyang King, Wong Kai-Kah, Liang Cheng, and Tang Shaoyi.

Jeme Tien Yau

Jeme "Jimmy" Tien Yau (Zhan Tianyou), one of the original thirty CEM boys dispatched to America in 1872, would go on to become one of China's most influential and honored engineers. Hailed as "the father of Chinese railroads," many of the industry standards Jeme established in China during his many years with the railroads are still in force today.

The eldest son of a tea merchant, Jeme was born in Anhui Province but grew up in Nanhai, Guangdong Province. He was only ten when he was selected to accompany twenty-nine other boys as part of the Qing imperial court's Self-Strengthening movement. Jeme's father had signed the required agreement, promising that his son would indeed complete his studies and return to China to accept his official assignment—a document that at the same time released the Qing government from any liability whatsoever. Like the others who were selected for the CEM, Jeme's formal status then became that of "government students" (*guansheng*), a ranking equivalent to students of the Imperial Academy (*jiansheng*).[61] They became, in effect, stipendiaries of the state.

In keeping with the CEM regimen, Jeme had been given a travel and clothing allowance of 790 taels, at the time equivalent to about 1,185 U.S. dollars. For special occasions he and the other boys were provided a set of official robes, including a long gown, jacket, and satin shoes, along with a shining "cadet button" to signify rank and status. Like the others selected for the first dispatch, the front door of Jeme's family home was adorned with an ornate poster, embellished with large gold letters, announcing to all who passed that a great honor had been bestowed on one of its members.

In America Jeme shared a room with fellow student Pawn Wing Chung (Pan Mingzhong) in the West Haven home of Luther H. and Martha Northrop. Jeme adapted easily and was a member of the Orientals baseball team at Yale, where he earned a PhB in civil engineering from the Sheffield Scientific School, along with two mathematics awards.

Returning home to China, Jeme had been first assigned to the Foochow arsenal school to study navigation and in 1884 became a naval officer after demonstrating great valor in the battle of Ma-wei. His naval career would be brief, however. Jeme had a fateful meeting with Wu T'ing-fang, the director of the New China Railway Company, who offered him a position in railroad construction and administration in northern China.[62] Jeme accepted the offer, and in this capacity would in 1895 become the first Chinese member of the English Institute of Civil Engineers.

His move into the top ranks escalated in 1902, when the government decided to build a railroad line between Kao-pei-tien and Liang-ke-chuang, to accommodate an upcoming journey planned by the empress dowager. The original plans were to employ a British engineer for the endeavor but the French objected, as the new line would tie in with the Peking-Hankow Railroad, a venture France had financed. To avoid any Anglo-French discord, the Chinese government decided instead to do something unprecedented. They assigned one of their own—American-educated engineer Jeme Tien Yau. Working extraordinarily long hours with his crews and borrowing available stock from other lines, Jeme successfully completed the project right on time, a remarkable accomplishment that brought him considerable acclaim in official circles in China and worldwide.

Just two years later, in 1904, the Chinese government decided to build another line, this time between Peking and Kalgan, and again tensions sparked between two foreign powers—Russia and Britain. Both countries had an interest in the region, and both demanded a stake in the project. Negotiations became so heated that once again China turned to Jeme. Neither the Russians nor the British believed Jeme and his Chinese crews had engineering expertise sufficient to build a railroad through the treacherous terrain of the mountainous regions. If it could actually be done, everyone agreed, it would be the most ambitious railway project ever accomplished in China.

Construction on the 250-kilometer track began in 1905, despite a litany of problems and some unanticipated hurdles, such as the refusal of one Manchu family to allow the laying of the line through their ancestral gravesite. Jeme assuaged their fears by conducting a ceremony dedicated to the ancestors of the family and by agreeing to create a creek between the tomb and the track. Despite these and many other complications, the railroad was successfully completed on May 17, 1909—four months ahead of schedule and at a cost considerably less than that of foreign-constructed lines.

The Chinese officials were elated. While the railroad itself was a critical triumph in China's quest for modernization, perhaps just as important was the achievement's psychological impact on the Chinese people. The Peking-Kalgan line had been the most difficult railroad construction in China's history. Most importantly, it was also the first railroad entirely financed, designed, and built completely by the Chinese.

Jeme never revisited the United States and the institutions where he studied, as some of his CEM classmates had, but he did send his two eldest sons to America to be educated. Both went as part of the entourage led by special envoy Tang Shaoyi (another former CEM student) in 1908.

Liang Dunyan

A member of the Orientals baseball team, southpaw pitcher Liang Dunyan (Liang Tun Yen) was a natural athlete. He also excelled at football (he liked football, he said, but he loved baseball)—talents that made him a popular figure on campus and in the community.

Born on November 4, 1858, in Langyan Village, Guangdong Province, Liang was the son of a merchant and at age thirteen Liang was among the thirty boys included in the CEM's first detachment. Liang was especially bright. He was allotted a period of two years after his arrival in America to learn English and other subjects sufficient for admittance to Connecticut schools. Liang learned quickly and after only one year of tutoring by his host family the Bartletts, he was admitted to Hartford West Middle School, where he attended until 1874. He then enrolled in Hartford Public High School.[63] At his graduation ceremony in April 1878 Liang demonstrated his fluency in English by reciting his own essay on the recent Russo-Turkish War (1877–78) titled "The Northern Bear." During the recitation he scolded Russia for being a "thief dressed in the uniform of the police"[64] and called upon European countries to unite against Russian ambitions. He was admitted to Yale soon afterwards and attended there until the time of the recall in 1881. In addition to his talents in English and on the athletic field, Liang was also a member of Kappa Sigma Epsilon Freshman Society and Delta Kappa Epsilon.[65] In 1881 he was reportedly disappointed not to be among those elected to join either Scroll and Key or Skull and Bones. Then as now, as historian Rhodes put it, their membership was supremely exclusive.

When Liang returned to China in 1881 he was among those assigned to the telegraph service, along with about twenty other students of the CEM.[66] One of his first responsibilities was to teach English in the government telegraph office in Tianjin, but in 1883 he returned to Guangzhou to serve as secretary and advisor to Zhang Zhidong, the governor-general of the provinces of Kuangtung and Kuangsi. In this position Liang rose in status along with Zhang.

In 1900 Liang was instrumental in helping to maintain relations with foreign consuls to secure peace in the Yangtze region and in 1904 he was promoted to Customs Daotai at Hankou, and then later assumed the position of Director of Beijing-Fengtian Railway. In 1904–07 Liang served as president of Beiyang University in Tianjin, and helped establish Tsinghua College to prepare students for study in the United States under the Boxer Indemnity program. In 1906 he was appointed chief commissioner to inquire into the causes of the Nanjing massacre and he helped resolve China's diplomatic split with France. By 1907 he had been appointed comptroller general of Imperial Maritime Customs, then later held the position of vice president of the Board of Foreign Affairs.

In 1910 Liang was sent on a special diplomatic mission to Europe before being appointed minister-at-large for Europe and America. In 1911 he was appointed minister of state in Yuan Shikai's cabinet for the first republican government and in this position held authority over all forms of communications in China, including railroads, steamship lines, and telegraph and telephone systems.[67] From 1914 until 1916 Liang served as minister of communications for the republic and was minister of Foreign Affairs during the Qing restoration. He worked in this capacity until his passing in 1924. Liang would leave behind two sons. His only daughter would marry the second son of his old friend and former CEM classmate Jeme Tien Yau.

Y. T. Woo

In ancient times, China was first to develop mining on a large scale and for centuries had created uses for the important metals. More recent excavations have unearthed evidence of China's tremendous skills in metallurgy, such as those used to cast the funerary bronzes made by the Shang peoples

Figure 3.2 Y. T. Woo; Thomas LaFargue Papers, Manuscripts, Archives and Special Collections, Washington State University Libraries.

in the second and first millennia BCE. Early Chinese invented bamboo drills fastened to the ends of long ropes, which could bore salt wells to a depth of several hundred feet. By the T'ang Dynasty China was prospecting by means of core boring or drilling, but despite their precocious metallurgy skills mining did not gain real importance to the Chinese until the nineteenth century, with the invention of steamships and steam engines. By midcentury large iron and coal resources were being mined to support these and other "modernizations" as part of China's self-strengthening program.[68]

Y. T. Woo (Woo Yung Tsang; Wu Yangzeng) was born in 1862 in Sihui, Guangdong Province. At about age ten he was sent to the United States with the first CEM dispatch, and moved in with David and Fanny Bartlett. He attended Hartford West Public High School and then enrolled in Columbia College School of Mines, but to his regret was recalled to China before he could graduate. He would later complete his training at the Royal School of Mines in London.

In 1881, as the recalled CEM students were being assigned to the various industries in China, the Kaiping mines were already well-developed and a section of railroad had been constructed to haul the excavated coal to a canal for shipment to Tientsen. With the return of the American-educated students the directors of the mines saw an opportunity to establish a school of assaying and mining at Tongshan. Seven of the returned students attended the new school, where they were taught by an American engineer, E. K. Buttles. One of those returned students was Woo Yang-tsang, better known as Y. T "Alligator" Woo among his constituents.

Woo's first official assignment in China was with the Tongshan mines, where he was commissioned by Governor Sheng Xuanhuai to make a survey of the mineral deposits in Hubei and Zhejiang provinces. In 1899 Woo was appointed assistant director and chief chemist at Kaiping Mining Company and the following year organized miners to resist the Russian invading forces that were attempting to take over the company. In 1906 he served as assistant examiner for returned students from Europe and America and as advisor to the Board of Education.

Woo is probably the most well-known American-educated contributor to China's mining industry, but several other former CEM students were also successful in establishing careers in mining after their assignment to the Tongshan school: Kwong Young-kong, who became engineer-in-chief at the Lin Cheng facility in Chihli and helped to establish valuation of the Pen His-hu coal mines; Tong Kwo-on, who would become president of Tsinghua College. Chun Wing-kwai, Lok Sik-kwai, Liang Pao-chew, and Kwong King-yang were also important contributors to the development of China's modern mining industry.[69]

Luk Wing Chuan

Born in 1859 in Xiangshan, Guangdong Province, Luk Wing Chuan (Lu Yongquan) also went to the United States with the first detachment, where he set up residence with his first American host, Julia Leavett Richards. He attended the Gunnery School and Norwich Free Academy in Connecticut as well as Yale's Sheffield Scientific School, where he studied civil engineering and was a member of Alpha Chi fraternity.[70]

Luk's first assignment in China was to attend the Foochow Naval School but he returned to the United States soon after, in 1882—one of only a handful of CEM students to find a means of finishing his American studies. Using a furlough he had obtained with the excuse that he wanted to visit his parents, somewhere along the way he diverted his path to America.[71]

After completing his degree at the Sheffield Scientific School in 1883, Luk held the position of Chinese vice-consul in Nevada (1898–1909), then served as vice-consul at the Chinese Consulate in New York. On July 31, 1909, during his term as vice-consul and after a scuffle in the consulate, Luk Wing Chuan was fatally shot by an unemployed Chinese man, identified by police as Wong Bow Cheung. He was survived by his American wife Margaret Lock Wing.

Ouyang King

Ouyang King (Ouyang Geng, Keng Owyang) was another CEM student who graduated from Yale's Sheffield Scientific School, earning a degree in dynamic (mechanical) engineering, along with Zhan Tianyou, who was awarded a degree in civil engineering.[72]

Ouyang was born in 1858 in Daling Village, Xiangshan district, Guangdong, and he was sent to America in 1872. He was first assigned to live with Guy B. Day, who ran a school in Bridgeport but was later relocated to the home of Luther Hopkins Northrop and his wife, who operated the Seaside Institute in West Haven. He also lived for a time with Henry A. Street in New Haven. Ouyang attended the school in Bridgeport and also the Seaside Institute and then later enrolled at Yale's Sheffield Scientific School, earning a PhB degree in 1881.

Quyang King was another of the students who managed to get back to the United States after the CEM recall.[73] After a brief stint at the Foochow Naval School and after graduation, Ouyang was put on board flagship *Yang Wu* for training. Here he applied for and was granted leave by the Chinese government to return to the United States in 1883 to continue his studies, for a period of one year. Upon completion he entered the Chinese Consular Service in New York City and in 1884 was appointed vice-consul for San Francisco.[74]

Reportedly, Ouyang was asked to resign from his post in 1894 by Yang Yu, Chinese minister in Washington, DC, for disobeying instructions and for an alleged criminal offense.[75] Apparently he had been linked with the smuggling of Chinese prostitutes to the United States. Another man, Hor Shee, had been accused of the crime, but Yang suspected Ouyang's involvement and ordered his dismissal. Ouyang refused to resign, however, and demanded an investigation to clear his name, a move that must have worked, as he continued in the position for several more years.

In 1895 Ouyang was sent to Mexico to investigate conditions there, with the aim of negotiating a treaty with the government that would allow the immigration of Chinese. His efforts culminated in the Sino-Mexican Treaty of December 1899.[76] He was also dispatched to Vancouver, British Columbia, to deal with local violence against the Chinese.[77]

In 1906, Ouyang and his family lost their home and possessions in the great San Francisco earthquake and fire, when large areas of the city were devastated, including parts of Chinatown. The Consulate building, where Ouyang and his family had lived, was completely destroyed. Living in a rented house in Oakland, Ouyang reportedly worked long days helping less fortunate Chinese families recover, and he served as a member of the Chinese delegation negotiating with the state and municipal authorities regarding the relocation of the affected Chinese, and the reconstruction of properties.[78]

In 1909 Ouyang was appointed China's first consul to Rangoon, Burma, and in 1912 he became consul general to Java. From 1917 until 1921 he served as first secretary of the Chinese legation at London and then his final service was as chargé d'affaires to Chile (1921–1927). Ouyang fathered seven children, two with his first wife Lillian Tian Loy, an American-born Chinese woman who studied medicine at Chicago's College of Physicians and Surgeons; and five others with his second.

Wong Kai-kah

A few former students of the CEM turned their successes in the workplace into diplomatic careers and some advanced to the highest ranks of government. Wong "Breezy Jack" Kai-kah (Huang Kaijia, Kie Kah Wong) was known for his gift of eloquence and his friends claimed he could make a flamboyant speech anytime, anywhere—even "when shaken from a sound slumber."[79]

Born on March 13, 1860, in Chenping, Guangdong Province, Wong went to America with the first CEM student detachment. His first host was David Bartlett, who had taken in many of the CEM boys, and he attended both West Middle Public School and Hartford High School, graduating in 1879. At Yale, Wong was a member of the Orientals baseball team, a member of Kappa Sigma Epsilon Freshmen Society, and in his graduation exercises was one of ten students appointed to give an oration.[80] His grand and eloquent speech on the life of French minister Jean Baptiste Colbert was received with hearty applause and a basket of flowers, according to an article in the *Hartford Daily Courant*.

Wong's first assignment upon returning to China was translator at Shanghai Water Conservancy Bureau and then later, for the personal staff of Sheng Xuanhuai, he would become managing director of China merchants Steam Navigation Company and Government Telegraph Administration and in 1898 Wong was appointed secretary of the Imperial Railway.

Wong worked with Shen Kung-pao, the managing director of the China Merchant's Steam Navigation Company, and he also served as secretary to various princely envoys that the Chinese government sent to America and Europe. In 1902, as secretary to the embassy, Wong was sent to England by the imperial government to attend the coronation of King Edward VII. Returning to China via the United States, he attended the Washington conference where he met President Theodore Roosevelt. Wong was decorated by the emperor upon his return to China.

In 1903, as China's vice-commissioner at the Louisiana Purchase Exposition, Wong brought his family with him to St. Louis, Missouri, to help with the construction of the Chinese exhibit. Wong's wife planned the interior decorations and helped supervise the work until its completion. As assistant imperial commissioner, Wong accompanied Prince Pu Lun to the United States in 1904 to the St. Louis Exposition and later to a visit to Washington, DC.

The following year Wong returned to the United States as a member of the Chinese delegation at the Portsmouth Peace Conference in New Hampshire, which concluded the Russo-Japanese War. He was on his way back to China from the conference when he lost his life in a freak accident. Suffering from what was diagnosed as nervous exhaustion, Wong had been advised to recuperate in a health resort in Japan. While at the facility he entered a bathroom and was overcome by charcoal fumes, causing him to fall against the stove, which overturned and burned him severely. He was rushed to Yokohama General Hospital but died in a matter of hours. He and his wife, Ji Su Tsung of Shanghai, had four children.

Liang Cheng

There exists only fragmentary information about the parentage of most of the CEM boys—only about one-sixth are well-documented. From this limited information it appears that only about four CEM boys came from scholar-official families, among them Liang Cheng, Li Enfu, Rong Kui, and Liu Yulin.

Liang Cheng was the son of a merchant and the nephew of Liang Zhaohuang, a metropolitan degree holder (*jinshi*) who had risen to hold the high-ranking post of prefect of Shuntian. He arrived in America with the fourth dispatch in 1875 at age eleven and later studied Greek at Amherst College, then attended Phillips Andover Academy, where he played on the baseball team.

Baseball rivalries between New England high schools at that time could be intense. At Exeter, New Hampshire, the June 1881 annual baseball game between Phillips Academy in Andover and Phillips Exeter Academy was no exception. Center fielder Liang Cheng hit a triple, driving in two runs, helping visiting Andover win the game, 13–5. There was great celebration.[81] When Liang and his Andover teammates returned home from their win over Exeter, a crowd was waiting at the station. "When the train arrived with the victorious nine, the whole school turned out. . . ." The team was greeted with torchlights and a brass band, along with an omnibus drawn by cheering students with a long rope. "Even Rome could not have received Caesar with greater enthusiasm. . . . "[82] Liang's hopes to attend Yale were thwarted by the 1881 recall—however, he did gain acclaim for helping to introduce China to American baseball.

All of the CEM students encountered problems when they were ordered back to their homeland, but Liang's initial return to China turned out to be especially difficult. In early March 1882, five months after returning to China with the second group, Liang still had not been allowed to see his family. Being a Christian brought with it additional problems. At Tianjin Naval Academy, where Liang had been assigned, he confided to an American friend that although he was compelled to work on Sunday, he tried his best to "keep it holy in my heart."[83]

Liang went on to work with the Ministry of Foreign Affairs and served in Europe and was knighted in England in 1897. A year later he accompanied Prince Chun to Berlin to officially apologize to the Kaiser court for the killing of German subjects in Shandong. From 1903 until 1907 he served as China's minister to the United States and to Germany from 1910 until the end of the dynasty. It was Liang Cheng, during his term as minister to the U.S., who was instrumental in convincing Theodore Roosevelt in 1907 to remit the excess portion of the American share of the Boxer indemnity (discussed further in Chapter 4) for educational scholarship.

Tang Shaoyi

Among the most influential of the former CEM students to gain a high position with the Chinese government was Tang Shaoyi (Tong Shao Yi), known by his American friends as "Ajax." Born in 1862 in Xiangshan, Guangdong, he had traveled to the United States with the third dispatch of CEM students when he was twelve years old. He first attended Hooker Street Grammar School in Springfield, then Hartford Public School, where he graduated with honors before enrolling at Columbia. His American hosts were Eugene and Harriet Gardner of Springfield, Massachusetts, and William and Virginia Smith of Hartford, Connecticut. However, after studying only a brief time at Columbia, the mission was recalled and Tang returned to China in 1881.

Upon his return he was first assigned to clerical work, but in 1882 became an assistant to the imperial customs inspector in Korea, P. G. Von Mollendorf. In 1884 Tang gained the approbation of Yuan Shikai, the imperial resident in Korea and garrison commander in Seoul. After serving as consul general for two years, he was recalled to China, where he became secretary to Yuan at the headquarters of the newly created army, and was charged with managing the Northern Railways. By 1899 he was chief political adviser to Yuan in Shandong and head of the provincial trade bureau. Tang was in Tianjin during the Boxer Rebellion and helped handle both the chaotic aftermath and the foreign claims for reparation throughout Chihli Province.

In 1901 Tang was appointed customs daotai at Tianjin; and from 1903 to 1904 served as superintendent of Beiyang University (now Tianjin University). In 1904 he was appointed as a special commissioner for Tibetan affairs and was made minister to the Court of St. James for negotiations with the British in Calcutta, and two years later he signed an agreement with the British recognizing Chinese sovereignty over Tibet. Around this time he also served as associate controller general of the new revenue council in the Imperial Maritime Customs, and was director general of Peking-Hankow. Then, as president of the Board of Posts and Communications, Tang replaced Yung Shikai's control over the telegraphs, railways, and China Merchants Steam Navigation Company.

In 1907 Tang signed an agreement with the British for the construction of the Canton-Kowloon railway, but was soon impeached by conservative enemies. In April of the same year he would be appointed governor of Fengtien and in that capacity negotiated with U.S. Consul General Willard Straight for currency reform and for the construction of a railroad to compete with the Japanese South Manchurian railway.

Apparently around this time Tang was officially degraded by the imperial government because he had practiced nepotism. However, he was later restored to full favor, according to an article in the *New York Times* in 1907.[84]

In 1909 Tang Shaoyi was appointed as imperial commissioner to visit Washington, DC, to officially thank the United States government for refunding a portion of the Boxer indemnity. Unfortunately his visit coincided with the official mourning period for the passing of the emperor and empress dowager, preventing him from attending any public functions or festivities—so many were unaware of his visit. "If they had been able to meet him, they would have been impressed by his intellectual keenness, by his suavity of manner, as well as by the appearance of forceful resolution," said the *New York Times*.

Tang lost his post as governor of Fengtien upon the retirement of Yuan Shikai. In 1910 he was appointed expectant vice president of the Board of Communications, but resigned early in 1911, before the outbreak of revolution and the reinstatement of Yuan Shikai as supreme military commander of the imperial forces. Tang, who was in support of the abdication of the Yuangong emperor, was instated as president of the Board of Communications and minister of communications in Yuan's cabinet. Tang went on to become an important contributor to the establishment of the new Republic of China.[85]

In 1911 the "Cantonese Clique" of Tang Shaoyi, Liang Dunyan, Liang Yu-ho, Wu Ting Fan, and other Western-educated officials commanded such a level of influence that they are credited for being a driving force behind the creation of the new government. Critic J. O. P. Bland believed that without the active aid of this group it would have been impossible for Sun Yat-sen and the other revolutionary leaders to establish the Republic of China.

In 1912 Tang was appointed premier when Yuan was elected president of the new republic, but clashed with Yuan over conditions governing the negotiation of foreign loans, among other things. In June he retired to Tianjin.

In 1916 Tang joined the opposition to Yuan's dissolution of the National Assembly and his new "dynasty," turning his support to Sun Yat-sen's political regime in southern China. Tang opposed, however, on constitutional grounds, Sun's taking of the "Extraordinary Presidency" in 1921 and during the 1920s refused several offers to return to government service. In 1929 he was named by Chiang Kai-shek as "superior adviser" to the national government at Nanking, but he ignored that appointment as well. It was not until 1934 that he assumed the position of the head of the Zhongshan district and helped plan the Zhongshan Port project to improve the local economy.

Tang Shaoyi retired at his home in Shanghai in 1934, but reportedly due to rumors that he was secretly negotiating with the Japanese (then in control of northern China) he was assassinated, reportedly with an ax.

OTHER NOTABLE CEM STUDENTS

The above list of former CEM students' accomplishments is by no means complete.[86] Other American-educated returnees whose occupations contributed to China's early modernization include Woo "Big Nose" Chung-yen, who helped in the formation of China's modern army and served as consul general to Yokohama. Chung "Munny" Men-yew, the "little coxswain" from the Yale rowing crew, went on to become secretary to the Chinese Legation at Washington, then chargé d'affaires to Madrid, and later consul general at Manila. Munny supervised the construction of the Shanghai-Nanking Railroad and finally became commissioner of the railway.

Liang Yu Ho "Charlie Cold Fish" rose to high positions in the Korean service and among other accomplishments helped to construct the twenty-seven-mile branch line of the Peking-Tientsin railway to the Western Masolea. Liang was later appointed to commissioner of customs at Newchang, the most important port in Manchuria, a post traditionally reserved for a Manchu of high rank. He also served as high adviser to the Chinese delegation to the Washington Conference.[87]

"Baby Ta Yeh," or Ching Ta Yeh, established telegraph lines connecting Peking with Mongolia and became the head of the telegraph service in Kyakhta and Manzhouli and Hei Monggol (Inner Mongolia). Chu "Flounder" Pao Fay became Managing Director of the Imperial Chinese Telegraph Administration, later serving as director of the Shanghai-Nanking Railroad Administration before being appointed to vice minister of communications in 1907, then vice president of the Board of Foreign Affairs.

Tong Yuen-chan, one of only two CEM boys who had been granted permission to cut off their queues during their time in America (presumably because the long braids interfered with their work in close proximity with certain machinery), became China's director general of the Imperial Telegraph Administration. Kee Ysu Yi was made director of the Mukden Electric Light Works in 1910 and later co-director of the Manchurian Mint. Liang Pe Yuk in 1903 assumed the Washington post as China's minister to the United States, then became director of the Canton-Hankow Railway, Canton section, and later was the Chinese minister to Berlin, representing China at the International Convention on the Prohibition of Opium at The Hague (1912).

Lin Yuen Fai became director of Beiyang Hospital, the first chief administrator of a Western-style hospital in China, and as Viceroy Li's personal physician Lin was credited for saving his life after an assassination attempt. Kwong King Yang became chief engineer for the Peking-Mukden Railway, the engineer-in-chief of Hankou Railway, Canton section, and then in 1912 was made chief engineer of the Peking-Kalgan-Shiyuan Railway. Kwong Pin Kong wrote a book, *The Metallurgy of Gold and Silver in China*. Tong Kwo On would become the first president of Tsinghua College.[88]

Given the remarkable record of achievements by the American-educated Chinese and their elevation in status, jealousy was bound to arise among the Mandarins. Although these Chinese-educated officials occupied high positions within the railway, telegraph service, mining industries, and most other critical arenas, these fields were becoming increasingly dependent on Western-trained engineers to conduct the actual business of developing and running the operations.

Thomas LaFargue makes the interesting point in *China's First Hundred* that almost without exception the CEM students never developed the revolutionary tendencies which had become so predominant in China at the turn of the century. They maintained their loyalty to the Qing Dynasty until the regime ended and only after the formation of the new republic did they change their allegiance. One of those students who changed his allegiance and joined the ranks of the new republic was former CEM student Liu Yu Lin, who became minister of the Republic of China to London.

Only one former CEM student was actively connected with any revolutionary party prior to the actual establishment of the Republic of China in 1912. Yung Sing-kew, better known by his Cantonese name Hoy Yung, had in 1891 met Sun Yat-sen, then a medical student at the Alice Memorial Hospital in Hong Kong. Sun later persuaded Hoy to join the Tung Ming Hui, Sun's revolutionary party, after which Hoy established the *China Daily News*, a publication designed to promote revolutionary sentiment in South China.[89]

Despite the shabby treatment the CEM students had been subjected to upon their arrival back in their homeland and the humiliating relegation to lower ranks during their first professional years, with time many contributed significantly to China's modernization, and several rose to high official ranks. On the eve of revolution, the fast-fading Qing court had the magnanimity to confess that it wished it had more of just such men as were turned out by the Chinese Educational Mission. To Yung Wing and others who had invested so heavily in the promotion of these first Sino-American education exchanges, the confession was a welcome sign that in the opening years of the twentieth century the Celestial Kingdom may have fully awakened to the idea of deep and comprehensive reform.

After the collapse of his educational plan in 1881, Yung Wing proposed several successive plans to the Qing government, for banking and railroad construction, but for various reasons none were adopted. Still very much "the runaway," the disappointed Yung once again leaned toward politics around 1898, when he hosted meetings for the leadership of the Reform Movement at his home in Beijing. It was an activity that would brand him as a criminal wanted by the Qing court. In fear of incarceration, or worse, Yung fled first to Hong Kong and then crossed the Pacific for the last time to the United States, where he would spend the rest of his years. While Yung may have considered himself a failure in his grand attempts to forever open China's doors to Western education, historians agree that his efforts were critical to the initiation of Sino-American academic exchange. Yung's work was a driving force behind two history-making changes in China—the introduction of machines and the imperial decision to seek Western education in the United States.

Those grand accomplishments would not be the sum of Yung Wing's legacy. While the CEM students were still in America, Yung had offered to bestow a collection of 1,237 volumes of Chinese texts on Yale if the school would consider establishing a professorship in Chinese languages and literature. "I hope Yale will not delay this matter long lest Harvard anticipate us," he urged. This laid the foundation for the university's East Asia Studies program and Yung's friend Samuel Wells Williams would become Yale's first professor of Chinese language and literature. Shortly before he died, Williams left a bequest to Yale earmarked to fund the teaching of the Chinese language or to assist "worthy Chinese students in the college who may be in need." The Williams Fund was created in 1903 and is Yale's earliest China-related endowment.

Yung Wing passed away in Hartford in 1912 and was buried in the local cemetery, and today his portrait hangs proudly alongside other prominent graduates in Yale's University Center. His prized collection of Chinese books, bequeathed to his alma mater, formed the nucleus of Yale's Sterling East Asian book compilation, one of the finest collections of its kind in the West, a continuing subsidy for enlightenment.

4 Righteous and Harmonious Fists

> " . . . now is the time for the West to implant its ideals in the Orient, in such fashion as to minimize the chance of a dreadful future clash between two radically different and hostile civilizations; if we wait until tomorrow, we may find that we have waited too long."[1]
>
> Theodore Roosevelt, 1908

After the recall of the Chinese Educational Mission in 1881, a few students still came to the United States under governmental or provincial scholarship, and following China's defeat by Japan in 1895 there was some renewed interest in the attainment of outside knowledge. The Self-Strengthening Movement, the late-century attempt to modernize China (which had included the CEM project) had fallen far short of the Qing government's ambitions. So to avoid a second disappointment, the Qing court's next approach to study abroad would be qualitatively different from the first. The movement had failed, most believed, because the elite had not taken Western learning seriously, and because the scope of study had been too narrowly confined to the acquisition of machines and military expertise. To truly modernize China the study-abroad program should be broadened to include students who would be groomed not just for the transfer of science and technology, but to become China's future political leaders.

The so-called failure of the CEM project was to some extent due to America's changing attitudes toward the Chinese, a downward spiral of public opinion that had been growing for years. Around 1875 the United States started to implement policies intended to regulate immigration—the first prohibiting entry of persons regarded to be of a "loathsome class." By 1916 the list of undesirables grew to include those with physical or mental defects sufficient to prevent them from earning sufficient wages, as well as paupers and others likely to become a public charge. Contract laborers (such as the aforementioned "coolies" Yung Wing had lobbied against) were prohibited, along with assisted aliens, criminals, prostitutes, or females "of immoral purpose," persons with contagious diseases, felons, anarchists, polygamists, and the illiterate.[2]

On May 6, 1882, the Chinese Exclusion Act was ratified, making the Chinese the first people ever to be singled out by the United States for restricted immigration. The new law was intended to stop the arrival of Chinese laborers and it was also designed to bar Chinese from naturalization. There were few exemptions—among them teachers, consular officials, tourists, and their spouses and children. Any Chinese who were already living in the United States when the act took effect were also allowed to leave and return. The act would be renewed ten years later and then in 1904 it was made permanent, until its repeal four decades after that.

In part due to growing tensions over immigration and other issues, between 1881 and 1909 Chinese enrollments in Western institutions were sporadic. In 1899 the university at Tientsin dispatched a number of students to the United States after making a direct appeal to Sheng Hsuan-huai, the sponsoring official in Shanghai. In 1903 Peking University sent sixteen students to various Western universities and Hupeh Province alone sent 103 students to Europe and America in 1906. The provincial scholarship students who went to America were placed under the direction of supervisors appointed by sponsoring officials. The Peiyang group sent to the United States in 1901 was for a time supervised by John Fryer, English educator and founder of the Anglo-Chinese College in Shanghai.[3]

Until around 1900, in addition to government and provincial scholarships were sponsorships by Christian groups. Christian organizations had in fact been influencing China's study-abroad programs for many centuries. Even as early as 1650 there is documentation of Chinese students who traveled to Roman academies under the aegis of the Catholic Church, and in the nineteenth century Yung Wing, the first Chinese student in America, was also mentored by Christians. After 1900 government scholarships, those awarded at both the central and the provincial levels, became the principal form of support for students going abroad until after 1909, when the Boxer Indemnity fellowships initiated the so-called second wave of Chinese student enrollments in America.[4]

It was China's defeat to Japan that had kept the Celestial Kingdom in modest pursuit of Western education—a necessary evil if they were to survive the onslaught of Western machines. Japan's victory, from China's perspective, was not just a defeat by some other country but a humbling submission to the powers represented by the West and their exported technologies—subjugation by people with the "morals of animals . . . by inventing powerful machines this outside world [Westerners] had overwhelmed the order of man and nature that created civilization and the good life."[5]

As usual the conservatives in China clung fast to isolationism. If the first Self-Strengthening Movement had not succeeded in shielding China from yet another barbarian encroachment, they reasoned, why should a second attempt bear a different result? Those in favor of reform understood that, to win the support of the conservatives, any further efforts toward change would have to be justified—not just in practical terms, but in the context of Confucian ideology.

SUPPORTERS OF EDUCATION REFORM IN CHINA

Changzhou scholar Kang Youwei was one who helped put the idea of reform into terms the empire could accept—a philosophical sanction that could justify the borrowing of foreign knowledge. Kang uncovered such a justification in Confucianism itself. Using the very tradition that had been historically cited to support the rejection of change, Kang was able to redefine the ancient tenets to justify China's need for reform.

Earlier Qing scholars had criticized the authenticity of the "Ancient Text" versions of the classics, which had buttressed Neo-Confucian orthodoxy since the Song Dynasty. The terminology seems oddly reversed because what is termed the "New Text" versions are actually the oldest, from the Earlier Han. The so-called Ancient Text versions followed and became the standard for the Later Han, remaining so as the Song philosophers established the synthesis called Neo-Confucianism. Repudiating the Ancient Text in favor of the New Text versions (they were older and presumably more authentic) presented a unique opportunity to escape the Neo-Confucian dominion and reinterpret the tradition.

In 1891 Kang published the *Study of the Classics Forged During the Xin Period* (CE 9–23). In this study, using the New Texts to back up his assertion, he argued that the Confucian philosophies honored by the Song scholars may not have been entirely those of Confucius.[6] Kang wrote that, according to the most ancient Confucian teachings, the world had three stages. The first was disorder and a period of chaos. The second an era of change, approaching peace and "small tranquility," and the third stage would be one of universal peace and complete tranquility. According to Kang, in the 1890s the world was unquestionably entering the second stage, a period calling for evolution and progress. In this way he justified for the empire, in acceptable Confucian terms, the changes in China that now seemed eminent.

Joining the voice of reform and likewise questioning the success of the Self-Strengthening Movement was Zhang Zhidong, the viceroy of Hubei and Hunan. This new show of support was a fundamental change of heart. Only a few years before, Zhang had entreated the emperor to rid China of all foreigners, first by setting all the Christian churches on fire, and then by educating the Chinese public of Westerners' propensity for evil.

But in 1898 Zhang abruptly reversed his plea to one of reform. In the tract *Quan Xue Pian* (An Exhortation to Learn) he proposed overarching modifications of just about everything except politics, using what he called combined knowledge—Chinese learning "for the essence" and Western learning for practical use. Dynastic rule and Confucianism were, Zhang believed, crucial for saving China and its rich traditions. But without the practical application of Western technology, he conceded, China seemed destined to perish. Zhang's tract was immediately endorsed by the young emperor Guangxu, who at once sponsored what he envisioned to be an important move toward modernization. His efforts would be cut short, however, at the hands of Empress Dowager Cixi.

The dowager Cixi had been ruling China from "behind imperial yellow curtains" for nearly four decades. Serving first as regent for her young son and then for her nephew, she had exiled, killed, or imprisoned all reformers she believed could be a threat to her supremacy. Zhang's life had been spared only because of their long friendship. During the Hundred Days of Reform, between June 11 and September 21, 1898, the Emperor Guangxu had issued decrees aimed at modernizing China, its administration, education, laws, economy, and military. But even as Guangxu's proclamations were officially sanctioned, they would remain largely on paper while everyone waited anxiously to see what the empress dowager would do.

Cixi's decision was a coup d'état. Fearing for his life, Kang Youwei managed to flee to Japan but the Emperor Guangxu was not so fortunate. He was captured and imprisoned, confined to an island in the palace lake surrounded by the imperial guard. Six other officials who had publicly supported the reform movement were found and executed. It was an episode that further helped to imbed the isolationist ideals of the die-hard Manchu princes, whose palace upbringing had rendered them ignorant of the world "and proud of it."[7] In a last-ditch effort to hang onto the ancient lifestyle to which they had become accustomed, many in the imperial leadership would become patrons of a secret group called the Boxers, whose influence was quickly taking hold among China's peasant society.

THE BOXERS

By the late 1890s northwest Shandong had become a hotbed for banditry and feuds. Located on the floodplain of the Yellow River, the dense population was so poverty-stricken that most of the gentry had moved away and feuds between the villages were commonplace. Some of the tension had been generated by the growing presence of foreigners. For years German missionaries had been coming to the region, aggressive and relentless in their efforts to convert the assumedly "lost" villagers to Catholicism, sometimes attracting them with food, education, services, or occasionally by offering support in lawsuits involving non-Christians. Many of the local residents resented what they viewed as unwelcomed manipulation and arrogance.

Resentment against Christian missionaries and anti-Western sentiment had been mounting in the region for years, and the discontent slowly spread to the interior. Reports of anti-missionary riots were increasing in number and frequency and the Qing government, fearful of foreign retaliation, ordered the magistrates to avoid provoking the Christians any further. The local antagonists had little interest in following such a directive, so they circumvented imperial authority by simply going "underground." Shandong peasants went quietly about the task of forming secret clubs that could defend their interests, groups like the Big Sword Society, which was formed to serve as a force against bandit suppression.[8]

The Boxers, another secret society that developed during this time, combined two peasant traditions—the ancient practice of martial arts (boxing) and the rituals of spirit possession or shamanism. Taking on the slogan

"Support the Qing, destroy the foreign," the society was first known as the Spirit Boxers, then later Boxers United in Righteousness. Some sources also give reference to the name Righteous and Harmonious Fists. During their rituals each of the Boxers would reportedly go into a trance, foam at the mouth, and then arise ready for combat, spirit-possessed and convinced of his invulnerability to swords or bullets.

The Boxer movement gained popularity and expanded quickly from its origins in Shandong across North China. Despite attempts at secrecy, stories of the society's colorful and sometimes frightening activities became topics of regional folklore, and it was not long before accounts of the Boxers' antics found their way to the imperial court. Believing these activists represented the voice of the Chinese people, and recognizing an opportunity for public support, the Empress Dowager Cixi and the imperial leaders elected to work covertly with the secret society, rather than against it, in a combined effort to eliminate foreign influence in China.

By early 1900 anti-Western and anti-Christian sentiments had reached uncontainable levels in China, and the Boxers decided it was time to take action. In May a group of the society's members damaged the railroad at Dongzhou in retaliation for the "steam dragon" having ended the town's tradition of stealing portions of the tribute rice. For centuries the rice had been transported by easily pirated boats—food that could be easily stolen, sustenance upon which those residing near the ports had come to depend. Then in June the American board building in Dongzhou, along with the college, the new church, and several homes of foreigners, were set ablaze, reportedly at the hands of the Boxers. Just a few days after that, the Imperial Post Office was destroyed and telegraph lines were severed.

Cixi officially declared war on the occupying powers—Japan, Holland, Italy, Belgium, Spain, Russia, Austria, and Germany—just before the Boxers entered the capitol to do even more damage. The Methodist Mission was the first building they demolished, followed by Catholic cathedrals, orphanages, hospitals, the electric and light plant, and the Russian bank, all burned to the ground. As the terrifying siege continued, the empress dowager authorized imperial troops to join and fight alongside the Boxers in their common battle against "anything foreign."

The result was a bloody eight-week siege against thousands of foreigners living and working in and around Beijing's legations (pre-embassies). The Boxer Rebellion, or Boxer Uprising, was an onslaught that had involved about 475 foreign civilians, 450 troops from eight nations, and approximately 3,000 Chinese Christians. An estimated 250 foreigners, mostly American and European missionaries and their families, were slain in North China before the fighting finally subsided and hundreds more were injured. Killed also were 150 racing ponies that reportedly were sacrificed to supply fresh meat for the warring parties.[9]

The uprising became the subject of newspaper headlines around the world. Eight countries, including the United States, implemented the China

Relief Expedition, which quickly dispatched three infantry regiments and one cavalry regiment from the Philippines to join the Allied forces. On August 14 the expedition reached the capital, to the great relief of the Westerners and Chinese Christians. Cixi was nowhere to be found. Disguised in common dress and with her long imperial fingernails cut, she had fled the city the day before, anticipating that the Imperial Palace would come under attack.[10] The sack of the Forbidden City itself was ultimately prevented, however, through the protective efforts of American and Japanese troops.

On August 28 the allies marched through the center of the Beijing, displaying their national colors, impressing to the Chinese the further establishment of foreign authority over China and its affairs. Reportedly, some of the allied troops were observed looting and pillaging the unprotected areas of Beijing, contributing even further to the terror of local citizens. American Board missionary Arthur Smith reported that it seemed the troops were there not just to rescue the missionaries but for the purpose of committing within the shortest time as many violations as possible.

It was months before the allied powers could agree on China's punishment for the consequences of the Boxer Rebellion and in the end it was Li Hongzhang, the viceroy who had sponsored the Chinese Educational Mission, who helped negotiate the treaty terms. The allies had wanted to reinstate the Guangxu emperor but it was Li who persuaded them to instead advocate that the Empress Dowager Cixi continue to hold the reigns of China's power.

To compensate for the loss of lives and property incurred by the Boxer Rebellion, the articles of the treaty required an indemnity in the amount of 450 million taels, to be paid by the Chinese government over a period of thirty-nine years. Of the total indemnity, the United States was to receive 7.5 percent, or about 25 million dollars. Russia's share was the largest (29 percent), followed by France, Great Britain, Japan, Italy, and others.

The amounts provided to the United States were not arbitrary, nor were they based on actual losses. Secretary of State John Hay had instructed the American delegation to ask for $25 million and had also requested that the total claim not exceed $150 million. He intentionally inflated the cost of the losses, hoping to later offer a reduction of the claim as a bargaining chip to encourage the other treaty powers to reduce theirs as well—together offering China scaled-down claims in preference for trade privileges. The bargaining ploy failed, however, and China was now in considerable debt.

In addition to the indemnity, penalties were ordered for nine Chinese high officials who had supported the rebellion, including Governor Yu-Xian of Shanxi. Punishment took a variety of forms—some of the convicted were beheaded, some exiled, a few were forced to commit suicide, and others were simply degraded. Around 119 provincial officials were convicted of lesser offences. Elites who had supported the rebellion (as well as their offspring) were banished from taking the Confucian civil service examinations for a period of five years in the cities where foreigners had been attacked or killed. And fortifications between Taigu and Beijing were to be immediately dismantled. On these terms, Li Hongzhang and Prince Qing signed the Boxer Protocol on September 7, 1901, in a somber ceremony witnessed by representatives from each of the eight allied countries.

Four months passed before the empress dowager and her party finally returned to the Forbidden City to reoccupy the palace and resume control. Acting on Li's sage advice, she immediately proclaimed herself a reformer, especially of education.

TEDDY ROOSEVELT AND THE INDEMNITY SCHOLARSHIPS

Not everyone in the West agreed with the outcome of the Boxer situation. There were a number of outspoken Americans who were vehemently opposed to the actions of the allies in China, viewing the Boxer Protocol as eerily similar to British imperialism in America. Crushing the revolution in China was, in their view, counter to the democratic ideals of the United States. Connecticut author Mark Twain (Samuel Clemens) was among the first to publicly rebuke the Boxer reparations as adulterated in light of the accepted foundations of civilization—love, justice, gentleness, Christianity, liberty, equality, and the quest for education. President Roosevelt called him a "prize idiot."[11]

In 1901, as Theodore Roosevelt assumed his duties as president of the United States, he was convinced that whoever controlled China also determined the future. America's relations with the Chinese were complicated, however, and vexed by contradictions. The Chinese Exclusion Act, for example, was an enforcement of what many considered discriminatory immigration policies. There were those who warned of potential consequences—one such admonition came from missionary Luella Miner, who had spent many years working in China. She cautioned that the students and scholars who were being rejected from entering the United States for education might someday "wield a trenchant pen" whose anti-American words could circulate worldwide. Minor also pointed out that Russia might be quick to take advantage of America's exclusionary policies and use the situation to attract China's study-abroad candidates to its own institutions. In time they could circumvent Western ideals by simply replacing them with their own, through education.

Sino-American policies were at the time an anomaly. As the United States advocated that China open its doors for American merchants and missionaries, at the same time it closed its own to Chinese merchants, travelers, and students. Supreme Court justice David Brewer warned Roosevelt that such incongruity was ample cause for China to change from being a friend to an antagonist.

It was partly Roosevelt's fear of angering American voters that caused him to sign the renewal of the Chinese Exclusion Act. He was in agreement

Figure 4.1 Theodore Roosevelt, circa 1910.

with keeping Chinese laborers out of the country and, like many in the voting public, feared social upheaval from racial mixing. But at the same time he reprimanded U.S. immigration officers for treating higher-class Chinese harshly and ordered that students be treated with respect as stated in the law. The inconsistent mandates unfairly targeted those without money, education, or status, and to some extent it was Roosevelt's recognition of the inequity of America's policies toward the Chinese that moved him to remit the excess Boxer Rebellion indemnity funds a few years later.

Two related events preceded the remission. First was the establishment of America's open-door policy toward China in 1899–01, a move initiated by Secretary of State John Hay and formulated by Chinese scholar and diplomat William Rockhill, who had himself served in the legations in Beijing. In accordance with the new initiative the other treaty powers were asked to adhere to a principle of equal tariff, collected by the Chinese government on foreign vessels at the port cities, regardless of each power's sphere of influence. The powers proved uncooperative regarding the request, however, and the attempt was eventually abandoned.[12]

Then in 1905 there began an anti-American boycott in China. Rockhill, now U.S. minister to China, was under pressure to correct this issue—it was the first time China had ever refused foreign goods. The boycott was launched largely as a remonstration against U.S. policy on Chinese immigrants, but it was also a protest against violence against Chinese citizens in America and its courts. Rockhill met in Shanghai with the Chinese merchant guilds that had orchestrated the boycott and warned that the Chinese government would be held responsible for any losses incurred from disrupted trade. After the meeting Rockhill reported back to the American government that he believed he was witnessing an undercurrent of impending change in China—a rising public voice and a nascent patriotic spirit.

It was in this spirit of impending change that China's minister to Washington, Liang Cheng (a former CEM student), approached the American government about returning some of the "excess" Boxer Indemnity funds to the Chinese. Liang trumpeted the justice of such a remission publicly—in newspaper interviews, civic speeches, and in discussions with high-level officials. He suggested that "perhaps a revision of the figures could be made by which the President would be enabled to obtain a clearer sense of the justice of the request my Government has made."[13] Liang then wrote a plan for the revision and presented it to Secretary of State Hay, who in turn recommended it to the president. Roosevelt was interested in Hay's recommendation, but had a question. How did China plan to use the returned funds?

Liang and the imperial leadership at first resisted the idea of any returned money being regulated or restricted by the United States. Yuan Shikai, the powerful commissioner of China's northern ports, envisioned using the funds to build railways in Manchuria to provide a defense against potential Russian and Japanese aggression.[14] But Rockhill was immovable.

When Liang met with Rockhill in 1905 to draw up further plans to present to President Roosevelt, they concluded that the wrong answer to the president's pointed question might give him cause to withdraw from the negotiations. So Liang advised that the American government " . . . return the indemnity so that it can be used for establishing schools and sending students abroad. The American government will be pleased to gain a reputation of being just and to bear witness of the development of talent through education. . . . "[15]

In July, even as the Chinese boycott dragged on, Rockhill called upon the Ministry of Foreign Affairs and then wrote to Roosevelt, further assuring each of them that any amount of the indemnity returned to China by the United States should be solely devoted to educational purposes. The boycott ended in September but Roosevelt would not act on the remission for another year and a half. It was only after Liang Cheng revived the request to the president, through the efforts of Secretary of Interior James Garfield and Secretary of Commerce and Labor Oscar Straus, that Roosevelt finally agreed to put a plan in motion.[16]

Other sources, an article in the 1922 issue of the *Chinese Students Monthly,* for example, give substantial credit to Arthur Smith, a dean of American missionary educators and one of the few China experts at the time. The article cited "Recollections of Theodore Roosevelt," in which Lawrence F. Abbott provided his account of what initiated the idea:

> In 1906 Dr. Arthur H. Smith long an American missionary resident in China . . . came to our office to enlist our interest in a plan . . . which he wished to bring to President Roosevelt. His Plan . . . was that one-half of the Boxer indemnity, say about twelve million dollars, should be given back to China on the understanding that she use the money . . . for sending Chinese young men to American collegiate institutions in China.[17]

When Smith met with the president in the Red Room on March 6, 1906, he firmly advocated the remission and its potential for positive outcomes.[18]

Many Americans appreciated the idea of remitting China's indemnity for the pursuit of scholarship. The University of Illinois' president Edwin James penned a congratulatory letter to President Roosevelt saying "The nation which succeeds in educating the young Chinese of the present generation will be the nation which for a given expenditure of effort will reap the largest possible returns in moral, intellectual and commercial influence. . . . " James believed that if the United States had succeeded thirty-five years earlier "in turning the current of Chinese students to this country . . . we should to-day be controlling the development of China in that most satisfactory and subtle of all ways—through the intellectual and spiritual domination of its leaders."[19] This strong ideal appealed to Roosevelt, who wrote in a later monograph:

> The awakening of China is one of the great events of our age, and the remedy for the "yellow peril," whatever that may be, is not the repression of life but the cultivation and direction of life. . . . Our Christian missions have for their object not only the saving of souls, but the imparting of a life that makes possible the kingdom of God on the earth. It seems to me that there is no place where there is better opportunity to-day to do this work than in China . . . "[20]

At Andover's 129th commencement in 1907, Liang Cheng was asked to address the alumni, and during his speech he told a lighthearted story of the forceful three-base hit he made as a youth in a championship game 26 years earlier—a hit that had won the game for Andover against Phillips Exeter. Reportedly, after the event Roosevelt approached Liang and questioned whether he was in fact the same person who had made that legendary hit in 1881. Liang assured him that he was, and from that moment, Liang later recorded, "the relations between President Roosevelt and myself became ten-fold stronger and closer." In June of 1907 Liang was officially notified of the finalized remission. The "magnanimous act has won the lasting gratitude of the Government and people of China," said an exuberant Liang. Six months later, in December, Roosevelt asked Congress for authority to cancel all claims on China that were in excess of the actual losses incurred. Congress initially reduced the indemnity by two million, but on May 25, 1908, it authorized the remission 12 million.[21]

Several former CEM students were involved with the remission of the indemnity funds, a process that would effectively initiate a second wave of Chinese student enrollments in American colleges and universities. In late 1908 former CEM student Tang Shaoyi was dispatched by the Chinese government as a special envoy to Washington, his mission to officially thank the United States for the remission.[22] He attended the ceremony held in December and watched as Roosevelt signed the executive order. In early 1909 former CEM student Liang Dunyan, now president of the Foreign Ministry, forged the agreement that would stipulate the funds for sending Chinese students to American colleges. Yet another former CEM student, Tang Guoan, would escort the first of forty-seven Boxer Indemnity scholars, officially launching a new era of education exchange with the United States.

The Boxer Rebellion Indemnity Scholarship initiative was similar to the earlier Chinese Educational Mission in that it was designed to send large numbers of Chinese to study in the United States over extended periods of time. News of the remission immediately won public and private praise. The *New York Times* printed that it was an example to the world for the "principles of right and justice and high-mindedness that prevail between honorable men." Sarah Conger, wife of the U.S. minister to China and a survivor of the Boxer uprising at Beijing, wrote that the American government's decision to cancel the indemnity was " . . . an attitude too deep, too broad, too high for word expression . . . [its] seed was brought over in the Mayflower; it was planted in the virgin soil of liberty . . . sustained in Truth's fortitude."[23] The Indemnity Scholarship funds were set up to continue for 31 years, with a portion of the money set aside for the building of Tsinghua College, an institute that would prepare China's students for study in America.

The indemnity scholarships and the establishment of Tsinghua College, both pivotal moves toward education reform, coincided with a monumental and almost inconceivable shift in China's history—the end of four thousand years of continuous dynastic rule. With its demise came further foreign intrusion and the once isolated country was now teeming with people from Europe, Japan, and the United States. It was the passing of "a magical era in which China had inspired true wonder in those who beheld it with an open mind," observed anthropologist Berthold Laufer in 1911. "The romance of China died away with the end of the Chivalrous Manchu dynasty."[24]

THE SECOND WAVE

Tsinghua (Qinghua) College was still under construction during this time of transition. Until its completion the Office for Students Going to the United States (OSGUS) would be in charge of administering the first indemnity scholarship examinations. The two agencies that had set up the office, The Ministry of Foreign Affairs and the Ministry of Education, were in some disagreement as to the exact purpose of the effort and the selection of students. Among the issues were the ages of students to be admitted, and whether the Chinese or the English sections would be the most important components of the examination process.

The first exams were held in 1909, at a central location in Beijing, for a period of five days. They were free and open to all male citizens, and 640 students took part in the process. Preliminary tests focused on the Chinese and English languages, as well as China's history and geography. The one hundred students who passed the first round of examinations then took the second, which included physics, chemistry, biology, algebra, geography, and world history. In addition to passing these tests, students were required to be in excellent health and have an upright character. They should exhibit no defects in physical appearance and have an unblemished background. Forty-seven young men from eleven provinces were finally selected for the first dispatch.[25]

The group departed China in 1909, two years before the fall of the Qing dynasty and the establishment of the Republic of China. From the Imperial Maritime Customs Wharf in Shanghai they boarded a steamer and en route the students spent time studying English and learning American etiquette, much as the CEM boys had done almost forty years earlier. The *China* sailed into the "harbor of Gold Mountain" (a Chinese name for San Francisco) on November 6, 1909 where they met with customs inspectors and then entered under a special student status outlined in the Chinese Exclusion Act of 1882. The students' luggage was scrutinized thoroughly, as the inspector said he suspected smuggling, but everyone was eventually cleared to leave (although some reportedly had to completely repack).

From San Francisco they continued by rail to Chicago through the Rocky Mountains and across the American plains. To help them pass the time they were provided copies of the *Book for Chinese Students Going Abroad*, a publication produced by the Young Men's Christian Association (YMCA) to help acclimate the group to American culture. Like their CEM predecessors, the youths witnessed many marvels. Some later wrote about things that surprised them the most, like standing in lines or the frequency of encountering automation. There were automated chewing-gum dispensers, machines to determine one's weight, and boxes to collect streetcar fare, to name just a few. The students were surprised by the large amount of paper used on the trains, especially the disposable commodities such as toilet tissue, cups, and towels.

From Chicago the group traveled on to Washington, DC, where they were met by Yung Wing's nephew Yung Swai, who had been serving there since 1890, first as an interpreter and later as secretary and chargé d'affaires in the Chinese Legation. From Washington the students were escorted on to their final destination in Springfield, Massachusetts. The entire journey from Shanghai to Springfield, a distance of 15,000 miles, had taken thirty-seven days. The students were then distributed among five preparatory schools in the area, as it was too late in the fall semester to begin a university program.

The "second wave" was officially under way. The next set of examinations would be administered in Beijing a year later, in 1910—this time considerably more demanding and requiring greater proficiency in English. From these exams an additional seventy students were selected to go to America. The following year (1911) another seventy-three were dispatched.

TSINGHUA COLLEGE

Tsinghua Imperial College officially opened for business on April 29, 1911, and from that point assumed full responsibility for overseeing the examinations and selecting the Indemnity Scholarship students. The college had been constructed on the outskirts of Beijing at the site of a formal royal garden belonging to a prince. Sometimes called the "American Indemnity College," Tsinghua began as a preparatory two-year school but would later become a four-year university. It was expressly designed to prepare students planning to attend United States universities by means of the indemnity funding—Tsinghua's graduates would transfer directly to American schools as juniors upon graduation.

In many ways Tsinghua was unlike China's traditional institutions. Its first faculty members were recruited almost entirely from the United States, although they would be gradually replaced by returning indemnity scholars. By tradition professors in China had typically remained at one school. At Tsinghua the instructors could not only be replaced, but they sometimes moved on their own accord to other institutions. So instead of close teacher-student relations based on familial, village, or provincial ties, relations at Tsinghua were less personal and temporary, an environment more akin to the culture of American colleges.

Teachers at Tsinghua also had more financial security, academic freedom, and physical resources than did their colleagues in other institutions, chiefly because of the indemnity funds. Schools in China that depended on national or provincial monies could find themselves short of cash any time the government deemed it necessary to siphon off assets in support of military or other expenses.

The daily schedule at Tsinghua was also unlike other Chinese institutions. Instead of beginning the school year after the lunar New Year, classes began each autumn on an American academic calendar. In China's traditional academies (*shuyuan*) students were offered classes that combined history, ethics, and general knowledge and they were allowed to come and go as they liked, learning according to their own speed. At Tsinghua students were offered a succession of different subjects during the day and regular attendance was mandatory.

The rules for Tsinghua had changed because the goals were different. *Sishu*, the system used in China's traditional institutions, had prepared students to take the imperial examinations for service in the dynasty's bureaucracy. It was the intention of Tsinghua to prepare students for United States universities, with the expectation that they would return and lead the republic. Both systems selected students using geographic quotas.[26]

Tsinghua's location also set it apart from other institutions. Tsinghua was the only college campus operating outside Beijing's city gate and remained so until Yanjing University opened in 1926, one mile away. In its early years Tsinghua was a forty-five-minute journey (by donkey) from Beijing and so the faculty and students resided on campus. Tsinghua became less isolated when a bus line was established (1926) between the school and the YMCA building in eastern Beijing. After that, on Saturdays the older students could take the bus into the city for the day to shop and eat, and sometimes city dwellers would journey to the Tsinghua campus to enjoy the tranquility of the college grounds.

The campus itself stood out in its environment. Most of Tsinghua's first buildings were designed by American architects and had a very different style from neighboring structures. Even so, in the Chinese tradition of constructing simple houses behind elaborate gates, Tsinghua's college grounds were set behind an imposing entrance built of white masonry supported by four grand columns—two Doric and two Corinthian. Called *Yong En Si* or the Temple of Forever Blessings, the beautiful gate opened into the former Tsinghua Park, a garden known for its lovely lotus pond and towering trees.

The American-designed buildings were equipped with materials shipped in from the United States, such as musical instruments, laboratory supplies, and something particularly unusual—an assortment of sports equipment. Sports had not been taken seriously at Beida (a colloquial term for Beijing University) but Tsinghua was able to incorporate them into their system almost immediately. The timing of the adoption of sports events at Tsinghua happened to fit well with the new wave of nationalism that was growing in China and soon the various teams would become symbolic of Chinese patriotism. Tsinghua students demonstrated their patriotism by supporting their sports teams and also by participating in patriotic marches and wearing Chinese clothes to symbolically cover their "Western-thinking bodies."

Tsinghua students themselves would shape the cultural elements of the campus, such as songs and flags, into new nationalistic forms. They established a student union, chose their own leaders for the school newspaper, and began a yearbook called "The Tsinghuapper," with Tsinghua's beautiful front gate gracing the cover of the 1916 issue. Alongside growing national pride was a considerable amount of prestige that came from attending Tsinghua, because it guaranteed its students a round of study in the United States.[27]

Between 1912 and 1929, after Tsinghua assumed the job of administering the scholarships, the college sent a fairly steady flow of students to the United States using the Boxer Indemnity remission. The first group of sixteen Tsinghua-trained graduates set sail in 1912, but in 1913 none was sent due to a problem with the funding.[28] Beginning in 1914 Tsinghua graduates would be sent regularly to America and by 1929 some 1,268 Tsinghua students had studied in the United States with the support of the Boxer Indemnity funds.

According to regulations established in the 1909 joint memorials of the Board of Education and the *Wai-wu-pu*, 80 percent of the students sent to the United States were supposed to study technical subjects, such as agriculture, engineering, commerce, and mining. Twenty percent were to study law, finance, and education.[29] During the years 1909–1929, 32.33 percent were enrolled in engineering, 3.63 percent in agriculture, 16.18 percent in science and medicine, about 11 percent in military and political science and 10.38 percent in economics. About 11 percent were enrolled in business, 2.77 percent in law, and 5.04 percent in education. The rest studied social sciences or the humanities.

Studies were difficult at Tsinghua and the grading system led to a high attrition rate. Between 1911 and 1921 only 42 percent of those who entered the school graduated (636 out of 1,500); 301 were expelled, 135 left for personal or health reasons, and 45 died. However, for those who completed the program, graduation day was cause for celebration—parties and receptions were held, given by school officials, families, and dignitaries. Sun Yat-sen, future president of the new Republic of China, hosted a reception for the class of 1919, where he took the opportunity to warn the students not to neglect their own superior cultural heritage in their enthusiasm for Western education.

Graduates went then to Shanghai for final preparations and were provided 500 silver yuan to purchase an appropriate Western-style wardrobe. The local YMCA provided a hostel where they could stay until their departure and a man was put in special charge of securing passports—a task that took everyone else two weeks was accomplished for Tsinghua graduates in about twenty minutes.

Other obstacles were more difficult to overcome. Soon after Indemnity students arrived in America, it quickly became evident that education in the United States would not be without challenges. Many students discovered that their English preparation was thoroughly inadequate, and, as they worked to comprehend the vernacular, were discouraged by the language's intricate rules and seemingly endless lists of exceptions. It was frustrating to be misunderstood in social situations, but it was worse not to understand all that was being said in the classroom. "Partially blind, deaf and dumb," the students compensated by reading daily newspapers or weekly magazines, or by convincing willing American volunteers to help them practice conversation—always with a dictionary at hand.

Aside from the challenge of learning "American" English, there were financial issues as well. Indemnity scholarship recipients were provided a stipend of $60, which according to most accounts barely covered the most basic of living expenses. Finding a means of subsidizing the meager allowance could be difficult, as foreign students were prohibited from working off campus, according to American immigration policy. Some did find jobs on campus while others fished or picked fruit during the summers. Some tried housework or worked in local restaurants illegally while others managed by borrowing money from friends or by ducking payments of bills. Still, the Indemnity Scholarship students were for the most part better off than Chinese students who depended on government or family stipends. In times of crisis the imperial government had oftentimes withheld funds that were allotted for education, as when the Qing dynasty fell in 1911, for example, and when the Republican government dissolved in 1917. Educational funding was diverted again in the mid-1920s during a period when China was facing a financial crisis. Through each of these lags in governmental support for education, funds generated from the indemnity remission continued as usual.

EARLY EXCHANGE ORGANIZATIONS AND PARTNERSHIPS

The resurgence of Chinese students in America, combined with a general increase in foreign enrollments, prompted the birth of several important agencies of education exchange. Over time these organizations and initiatives would strongly influence academic trade with China.

Since its founding in 1901, the Yale-China Association contributed substantially to the "furtherance of understanding and knowledge between Chinese and American people." Although separately incorporated, the Yale-China Association is a close affiliate with Yale University. Its projects have included programs in a variety of fields, among them public health and nursing, legal education, English-language instruction, American Studies, and cultural exchange for Chinese and American students. Yale-China has been responsible for programs in Beijing, Changchun, Changsha, Chengdu, Guangzhou, Guiyang, Kunming, Ningbo, Tunxi, Urumqu, Wuhan, Xiamen, Xi'zn, and Hong Kong. Many of Yale-China's projects were intentionally situated in remote areas, distant from the prosperous coastal cities that had been traditional venues for most educational opportunities.

First incorporated as the Yale Foreign Missionary Society, the nondenominational association became popularly referred to as Yale-China around 1913. By the 1920s the society had ceased to be an overtly missionary initiative and in 1934 it was re-incorporated as a secular organization known as the Yale-in-China Association, until 1975 when the name officially changed to the Yale-China Association.

Founded by a group of Yale graduates and faculty members who were intent upon establishing a Christian missionary presence overseas, Yale-China was born in an era of religious fervor that swept American college campuses at the end of the nineteenth century. China was their first focus, chosen in part to honor 1892 Yale graduate Horace Tracy Pitkin, who served as a missionary in China and died tragically during the Boxer

Rebellion. The city of Changsha in Hunan Province, the founding members decided, would be Yale-China's base of operations.

Yale-China had been conceived for Christian purposes but under the influence of Dr. Edward Hume it grew to assume a more educational than evangelical function. By 1905 Hume's medical clinic in Changsha had grown into an extensive educational compound that would become the site of several preparatory institutions—the Yali Middle School (Yali is a Chinese transliteration of the word Yale), the College of Yale-in-China, and the Hsiang-Ya Medical College—a facility that developed a reputation for providing the most advanced training in Western medicine in all of central and southern China. The College of Yale-in-China later relocated to Wuhan and joined two other missionary colleges to form Huachung University.

Initially staffed almost entirely with Westerners, from the beginning Yale-China made an effort to bring in as many Chinese as possible. By the late 1920s all major leadership positions were held by Chinese, making Yale-China very much a joint Sino-American enterprise. As with most enterprises there were a few extraordinary individuals associated with the association's early history who earned a permanent place in Yale-China lore. Two examples are Frances Scherer and Tierong "Sophie" Zhu.[30]

Frances Scherer was born in Shanghai to American missionaries George and Mary Schlosser in 1929, about the time the United States was falling into deep economic depression. *To Be a Pilgrim,* Mrs. Scherer's self-published memoir, recounts her childhood years in China, describing her isolation as an offspring of foreign missionaries and the daily realities of China's struggle with poverty. She graduated from Yenjing University in 1936 but did not go on to medical school due to a serious illness, but also because the American depression had restricted available funding. In spite of these setbacks she went on to become a champion of helping others, both in China and in the United States.

In her book Scherer writes about her wartime experiences in Kaifeng as a member of the Free Methodist missionary staff. "Young men in ragged dirty uniforms were shattered for life," she recalled. "We had no antibiotics, no analgesics, not even enough aspirin to go around. Trains were coming in at the rate of three or four a day, sometimes with 200 to 600 men . . . we saw not one single weapon among them, nor even an officer who appeared to be in charge . . . the situation was one of total chaos." [31]

Three years later while in the United States Scherer was again inspired to help the wounded after Japan's attack on Pearl Harbor, and she enrolled in the Johns Hopkins School of Nursing. Shortly after graduation she was recruited by Dr. Edward Hume for the Yale-in-China program and found herself right back in China. This time she was asked to serve in Changsha—as the sole Western medical employee in a city that was nearly in ruins.

When Scherer arrived she found that many of the buildings and facilities had been destroyed by the war. In the medical units linens and scrubs were rarely washed, even more rarely sterilized. The nursing students that had remained were living in an attic with holes in the roof, providing them little or no protection from the torrential rains. Letters in the Yale-China Association archives document Scherer's impassioned appeals for support of any kind. "The work goes on . . . ideals are still high and now that peace is here again the standards are rising and there is new hope. . . . "[32] But any hint of optimism would disappear in 1948 as the situation further deteriorated, forcing Scherer and her husband to evacuate Changsha. With the help of Dwight Rugh, Senior Yale-China field representative, they were allowed to return for a brief time but in June 1949 they retreated permanently to the United States, leaving behind them a legacy of service and goodwill.

Tierong "Sophie" Zhu was another Yale-China Association pioneer and her impact on Yale-China staff and scores of Yale-China teaching fellows, according to the association's archives, "cannot be measured." She is especially known for her selfless service at Hsing-Ya (now Xiangya) School of Nursing and Yali Middle School. Born in 1915 in Shanghai, her association with American education began early when she attended the Mary Farnham School. Her best friend was Edith Millican, the daughter of an American missionary, who, according to Sophie, spoke "very fluent Ningbo dialect and we chatted very fast, like two little birds."[33] Sophie later graduated from the University of Shanghai, where she majored in chemistry and also exhibited skill as a pianist. In 1937 she married Zhang Yifan, graduate of Suzhou Law School.

Like Frances Scherer, Sophie contributed remarkably to the relief efforts during the Sino-Japanese war through her work with the United Nations Relief and Rehabilitation Administration, the Chinese National Relief and Rehabilitation Administration, the YWCA, and others. In 1946 her humanitarian efforts were suspended briefly when she moved with her husband to the United States to study at Yale (Zhang carried the baton at the Yale Law School graduation of 1948). After graduation Sophie and Zhang returned to their homeland.

For the next thirty-eight years Sophie Zhu taught at Hsiang-Ya, serving tirelessly as mentor, teacher, and loyal friend to many dozens of Yale graduates in Changsha. "During my two years in China, Sophie was the person who advised, taught, cared for and worried about me the most," remembered Soren Rottman in a 1998 *Yale Review* article.[34] Zhu experienced considerable hardship after the death of her husband in 1955, as Mao Zedong's revolutionary plans were taking effect. Zhu's association with Yale-China undoubtedly complicated her situation, but she never wavered in her support. After Sino-American relations "normalized" under Deng Xiaoping's leadership around 1979, the Yale-China Association returned again to Changsha and Zhu worked again with the fellows for a short time.

Another important organization that made its debut during the time of the "second wave" was the Institute of International Education (IIE), an organization at the forefront of global education exchange today. The IIE was established in 1919 in the aftermath of World War I by Nobel Peace

Prize winners Nicholas Murray Butler, president of Columbia University, and Elihu Root, former secretary of State. Stephen Duggan, Sr., the third founder and a professor of political science at the College of the City of New York, would become IIE's first president. The three men were convinced that world peace could only be achieved through greater understanding between nations, and international educational exchange was the most effective way to achieve such a goal.

The Institute's new president Stephen Duggan helped persuade the U.S. government to create a new category of non-immigrant student visas, bypassing postwar quotas set by earlier legislation. Other early IIE efforts included the publication of the first reference guides to international study, and the facilitation of a network of International Relations clubs. The American-Chinese Student Exchange, which offered some of the first study-abroad opportunities for Americans in Asia, was established in 1936—the first of many important IIE alliances with China to come.

FEMALE STUDENTS AND SCHOLARS

Educational prospects for Chinese females, especially at advanced levels, were exceptionally limited in China's institutions prior to the twentieth century, and opportunities to study abroad fewer still. Those circumstances began to change with some rapidity during the Indemnity Scholarship era, however. In the early years all Tsinghua students were male but beginning in 1914 the college began offering a few scholarships (ten every other year) to women students from other schools. Between 1914 and 1929 Tsinghua sent fifty-three female students to the United States, most at the undergraduate level.[35] The young women had to have the same academic credentials as the men, with one additional requisite—they were to have natural *tian zu* (not bound) feet.[36]

The awarding of indemnity funds to promising female students generated considerable public interest and support, so when the scholarships were temporarily halted in 1920, protests were heard across China. Several hundred citizens, mostly female students, petitioned the government, condemning the unfairness of women being denied admission to Tsinghua. Qualified females should be provided more opportunities for higher learning, the protesters declared, and the offering of a few indemnity scholarships was a small contribution compared to what was really needed. They were quick to point out that victories had already been won because of female scholarships.

One of those victories was Boxer Indemnity scholarship recipient Chen Hengzhe (Sophia Chen), who in 1914 became one of the first two Chinese women to study at Vassar College in Poughkeepsie, New York. Chen had been born in 1890 to a family of magistrates in Jiangsu Province who were well-known scholars and poets. At an early age her maternal uncle encouraged Chen to model herself after Western women, and she was introduced to Western science and medicine. At age twenty-two, after refusing to marry the man her father had chosen for her, Chen decided to live with her aunt, a woman who studied traditional medicine, in her home near Suzhou. Chen credits her aunt for convincing her to make a bold move—to travel to Shanghai and take the Tsinghua examinations for women.

Chen passed the examinations and joined the first group of women students sent to America with indemnity funds. The dispatch was a historic accomplishment and a source of pride not just for Chinese women, but also for China. A news article in 1914 praised the efforts of Chen and the other women scholars, saying that China "needs women physicians and teachers more than any other civilized country in the world."[37]

Sophia Chen liked to write and served as a contributing editor to *Youth,* a magazine of poetry published at Cambridge, where she introduced many Americans to Chinese poetry through her lively articles in the *Vassar Miscellany Monthly.* In 1919 Chen graduated Phi Beta Kappa and was awarded a Vassar scholarship to study at the University of Chicago, where she would also serve as president of the Chinese Students' Club. Completing her studies, Chen returned to China in 1920 to become the first woman professor at Beijing University, teaching Western history and English. She would later serve as a delegate to the Institute of Pacific Relations conferences in 1927 in Honolulu and in Kyoto in 1929.

Chen's writing continued throughout her career. She wrote a two-volume book, *History of Western Countries,* as well as essays and articles describing new educational and occupational possibilities for Chinese women. One such article was "A Non-Christian Estimate of Missionary Activities" published in the *Chinese Recorder,* a missionary magazine in Shanghai. Chen and her husband, the now-influential Hu Shi (an Indemnity scholar who had attended Cornell), were two of the eight founders of the *Independent Critic,* a privately published magazine that encouraged democracy and warned against authoritarianism. In 1947 she moved to Cambridge, Massachusetts, to be with her oldest daughter, who was studying at Radcliff, but returned again to China following the 1949 takeover of the Communist Party. After a lifetime of critiquing the government, she and her husband stopped making any public political comments whatsoever.[38]

Tsinghua's early scholarship opportunities for women gave rise to others, such as the Barbour Scholarships for Oriental Women, a creation of Levi L. Barbour, former regent of the University of Michigan. The Barbour Scholarships provided funding for the education of women from 1917 until 1941 and about half of the 212 recipients were Chinese. Many returned to China to serve as educators or doctors.

One of the Barbour scholars, Wu Yifang, served as president of the University of Michigan Chinese Club (1923) and president of the Chinese Students' Christian Association in 1924–25. She served as vice president of the Chinese Students' Alliance in 1925–26. After receiving a PhD in biology in

1928, Wu returned to Ginling College in Nanjing, where she became the first Chinese woman ever to hold a college presidency in China. She served two terms as chairman of the National Christian Council of China in the 1930s and was the only Chinese woman delegate to the United Nations conference in 1945.

Another noteworthy University of Michigan female graduate was Ding Maoying, an indemnity student who studied there from 1916 to 1920. After serving as chief resident at Beiyang Women's Hospital in Tianjin, Ding received a Barbour Fellowship for a year at University of Michigan and then studied at Harvard Medical School. She would become the medical director at Beiyang Women's Hospital.

The May Fourth Student Movement of 1919 had helped signal the final destruction of barriers to female education in China. The following year two female students entered Beijing University under the chancellorship of Cai Yuanpei, a strong advocate for educational equality.[39] Other institutions slowly followed suit.

From 1916 to 1929 Tsinghua further expanded scholarships to females and also to male students at large—no longer were candidates for indemnity funds restricted to its own graduates. This new population of applicants was required to have earned university degrees and those receiving scholarships were obliged to apply them strictly to graduate work in the United States. These grants were usually limited to two or three years of study. In addition to scholarships for this new pool of applicants, Tsinghua also designated funds to help needy Chinese students who were already studying in America. By 1929, soon after Tsinghua College became Tsinghua National University, remission scholarships were opened to all candidates.[40]

All indemnity scholarship grants had been administered by a supervisor of studies appointed by the Chinese minister of foreign affairs, until September 1933, when its affairs were turned over to the China Institute in America. The Boxer Indemnity scholarship program would later serve as a model for the Fulbright program's grants for international educational exchange.[41]

This second wave of students would diminish as China advanced toward communism in the 1930s. Nonetheless, not since the 1870s, when Yung Wing's CEM program was in full operation, had America witnessed such a large migration of Chinese students to its colleges.

THE CHINESE STUDENTS' ALLIANCE

An important vehicle of allegiance and communication among Chinese students in America during this era was a student-led organization called The Chinese Students' Alliance. The Alliance began with a meeting of twenty-three students from Berkeley, Oakland, and San Francisco in a Congregational church in the fall of 1902, a group whose goal was to find a way to establish a sense of "community" among the Chinese who were studying in the United States. Such an alliance would serve also as a provision for communication and would strive to arouse patriotism for China.[42] The following year a similar association was founded by Chinese students in Chicago and another in Ithaca, New York, in 1904—then at Berkeley the year after. In 1905, thirty-six students met in Amherst, Massachusetts, and founded the Chinese Students Alliance of the Eastern States. By now these organizations had together attracted an estimated 115 members.

Aside from a device for communication, unity, and encouragement, these alliances also sought to bridge cultural and linguistic divisions between southern and northern Chinese students—as well as between Chinese-born and American-born Chinese. Similar in purpose, the alliances also sponsored many popular Sino-American activities. In 1911, former indemnity student (graduate of Cornell University) V. K. Wellington Koo united all five groups to form the Chinese Students' Alliance, an organization that would operate until 1931.

Under the umbrella of the alliance, many local clubs developed, on both college and high school campuses. Several of the clubs were especially active. Among the most successful was the group established at the University of Michigan, an institution that already had a strong affiliation with China, in part through the efforts of its president, James B. Angell. Among other things, Angell arranged for his institution to host a delegation of commissioners from China who were studying constitutional government in 1906, placing them with local host families and enlisting businesses in Lansing to provide tours of their facilities. By 1913 the University of Michigan had enrolled fifty-nine students from China, the largest population of Chinese students in the United States. Thirty-three were there on indemnity scholarships. Fifteen were Christian, representing the largest number of Chinese Christian students on any American campus.[43]

A critical component of the Chinese Students Alliance was the *Chinese Students' Monthly,* its chief publication. A platform for expressing goals and opinions, the *Monthly* helped keep students informed of important news and activities in both America and China, and served as an outlet for Chinese students to publish poetry, short stories, or opinion pieces. The *Monthly*'s readership included most Chinese students in the United States. Professors, American students, businessmen, and missionaries added to the readership roster, and copies were sent to Chinese students in Europe as well.

The *Chinese Students' Monthly* would eventually encounter financial problems, and there was administrative instability and high turnover due to the transient nature of academic life. When expenditures fell short, such as in 1918 and 1919, when editors were facing new postal laws and rising costs, it grew increasingly difficult to keep the publication in operation. Keeping up with subscriptions was another ongoing concern. Student addresses could change every year or two, so maintaining contact with the badly needed subscribers was difficult.

The *Monthly*'s demise began around 1927, the result of waning funds, but also of politics. Increasing numbers of articles were appearing in the *Monthly* that focused on the growing turmoil in China and on escalating Chinese discontent with the West. Some articles praised the Soviets and their influence in China while others condemned the United States for barring Chinese students from white schools in Mississippi. Inflammatory cartoons appeared, one depicting the West as evil "behind a mask of civilization."[44] Offended American advertisers began canceling their orders.

The deathblow to the *Chinese Students' Monthly* may have been the 1929 printing of "American Imperialism, Enemy of Chinese Independence," an article that openly advocated Marxism. It was written by Earl Bowder, editor of Labor Unity in Chicago and the future head of the American Communist Party. Outrage over the article resulted in the firing of the *Monthly*'s editor Hu Dunyuan and the alliance's president Yu Zipei. Hu was charged with "deliberate red editorial policy." Grievances against Yu, a woman and a member of the Communist Party, included abuse of power and illegal use of the alliance for propaganda.[45] Three men were appointed to continue the administration of the publication, but the organization had been dispirited beyond repair. The *Chinese Students' Monthly* printed and distributed its last issue in April 1931 and the alliance came to an end.

The charges of propaganda leveled at the *Monthly* might have convicted some American publishers as well, had they been applied. The first decades of the twentieth century offered similarly skewed stereotypes of China in dozens of American magazines, newspapers, and movies. Stories about wars, floods, earthquakes, bandits, and corruption in China, designed to attract American audiences, rarely mentioned the signs of progress in its education systems, commerce, and industry. Some even alleged that the publishers' motivations were to influence American public opinion in anticipation of military intervention against China. Lowering the public's opinion of the Chinese could prove useful in the promotion of public support for the continuation of immigration laws and treaties, charged the critics, policies considered unfair by most Chinese.[46]

The "backwardness" of China was still promoted by the press and it was true that many Americans continued to think of Chinese as laundrymen or operators of ethnic eateries. The idea of intelligent students with bright futures as leaders in their midst still seemed foreign to many. It was a common misperception that most Asian students were Japanese. In fact, in 1915 there were 594 Chinese students in America, compared to 336 from Japan.

THE REST OF THE MONEY

By 1922, according to a report by the American Council Institute of Pacific Relations in New York, there were 1,507 Chinese students enrolled in accredited United States colleges and universities. Slightly larger figures were reported by the Committee on Friendly Relations among Foreign Students due to its expanded list of institutions.[47]

That same year discussions began about what to do with the remaining portion of the excess Boxer Indemnity, an amount totaling about $6 million. To help determine its best use, in April 1924 a congressional hearing was scheduled to review the results of the first indemnity remission. A State Department representative described for the group the benefits, not least among them the opportunity to train and influence future Chinese leaders. Others pointed out some problems, however. John MacMurray, chief of the Division of Far Eastern Affairs in the State Department, reported that in his opinion the indemnity scholars often set themselves apart from their fellow Chinese by their new living standards and new preferences. Princeton professor Robert McElroy, who traveled and lectured in China, advised that in the future Chinese students should be trained with reference to China, not America, in order to translate their skills for use in their homeland.

In 1924 Congress voted in favor of establishing the China Foundation for the Promotion of Education and Culture and in July 1925 President Calvin Coolidge signed an executive order remitting the rest of the excess from the indemnity to the newly created foundation.[48] Ten Chinese and five Americans comprised the China Foundation Board, a group designated to administer the remaining portion of the Boxer Indemnity. Members included Premier Yan Huiqing; Foreign Minister V. K. Wellington Koo (a former indemnity student); Jiang Menglin, president of Beijing University; Zhang Boling, president of Nankai University; and philosophy professor Hu Shi, a former indemnity scholar. Americans included John Dewey and Paul Monroe from Columbia University, Roger Greene of Peking Union Medical College, and J. E. Baker of the Ministry of Communications in Beijing. Zhou Yichun, former president of Tsinghua, served as the first executive director.

The 1920s was a time of turmoil in China. The Chinese Communist Party and Sun Yat-sen's Nationalists cooperated in efforts to finally and forever roll back warlordism and imperialism, and the new Nationalist government was set up in Nanjing.[49] Russia and the United States vied for authority in China's future—some speculated that the move to administer the second remission was in part due to rumors that Russia had canceled its Boxer debts. Sun Yat-sen remarked that America's true motivation may have been concern about Russia's growing influence in China, rather than generosity.

Whether or not rumors were an influence, higher education reaped the benefits. The foundation allotted money from the second remission for additional scholarships and also used some of the funds to support other educational efforts, broadening its venture beyond Tsinghua. Funds were used to support twenty graduate scholarships per year for top students from universities across China, and also paid for the national library of Beijing, a facility that would translate Western scientific books. Research institutes in the fields of biology and social research were also subsidized by the second remission. As with the first indemnity remission, some complained about the restricted use of the money—but had the funds been under the control of the Chinese government, the board told their critics, it may very well have been spent for military rather than educational purposes.

Nationalism was rising in China and after the Guomindang (Nationalist Party) gained power in 1927 the Ministry of Foreign Affairs and the Ministry of Education again competed for control of Tsinghua. Experiencing a period of growth, its name officially changed to Tsinghua University, new buildings were added, and women students were no longer a rare sight on campus.

In 1929, the government, now under control of the Guomindang, Tsinghua sent its last group of indemnity scholars to the United States. The same year, on August 20, the American minister reluctantly turned over control of Tsinghua to the Chinese Ministry of Education, as the college's assets were turned over to the China Foundation. After two decades of operation the Chinese simply did not need its advice, reported the U.S. State Department. The only vestiges of control were the few remaining American teachers and the American textbooks still in use, as Tsinghua struggled to maintain control of its academic freedom.

A SECOND WAVE OF CONTRIBUTIONS

Many important and influential scholars emerged from China's second wave of education exchange with the United States, and, like their CEM predecessors, the indemnity students' accomplishments would be important to China's continuing modernization. Among the most influential and well-known of these scholars was Hu Shi , a philosopher, essayist, and a leading liberal in the May Fourth Movement.

Hu Shi had grown up in a fatherless home, under the strong influence of a traditional mother who also supported "modern" education for her son. In 1910 Hu won a Boxer Indemnity scholarship to study at Cornell University in New York, and then later studied philosophy at Columbia, where he was influenced by liberal John Dewey. Hu would become a leader in the New Culture movement. As a professor at Beijing University, he wrote for the journal *New Youth*, a publication edited by one of the founders of the Chinese Communist Party, Chen Duxiu. From 1938 until 1942 Hu Shi would serve as China's ambassador to the United States. He later was chancellor of Beijing University (1946–48) and then served as president of the Academia Sinica (now the Chinese Academy of Sciences) in Taiwan.[50]

Hu became a leading critic and analyst of traditional Chinese culture and thought. His writings helped to replace the classical style with the vernacular literature—perhaps his most important contribution to China's modernization. Even today Hu's contribution to writing and scholarship in China's literature and history continues to play an important role, especially as an inspiration for other writers. However, because of his criticism of the Communist Party, today his work is seldom taught in schools in mainland China.

Another "second wave" scholar was Tao Xingzhi, who studied at Columbia in the Teachers College and returned to his homeland to promote modern education. Tao's synthesis of Deweyan and Chinese approaches to progressive education, a text based on his analysis of Chinese life and society, would make him one of the most renowned educators in Chinese history.

Chen Hegin, after studying at Teachers College in 1917 and 1918, returned to China to become the first Chinese theoretician of early childhood education. Alongside his promotion of early childhood educational opportunities, Chen developed teacher-training programs that emphasized child psychology, education for handicapped children, and family education.

One of the first Chinese students funded by the Boxer Indemnity Scholarship program in 1909 was Wong Chin (Wang Jin), from Zhejiang Province. After completing his bachelor's degree in chemical engineering at Lehigh University, he returned to China to serve as the dean at two major Chinese universities—the College of Sciences at Southeast University and the National Central University. A renowned scientist, Wong was invited to form the Academia Sinica and became the first director of its institute of chemistry. He was also one of the original members of the Chinese Science Society, the earliest comprehensive scientific organization in China, and in the 1920s served as editor in chief of a major Chinese scientific magazine. After the Communist Party assumed control, Wong was assigned to Zhejiang Normal College, to conduct research in analytical chemistry. Here he edited and reworked the most widely used chemistry textbooks at the time, volumes originally written by Russian scientist Vladimir Nikolaevich Alekseev. Wong also co-founded the Chinese Chemical Industry Society and the Chinese Chemistry Society.

Yeh Tingshien (Yi Dingxin) from Hunan province graduated from New York University in 1915 with a master of science degree. After his return to China he was employed by Hanyeping Company, a large coal and steel conglomerate, where he contributed to the design of the power-generation system in steel production, and also the transformer substation system used in coal mines. In 1926 he joined Hunan University as a professor and later was provost of the Engineering School of Zhejjiang University. In 1929 he returned to industry, serving as the director of the Hangzhou power plant, then as chief engineer at the Hunan Electric Light Company. A new 20-kilowatt electric power plant was built under his leadership, an accomplishment that made Yeh famous throughout central China. A fire in 1938 burned the company to the ground, however, and Yeh returned to Hunan University to work as a professor, dean, and then provost. While serving at Hunan, Yeh taught courses in hydrodynamics, pyrology, and power plant design and published two of the earliest textbooks in the field.

Ho Chieh (He Jie) from Guangdong Province became a renowned geologist and one of the most senior academics in science, technology, and modern higher education in China. In 1909 Ho came to the United States on an indemnity scholarship, first studying coal mining technology at the Colorado School of Mines, then at Lehigh University, where he studied advanced geology and earned a master of science degree. When he returned home in 1914 Ho joined the faculty of Peking (Beijing) University, first as a professor of engineering and then as director of the Department of Geology, one of China's first departments in that field. Ho's career included faculty appointments in mining and metallurgy at major universities in China. Outside of academia, Ho Chieh held positions as director of Geological Surveys for Guangdong and Guanzxi, and he created many of the mineral and geology maps for these provinces.

In 1918, when most Chinese still believed in astrology, Yu Ching Sung (Yu Qing Song) was studying at Lehigh University to find "truth beyond the sky." After earning his bachelor's degree he studied astronomy at the University of California, where he focused on star spectrums. Back home he would use his knowledge to build the first observatory in China. A research scientist at the Berkeley Observatory before he was appointed full professor at Xiamen University in 1927, Yu was later made director of the Chinese Academy of Astronomy. In this capacity he designed the Purple Mountain Observatory in Nanjing and the Phoenix Observatory in Kunming. Later in life Yu took positions outside China, at the University of Toronto and also at the Harvard College Observatory. He was professor and chair of the Williams Observatory at Hood College, and was a member of the Royal British Academy of Astronomy.[51]

Chang Poling, who studied at Columbia Teachers College, returned to Tianjin to found Nan Kai University—and there are many more examples. The second wave of Chinese student enrollments in America's universities, like the first, was short-lived, and it took place during a time of governmental transition and instability. Chinese higher education in the early decades of the twentieth century was in a period of change as well and, just as the second wave of returnees had been, was deeply affected by American educators John Dewey and Paul Monroe.

5 A Random Grafting of Twigs

In the first years of the twentieth century Japan had been China's preference for study abroad not only because of its proximity but also because of its strong influence, a combination of Japan's successes on the battlefield and of shared Confucian values. Japan's influence reached its peak around 1911, as the Boxer Indemnity scholarships initiated America's second wave of Chinese enrollments. After that, and until Sino-American diplomatic relations were severed in 1949, the United States held more influence over China. By the beginning of World War II the U.S. had become China's chief partner in educational exchange and both countries had come under the influence of the American educator John Dewey.

DEWEYAN PHILOSOPHY AND CHINA

It is difficult to overstate the importance of John Dewey's influence on China's educational perspective during this time period, especially through the decade of the 1920s, as the indemnity scholarship era and the second wave of Chinese enrollments in America was underway.[1] Dewey's writings and teachings were already profound influences on modern education in the United States. Ideas like "education as growing," "education as life," "school as society," and "learning by doing" attached critical importance to the intimate connection between the school and society, and emphasized the central ideal of pragmatism. What would become known as Deweyan philosophy was based on a thorough study of academic history ranging from the ancient Greek classics to modern Europe, deeply rooted in the modern ideals of science, democracy, and industry.[2]

Dewey's influence had also been introduced to Japanese academic circles. In 1888 a Japanese journal published one of Dewey's essays on psychology and in 1900 his early work *Outlines of a Critical Theory of Ethics* was translated into Japanese. By 1918 two of Dewey's most important works on education, *School and Society* and *Democracy and Education*, were made available to Japanese readers, giving rise to the opening of around a dozen experimental elementary schools modeled after Dewey's school at the University of Chicago.

On May 30, 1919, Dewey visited China. Arriving in Shanghai, he was surprised to learn that over one thousand leading educators in central China were waiting to hear his opening address, scheduled for three days later. Dewey spent the next two years and two months in China, giving lectures that drew legions of fervent young admirers, and the contents of his speeches were carried in numerous journals and articles. Around five book editions with different series of lectures were published, as he left his footprint in thirteen provinces. An article in the *New York Chinese Students' Monthly* described some of the fervor surrounding Dewey's visit, saying "Mr. Dewey's career in China is one of singular success . . . teachers and students flock to his classrooms . . . clubs compete to entertain him, to hear him speak; newspapers vie with each other in translating his latest utterances."[3]

Why was this Yankee scholar followed so enthusiastically? Some attribute Dewey's impact to the social and intellectual upheaval of the May Fourth Movement. The movement refers to the student demonstrations in Beijing in 1919 that began as a protest of the Versailles Peace Conference, but in a broader sense it represented a period of change that took place between 1917 and 1921, a renewed attempt to reform China through intellectual and social means.

After the collapse of the Qing Dynasty, Chinese intellectuals soon came to realize that, rather than making China a modern nation-state, the founding of the republic was "merely the culmination of the process of the disintegration of the traditional sociopolitical and cultural-moral orders."[4] This intellectual crisis had resulted in an alliance of "new intellectuals" and from 1917 to 1919 Beijing University was their base of operations. Supported and promoted by publications such as *New Youth* and *New Tide* magazines, these New Culture intellectuals, among them Hu Shi, Ch'en Tu-hsiu, Ch'ien Hsuan-tung, Li Ta-chao, Kao I-han, Luo Chia-lun, and many others, began an attack on "old literature" and "old ethics" as they upheld new thinking and vernacular writings.

Dewey has been frequently linked with his disciple Hu Shi, the former Boxer Indemnity scholar who was himself a well-known reformer. However, it was neither Dewey nor Hu Shi who initiated the New Culture Movement or the New Thought Tide, according to writers such as Chow Tsetsung, who commented that this approach was "neither planned nor directed by any one person." It represented a "common meeting ground" for people with different perspectives and ideas.

Dewey had arrived in China just in time to convey his ideologies to an audience already receptive to change. He was warmly welcomed because what he was saying was more or less what the new intellectuals had been propagating—ideals they were hoping to strengthen. The Chinese liberals were skeptical about the possibility of reforming even politics until a new generation came on the scene, and were now putting their faith in education and in social changes, both of which would take some years to consummate.

After the May Fourth incident in 1919, alliances among the various groups of new intellectuals began to dissolve and the cultural reformist

Figure 5.1 John Dewey, circa 1925.

movement was starting to decline. A month after Dewey lectured at Beijing University, Hu Shi and Li Ta-chao began what would become a famous debate over problems and "isms" designed to reflect the conflicts within the new intellectual circle. In agreement with Hu, Dewey made several attempts to persuade these audiences to adhere to a "step-by-step" cultural reconstruction, holding fast to the reformism of the first period of the May Fourth Movement. In the end his efforts were futile, however. The cultural-intellectualistic approach of the earlier period gradually lost its appeal and was replaced by the Marxist-Leninist revolutionary ideal.

Even still, Dewey's influence in China in the 1920s went beyond the bounds of Chinese liberalism and education reform. His experimental methodology influenced not just liberals but also leftists. Hu Shi commented that his two greatest influences had been John Dewey and English biologist Thomas Huxley, a man known as "Darwin's bulldog" because of his strong defense of evolutionary theories.[5] Huxley taught him to doubt and to believe in nothing without sufficient evidence; Dewey taught him how to think, taking into account the immediate problems and the effect of thoughts. Hu would go on to translate many of Dewey's works.

Another who fell under the influence of Dewey's pragmatism was Mao Zedong. While he was working as a librarian's assistant in Beijing University (from 1918 until 1919) Mao attended Hu Shi's courses and also had private talks with Hu, seeking his advice about studying abroad. Hu suggested Mao remain in China and do on-site investigation and research. Hu also suggested the creation of a "Self-Study University" in Mao's home province, an idea that would be later implemented. Many of Dewey's books, *Five Major Lectures, Trends in Modern Education, On the Development of Democracy in America*, among others, frequently appeared on the "important books" list and on the roster of books distributed by the Cultural Book Society, of which Mao was a founder. In a 1920 letter to a friend, Mao wrote that he was in the process of reading three great contemporary philosophers—Dewey, Bertrand Russell, and Bergson. In his "Manifest on the Founding of the Xiang River Review," Mao listed pragmatism, a decidedly Dewey philosophy, as the most progressive thought.[6] Despite its decline, Dewey's pragmatic philosophy for the connection between society and life continued to influence the setting of educational aims, the development of education theory, and the reform of curriculum and teaching methods, even in the 1930s and 1940s.

PAUL MONROE

For a long time, academic circles in China and in the United States paid little attention to another important educator, Paul Monroe, largely due to Dewey's monumental celebrity. Nonetheless, Monroe's influence was considerable during the same period. A review published in *China Papers* in 2010, which investigated Monroe's impact on returned Chinese students and middle-school reform, asserted that his contribution to the educational development in modern times was nothing less than profound—especially in the areas of talents cultivation, reform, social transformation, and educational exchange.[7]

A 1921 *New York Times* article titled "To Show China How to Run Her Schools" reported that "Professor Paul Monroe, now on his way to the Orient with John D. Rockefeller, Jr. and party, to take part in the formal opening of the $10,000,000 Peking Union Medical College . . . has been assigned the task of improving the methods of administration in educational matters in China. . . . "[8] Monroe, professor of educational history and director of the School of Education of Teachers College at Columbia University, would remain in China to work toward that mission. While his efforts focused on the methods employed in the vast provincial area outside Peking, his ideas would be extended to the whole national system of education in China. Between 1920 and the end of the 1940s, Monroe visited China more than ten times to investigate education, lecture, and conduct cultural exchanges. His visits encouraged educational research in China and his work also helped to facilitate the "6–3-3" public schooling system.[9]

In Monroe's 1927 book *China: A Nation in Evolution,* his assessment of the country and its educational future with the United States was remarkably perceptive. Written almost ninety years ago, Monroe's insights demonstrated both understanding and foresight: " . . . the Chinese problem is not one to be quickly solved, but long to remain with us; that beneath the political revolutions and conflicts, economic, industrial and cultural changes far more significant are going on; that to effect these changes will take time measured in decades and generations." He added a Chinese proverb: "He who would understand the past and the present must read five cartloads of books."[10]

CRITICS AND DECRIERS

The second wave of American-educated students and scholars who returned to China developed their careers in the shadow of the influence of Dewey and Monroe. Chinese students from the early CEM project had returned to their homeland to successfully modernize many of China's industries but this new wave of returnees was expected to develop China further—this time with a strong dose of Deweyan pragmatism. By the 1920s it was clear to everyone that American-educated students would continue to affect the ebb of change in China—on this basic point almost everyone could agree. Whether or not these changes would be completely beneficial to China's modernization was, in some circles, a topic of heated debate.

Even as American newspapers were printing glowing, often sentimental reports of the Chinese students' academic achievements and the promise their training held for China's modernization, many were at odds with the assumption that such changes were good for the country. Among the Chinese public were many outspoken critics who voiced dissatisfaction with China's system of education, study abroad in particular.

An early work reflecting this disenchantment is *Jindai Zhongguo Liuxueshi*, or *History of Studying Abroad in Modern China*, by Shu Xincheng. Shu faulted both the Chinese government and the returned students for what he viewed as the failure of education exchange, accusing the latter group of forming a "kind of special class" who "enjoyed the fruit without the toil."[11] Shu charged that these students were using their degrees more to achieve personal success and distinction than to serve or modernize China, accusing them of behaving more like foreigners, trying to seize more power than they deserved.

Shu's harshest criticisms were saved for the Chinese government. Since the beginning there had been no definitive purpose or policy regarding study abroad, he charged, citing the lack of coordination among institutes that sent students abroad and the absence of a uniform set of policies to guide procedures or admissions. Sometimes students were admitted to study-abroad programs because of their wealth rather than ability, and those who were self-supported were often exempted from the screening examinations, creating a population of students who were "seeking only empty names and not practical knowledge."[12] To add to the imbalance, many of the self-supported students, who were favored by the government, had studied at Christian institutions in China and thus were already somewhat

"Westernized." According to Shu, this early training further dimmed their potential for academic success when they returned to China.

Shu criticized that the concentration of Chinese students educated in the United States and in Japan was contributing to both the Americanization and the Japanization of Chinese society, and he condemned Tsinghua for investing too much money for too few returns. Even if all the students turned out to be high achievers it was still not cost-efficient, he claimed. This was because what the students had learned in America was simply not readily applicable to China's needs. Shu was convinced that China's efforts to promote and finance study abroad in the West would in the long run be a hindrance to China's modernization, not a benefit.

In *Chinese Intellectuals and the West* (1966), Y. C. Wang supported many of Shu's arguments against study abroad.[13] Wang especially disagreed with the uneven distribution of Chinese social resources, claiming that in many cases an education in the United States was a privilege of the rich. Most study-abroad students were recruited from the coastal provinces, such as Jiangsu, Zhejiang, and Guangdong, which from the beginning had monopolized the opportunities. The effect of that imbalance introduced problems more far-reaching, Wang alleged. The poorer provinces, which already suffered from a lack of educational opportunities and meager conditions, had little chance of sharing in the resources for studying abroad. Most returned scholars, even those few from remote regions, also tended to settle in the coastal cities after their education, he added, completely deviating from the traditional ideal of scholar-officials returning to their native region. But the draw was understandable. Not only were there more occupational choices but in many cases it was the familiarity of the more-Westernized coastal cities that appealed to the newly "Americanized" returned students.

The fact that most Western-educated Chinese tended to return to the coastal cities may have been a particularly egregious situation in the case of returned agriculture students. According to statistics for 1925, 70 percent of students returning from the United States with agriculture degrees had remained in education, some worked in the political sector, and others were unemployed. According to the report, none was actually engaged in rural agricultural production.

There were American-educated returnees who attained high achievements in business, finance, or engineering or in the political sector, but according to Wang many, perhaps most, were not directly applying the education they had attained in the United States. Returned business scholars went to work in banks for the most part and few founded or developed businesses, according to Wang. Of the 564 Chinese business "celebrities" he surveyed, only ten were returned scholars and nine of those were in banking. Of the forty industrial leaders in Wang's survey, thirty of them were engineers and eighteen of those were returned scholars. However, all of them had become directors of state-operated businesses and no longer worked as engineers, observed Wang.

What Wang believed he had revealed from the survey was a disconnection between education and employment. It demonstrated a general unwillingness among the returned scholars to work in humble positions, or in the rural areas of China. At the same time, the survey's results had shown, Wang concluded, that returned students had little Western knowledge that was genuinely applicable to Chinese society.

Shu and Wang were in agreement that China's emphasis on higher education in general during the period had been supported at the expense of elementary education. In 1931 China spent two hundred times as much on an individual college student as it did on an elementary school student. As a point of comparison, in Europe the ratio was about eight to one.[14]

Wang acknowledged the returned scholars had accomplished some things, but also criticized their arrogance. Their Westernized ways and their foreign-acquired education simply did not correspond to China's needs, he contended, tracing the weaknesses back to Yung Wing and the CEM. Yung never intended, Wang believed, to provide the CEM students with both an American and a Chinese education, as Li Hongzhang had prescribed. Wang was convinced Yung was secretly intent upon the students abandoning their culture. He argued that by Yung becoming an American citizen in 1852, he had served as a role model for the several CEM students who had elected to remain in the United States permanently. Wang's belief was that most of the Chinese students wanted to naturalize from the beginning—a trend that continued and increased over the decades. Wang went on to criticize the graduate rates of Chinese students in America. According to his calculations, between 1854 and 1954 about twenty-two thousand Chinese students had come to the United States, but only about 50 to 60 percent had earned a degree.

Criticism of Sino-American education exchange was by no means confined to the Chinese. Influential American critics in the early twentieth century launched attacks on two fronts—the condition of Chinese education in general, and on study abroad in particular. Among the more outspoken critics were Thomas Read of Beijing University, Tsinghua University exchange professor Robert McElroy, and Nathaniel Peffer, who worked as a journalist in Beijing and in Shanghai. Another was Selskar M. Gunn, vice president of the Rockefeller Foundation. Well-known liberals such as John Dewey and Bertrand Russell also voiced apprehension about the long-term effects of Sino-American education exchange.

Gunn charged that American-educated Chinese students, assumedly working to modernize China, were guilty of "blind copying," engaged in what he described as the "random grafting of Western twigs onto Chinese trees of which the Westerners had little knowledge."[15] Further criticism came from Nathanial Peffer, who reported from Beijing and Shanghai:

> From what I saw and heard in China during the five years I stayed there, I have to conclude that as a class the returned scholars were not

only a sad disappointment as representatives of their nation but were also not successful despite having favorable opportunities . . . their worst faults are their glib tongues, the mere lip service they give to patriotism. . . . [16]

PROGRAMS, ORGANIZATIONS, AND INITIATIVES IN THE 1930S AND 1940S

Even in light of the criticisms and the unsteady political climate that existed in the 1930s and 1940s, most supported the idea of education exchange, and a number of important U.S.-China educational exchange efforts were either introduced or enhanced during this period.

The second remission of Boxer Indemnity funds would for a time continue to provide scholarships for study in the United States. To guide their administration, as mentioned in the previous chapter, the Chinese government had appointed ten Chinese and five Americans to form a board of trustees, with a constitution stipulating that the board would be self-perpetuating, guaranteeing a future relatively free of government interference. The China Foundation for the Promotion of Education and Culture spent the next several decades carrying out its mission.[17] Among other things, between 1924 and 1949 the foundation helped save National Peking University from financial ruin by subsidizing the payroll for its teachers and staff, and it provided science fellowships in teaching colleges. Grants and subsides were offered through the China Foundation for 233 universities and colleges, 139 research institutes, and 147 cultural and other organizations. Research professorships and fellowships were provided for many prominent professors, as well as outstanding young professors, to conduct research domestically and abroad. The Foundation also established the National Library of Peiping by funding its building and the purchase of rare books.

Institute of Pacific Relations

Another important organization during this period was the Institute of Pacific Relations, established in 1927. Lauded in the 1920s as the "lily in the barnyard of politics," but denounced by a Communist journal in the 1930s as an "institute of pirates and robbers," the institute would operate in an environment of controversy. Formed in Hawaii with delegations from eight countries, it offered a forum for nonpartisan and confidential exchanges between national figures, an effort designed to help deliver information to the decision-making circles of the respective governments represented in the group.

As early as 1923 leaders from the Young Men's Christian Association (YMCA) were concerned by the growing tension between the United States,

Japan, and China over America's restrictive immigration laws, and called for a means of discussion to improve the situation. A conference was held in Hawaii in July 1925 and a new organization was founded, with former indemnity scholarship graduate Hu Shi among the Chinese delegates. During its tenure the institute contributed substantially to Asian cultural, educational, and political understanding through its stockpile of research and publications, including its quarterly journal *Pacific Affairs*. The institute was closely aligned with study abroad. In addition to Hu Shi, Boxer Indemnity scholar Chen Hengzhe (Sophia Chen) also served as a delegate in 1927 as an interpreter. In 1931 she contributed to the *Symposium on Chinese Culture* held in Hangzhou.[18]

The Institute of Pacific Relations prospered between its inception and 1944, when it came under a much-publicized investigation from the U.S. Senate Subcommittee on Internal Security, resulting in the loss of most of its support from foundations and corporations. Senator Pat McCarran, suspicious of its promotion of cultural and educational ties with China during the anti-communist "McCarthy era," even accused the Institute of having caused the "loss" of China.[19]

Yale-China

Even in an environment of McCarthyism, many in America hoped to repair academic ties with estranged countries and to rebuild educational exchange programs that had been suspended during the several years of conflict. The war years had been generally difficult ones for long-established collaborations operations such as the Yale-China Association, which had successfully worked with educational and medical partnerships in China since the turn of the century. One of Yale-China's institutional casualties was the Hsing-Ya Hospital, whose staff had assumed the overwhelming task of providing as much care as they could for legions of wounded soldiers and refugees. As the Chinese Nationalist armies retreated towards the southwest, the institutions were forced to follow, to escape the advancing Japanese. By July of 1938, Huachung University had moved to Guilin, until bombing raids forced it to retreat even further to the remote region of Xizhou in Yunnan Province. Meanwhile, Yali Middle School had relocated to Yuanling in western Hunan as the medical college and nursing school sought safety at Guiyang, in Guizhou. Many of Yale-China's Changsha facilities were damaged by Japanese troops, but the intrepid staff who returned to Changsha in September of 1945 resolved to rebuild the campus and resume fully is prewar operations.[20]

NASFA

The Institution of International Education, in operation since 1919, would spawn other important organizations that would become cornerstones of academic exchange. One was the National Association of Foreign Student Advisers, now known as NAFSA: Association of International Educators. Another was the Council on International Educational Exchange, which would become an important contributor to Sino-American academic exchange after 1979.

In 1942 there were only a few persons formally identified as foreign-student advisers (FSAs) in the United States. By 1947 the number of FSAs had risen to about thirty, who were finding their service in increasing demand due to booming postwar foreign enrollments. Therefore at the Chicago conference that year, which was sponsored by the IIE and the Department of State, on the agenda was the creation of a Conference Steering Committee to guide future meetings. The attendees adopted a resolution to establish a Committee on By-Laws for a "National Association."

The decisions about what to name the new association and issues regarding membership qualifications and the organizational structure would be finalized at the Ann Arbor Conference on International Student Exchange the following year, in 1948. The National Association of Foreign Student Advisers (NAFSA) was officially founded and for the first time attendees could be identified officially as "foreign-student advisers." Bylaws were established and Clarence Linton, adviser to students from other lands at Teachers College, Columbia University, was named president. Set in place in the upheaval of the 1930s and 1940s, NAFSA would in later decades become an important supporting agency for the logistics and mechanics of Sino-American education.[21]

The United States Information and Education Exchange Act of 1948, also known as the Smith-Mundt Act, served as the postwar charter for peacetime overseas information and educational exchange activities.[22] The object of the act was to enable the United States government to promote a better understanding of America around the world, the intention to promote intercultural education and mutual respect.

The Fulbright Program

At the core of the new Fulbright Program was the goal of promoting intercultural understanding. Two years before, in 1946, the U.S. Department of State had invited IIE to administer the initiative, an ambitious project proposed by Arkansas senator William J. Fulbright just one month after the United States dropped atomic bombs on Japan. Fulbright proposed that the U.S. government appropriate proceeds from the sale of war surplus to finance education exchange. It was a cost-effective and creative idea perfectly suited to the ideals of efficiency and diplomacy in postwar America. Fulbright's proposal was ratified the same year, and China was among its first participants. On November 10, 1947, a Fulbright accord had been signed by the Nationalist Chinese Foreign Minister, Wang Shiqie, and American ambassador J. Leighton Stuart. By August 1949, fifty-one students had taken part in the exchange—twenty-seven Americans and twenty-four Chinese.[23]

The Fulbright exchanges would be abruptly suspended with the rise of Mao Zedong and the founding of the People's Republic of China. U.S.-China diplomatic ties, as well as academic collaborations, would cease operation after 1949 and would not resume for another thirty years.

6   The Mao Years

> One watches the unyielding pines in the vast azure sunset
> And the fleeing clouds below in seeming chaos yet majestically moving.
> Here beside the cave of the Taoist Immortals one sees that boundless beauty
> Is to be found only among the most dangerous peaks.
>
> Mao Zedong

Between 1945 and 1949, civil war ensued in China. In the end, Chiang Kai-shek and the Guomindang fled to Taiwan as Chairman Mao announced the founding of the People's Republic of China.

Postwar years in China were unsettled. Chinese universities during the civil war period had been nominally connected to the established Nationalist (Guomindang) government, but the new Communist Party was gaining strong support among university students. Anti-American (and by extension anti-Nationalist) protests on university campuses in 1946 and 1947 had played a significant role in the erosion of public support for the Guomindang. When the Chinese Communist Party (CCP) took control in 1949 it was evident that student sympathy lay with Mao Zedong and the new leadership.

In the uncertain period following the regime change, the CCP was hesitant to interfere with the affairs of China's universities, seeing them as important bases of support and the party's leader Mao Zedong himself gave orders to shield Yenching and Tsinghua Universities from any harm during the military takeover of Beijing.[1] Mao was supportive of providing Chinese citizens with good universities; however any endorsement of Western educational ideals, or academic exchange with the United States, would not be forthcoming.

In 1936, a year before China's War of Resistance against Japan, 1,002 Chinese students were enrolled in United States colleges and universities. During the war years (1937–1945) the number dropped to less than one hundred per year and after 1949 the flow of students from mainland China to America stopped almost entirely, and would not resume until after Mao's death, three decades later.

THE POET

A cheering crowd gathered in Tiananmen Square on October 1, 1949, to hear Mao Zedong announce the founding of the People's Republic as the closing of China's "doors" resonated across the globe. China's state-sanctioned apartheid against the inequities of Western capitalism would effectively terminate official Sino-American diplomatic relations for the next thirty years, and academic collaborations were provided few exemptions. Mao and his party were reinventing China, imposing a form of government intended to "equalize" the Chinese people while maximizing the efficiency of its workforce, a plan for universal socialization that did not include a Western education.

Mao Zedong had emerged from obscurity to become a charismatic and dynamic leader who was respected to the point of reverence for his governmental and political talents, but he had endeared himself to the Chinese people through his poetry and his many writings. Mao appreciated literacy and the arts but he also respected the power of organized labor. During his reign of power, Mao often used visual images, songs, and poetry to advance political and social ideals among the people.

After he assumed power, one of the first things on Mao's to-do list was a reorganization of China's higher education according to the Soviet model, a system that emphasized specialization rather than comprehensiveness, in step with the ideology of the Communist Party. All of China's private universities, including those sponsored by foreign missionaries, were quickly placed under the authority of the state, along with a new directive—they were to train a fresh generation of intellectuals who would build a new China.

Adopting the Soviet model represented a dramatic shift in modern Chinese education. In the early twentieth century China's universities had emulated their Western counterparts. Between 1910 and 1949 traditional academies (*shuyuan*) were increasingly obsolete while institutions such as Beijing University's Cai Yuanpei led efforts to import what were essentially German and French conceptions of the university.[2] When the Chinese Communist Party overtook the Guomindang in 1949, tertiary education in China consisted of 205 public, private, and missionary universities with a total enrollment of about 117,000 students, or approximately .002 percent of the population.[3] A persistent concern at the time was that college education, study abroad especially, had remained the domain of a select few.

STRANDED IN AMERICA

Mao's 1949 proclamation at Tiananmen Square began a period of separation between China and the United States, as the two countries viewed each other from afar with growing mistrust. Circumstances that followed would only deepen the divide. Just eight months after Mao's speech and as war escalated between the United States and Korea, the American government imposed a blockade on China, effectively preventing any Chinese who then lived in the United States from returning home.

With the advance of communism in 1948 and 1949, most Chinese students in the United States had been cut off from their financial support in

China and some were declared to be in acute distress. Much of the burden had fallen upon the colleges and universities in which they were enrolled. Institutions made scholarship funds available, tuition payments were postponed, and some emergency funding was granted. Sometimes local businesses provided credit, and many religious and civic organizations stepped up to offer assistance. But the combined efforts proved inadequate and institutions turned to the government for help.

The United States government, assisted by the Institute of International Education and the China Institute in America, began providing aid for the stranded students in 1948, with an initial allotment of $8,000. In 1949 at the request of the Chinese government another half million was transferred to the Department of State from the Aid-to-China program of the Economic Cooperation Administration. Later that year an additional four million dollars was made available as part of the Foreign Aid Appropriation Act of 1950 and six million would be provided under the China Area Aid Act of 1950. In a seven-year period the State Department would allot another eight million in aid to 3,517 Chinese students, and 119 Chinese scholars and professors. The aid was restricted to tuition and "maintenance adequate to achieve an immediate educational objective," plus emergency medical treatment and, if requested, a return ticket to China.[4]

There were several newsworthy incidents relating to the "stranded" Chinese during that period. One was the removal of nine Chinese students from the *S.S. President Cleveland,* a ship bound for the Far East via Honolulu—an event that received worldwide attention. China's newspapers filled with stories of such incidences, charging the American government with unauthorized detention of Chinese citizens, as sentiment darkened on both sides. By 1955 Sino-American tensions were high—the bombing of offshore islands in the Taiwan Strait the year before had brought China and America to the brink of war. When the Chinese foreign minister suggested that China would be willing to meet with the Americans for a series of bilateral talks, the two countries arranged meetings between governmental representatives of ambassadorial rank, to take place in Geneva, Switzerland. These ambassadorial talks would be the principal form of contact between the PRC and the United States for the next sixteen years.

Among the issues addressed by the ambassadorial representatives in Geneva was the repatriation of nationals, including students and scholars, in either country. Present at the first meetings were U.S. ambassador to Czechoslovakia U. Alexis Johnson and Chinese ambassador to Poland Wang Bingnan.[5] Repatriation had been an ongoing issue since the Chinese Communist victory in 1949 and the outbreak of the Korean War. When it was clear that the United States would officially recognize Taiwan rather than the People's Republic of China, the mainland Chinese authorities retaliated by denying exit permits to American missionaries, business owners, and scholars who resided there. Quite a few were arrested, some never tried or informed of how long the detention would continue.

As Americans were being arrested in China, the United States government declared a state of emergency and issued an order—that any Chinese students or scholars considered capable of aiding China's efforts with their expertise would not be allowed to return home. At the time of the mandate an estimated five thousand Chinese students were still in the United States, and more than one hundred would be detained for a number of years.

It was not until September 10, 1955, after several weeks of discussions, that an agreement was made acknowledging the right of Americans in China and Chinese in the United States to return "freely and expeditiously" to their countries of origin. Complications were anticipated, so in the event a student believed he or she was being prevented from returning, "third parties" were designated to intervene and provide mediation. For the Chinese in the United States, the third party was the Indian Embassy, and for Americans detained in China the designated third party was the British Embassy. Arguments ensued nevertheless. American officials accused the Chinese of continuing to hold U.S. citizens on false charges and at the same time Chinese representatives questioned why many of its citizens were still in America. The United States assured China that their citizens were no longer being barred from leaving the country—some were simply choosing to stay. Of those Chinese students who were stranded in the United States only about 150—students or scholars whose technical skills might have aided the Communists—were actually detained by the American government after 1951. When the orders were lifted in 1955, only thirty-nine of those detainees chose to leave.[6]

After sixteen years and 136 meetings, the ambassadorial discussions finally ended when President Richard Nixon traveled to China to set the stage for American recognition of the People's Republic of China. While the group accomplished little in terms of formal agreements, the discussions in Geneva did provide the two countries with an avenue for negotiation, helping to calm tensions that may have otherwise escalated.

MCCARTHYISM

As China was reshaped under the tutelage of Mao Zedong, there were those in the United States, Senator Joseph McCarthy chief among them, who were determined to mold American popular opinion to mirror a conservative anti-communist perspective. The social effect of "McCarthyism" in the late 1940s and 1950s has been widely publicized; however, little is documented about its influence on higher education exchange, although it is evident that universities were among the main concerns—prime targets for anyone wanting to root out communism.

A case in point was Sherman Wu, the son of a Chinese politician and a communist, who in 1956 was rejected from a Northwestern University fraternity. The group justified their decision by claiming that his presence as a communist would "degrade their house."[7] There were attacks on professors as well, some carried out by state and local authorities, following the example set by the McCarthy-sanctioned House on Un-American Activities Committee. However, state governments, unlike federal, more often applied symbolic legislation or economic sanctions to the universities rather than criminal prosecutions.

Responding to the possibility of state or federal investigation, many American universities began imposing oaths of allegiance on their faculty and administrators—a pledge of loyalty to state and national constitutions and a disavowal of membership in any organization with an aim to overthrow the government by force or violence. The practice was not without controversy. The University of California was one institution that suffered considerable criticism over its imposition of such a pledge, and many questioned the right of the institution to demand such a statement. No matter how the oath of allegiance was worded or presented, everyone understood its meaning—if you supported communism, your career was at serious risk.

Evidence of McCarthyism was everywhere. At the University of Washington two faculty members who admitted to being members of the Communist Party were fired and another was dismissed because of what was termed an "ambiguous relationship" to the party and for violations of the university's administrative code. University president Raymond B. Allen defended the actions of his institution in an article published in the May, 1949, issue of *Educational Forum*. A member of the Communist Party is not a free man, Allen alleged, "because he is a slave to immutable dogma and to a clandestine organization masquerading as a political party."[8]

Most of these "intellectual purges" in the United States occurred between 1952 and 1954, when an estimated one hundred academics lost their jobs for belonging to the Communist Party. Others were dismissed for having suspected affiliations with the party, or for refusing to pledge a loyalty oath disavowing such accusations. Social and political pressure was such that even the American Association of University Professors (AAUP), historically a mainstay for faculty support, failed to come to the defense of academic freedom during those years. Like those who were put on the "Hollywood blacklist" of suspected communists in the film industry, many professors would find it impossible to reestablish their professions until the policies of McCarthyism degenerated with the liberalism of the 1960s.

EAST-WEST EDUCATIONAL COLLABORATIONS IN THE MAO YEARS

When the Communist insurgency toppled the Nationalist government, collaborations and partnerships such as Yale-China faced an uncertain future in the face of growing hostility. The new Communist government predictably took possession of its Changsha properties in 1951, renaming the Yali

Middle School "Liberation Middle School." Dr. Dwight Rugh, Yale-China's last representative in Changsha and the only American on campus, had spent most of the previous year under house arrest.[9] With a new government now firmly in control, for the next three decades ties between Yale-China in New Haven and the institutions in Changsha and Wuhan would be essentially severed. From 1951 until 1954 the association devoted its resources to financing the education of Chinese students in America, as it looked to other parts of Asia for new projects.

A refugee college in the British colony of Hong Kong soon became Yale-China's focus of attention. A group led by Ch'ien Mu and other Chinese intellectuals wanted to preserve traditional Chinese learning and values in the face of mainland communism, and after months of negotiations the result was a Yale-China affiliation with New Asia College. This time the relationship would be one of support and assistance rather than direct administration, as it had been in Changsha. Funding for the affiliation, provided through the generosity of the Ford Foundation and others, enabled New Asia faculty to study in the United States. In 1956 Yale-China reinstated its practice of sending two recent Yale graduates annually to teach English in China—this time they would be sent to New Asia College instead of Yali Middle School.[10]

In 1959 the possibility of founding a university in Hong Kong was explored, an institution that would use Chinese as the medium of instruction. The Council of British Universities selected New Asia, United, and Chung Chi colleges to federate and form the new Chinese University of Hong Kong, which was formally inaugurated in 1963.[11] Yale-China contributed to its new campus by securing funds to construct numerous buildings, among them the university's health clinic, the Yali Guest House, Friendship Lodge, and a student dormitory. Soon to follow was the New Asia-Yale-in-China Chinese Language Centre and the International Asian Studies Program, which continues to host hundreds of international students each year.

FORMOSA

European navigators in the sixteenth century had recorded the sighting of an island off China's coast. They were struck with the island's splendor, and called it Formosa, meaning beautiful. "Peaks, crests, rugged crags, rounded domes, follow in endless variety . . . while the mountain torrents everywhere break into foaming waterfalls, or rush through dark gorges amidst the bright tints of dense sub-tropical vegetation . . . native villages suspected rather than seen."[12]

The civil war between Chiang Kai-shek's Nationalists (Guomindang) and the Chinese Communist Party was a conflict that had started in China well before World War II. When the civil war finally ended in October 1949 and as Mao Zedong assumed power, an estimated two million refugees, predominantly from the Nationalist government, military, and business community, gathered their possessions, left everything that was familiar, and fled to the island of Formosa (Taiwan) to set up a new center of Chinese government. For the fifty years prior, Taiwan had been under the authority of Japan, and had enjoyed a period of peaceful development. Under Chiang's leadership the Guomindang established a "provisional" Chinese government on Taiwan, calling it the Republic of China (ROC) and its capital was set up in Taipei. They declared themselves the official rulers, the "sole legitimate government of all of China, including the mainland"—a claim they finally abandoned in 1991.

DIVIDED DEMOGRAPHICS

Soon after the establishment of the ROC in Taiwan, the IIE conducted its first *Open Doors* international student census, published in 1951, a report that has since become the principal resource for foreign student-enrollment statistics. According to that first census, 3,549 Chinese students were enrolled in American colleges and universities that year—mostly those who had begun their studies before the Communist takeover. "The Chinese program is now in a state of dissolution," read a statement published alongside the report. "With aid from the U.S. government Chinese students and specialists are returning to Formosa (Taiwan) or, in some cases, to the Chinese mainland, or are rapidly completing their studies in American institutions."[13]

It is difficult to provide an accurate count of Chinese students in American institutions during the 1950s because the countries of origin become blurred. In the 1952 count, the total number of Chinese students in the United States was reported to be 2,960 and for the next few years IIE combined the sending countries (PRC, ROC, and Hong Kong) in their final count. By 1959 the total number of students from the three countries was 3,837. By 1965 IIE began separating the census by individual country and that year reported 4,620 students from the ROC, 3,279 from Hong Kong, and another 2,160 were "unspecified," for a total of 10,059. A decade later in 1975, there were 8,229 students from the ROC, 8,884 from Hong Kong, and 22 from the People's Republic of China, according to IIE reports.

THE SOVIET MODEL

As is clear from the enrollment numbers, mainland China was not in the market for American education—it looked to the Soviet Union instead. China's interest in study abroad had always been driven by its quest to improve its economy and military. In the decades before China's market-oriented reforms, mainstream modern economics were harshly criticized as "reactionary Western doctrine" and economists who proposed to introduce modern economics to universities in China were also repressed until the field in China, by one description, was "fully deserted."[14]

"I started my career as a student of economics in Jinling University, a missionary university in Nanjing in 1950," wrote Wu Jinglian, "studying the works of Alfred Marshall."[15] Within a year, before Wu could learn about Keynesian economic theories, his studies were interrupted by a series of political campaigns—the crackdown on counter-revolutionaries and the campaign to re-educate intellectuals in particular. In 1952 the government began a massive re-organization of higher education in China that started with the replacement of all teaching materials with those from the Soviet Union.

Under Mao's leadership and in sync with the Soviet model, in the 1950s specialized subject colleges were established independently, while others were separated out from existing programs in comprehensive institutions. Research in the new People's Republic of China was essentially separated from teaching, an anathema to the American system. A central plan was introduced in China that nationally unified instruction plans, syllabi, and textbooks at every level of education. Materials were subject to the scrutiny and approval of the Communist Party and all instruction was to reflect the party's official perspective.

In the new Chinese classroom, the emphasis on Soviet cultural supremacy was accompanied by the repudiation of all Western influence and of China's past educational heritage—the former condemned as bourgeois and the latter as feudalism. The First All-China Conference on Higher Education (1950) in Beijing had included on its agenda the necessity for education to serve the state, the need for more centralized control over education in general, and the refocusing on science and technology. Historian John Fairbank described the shift from liberal arts to technical subjects as a change from a "program that produced broad-gauged people for top government jobs to a more practical one that produced technicians. . . ."[16]

The new government's justification of the dramatic and costly revisions appeared in an article in the *Guangming Daily*:

> In the current process of revising and adopting teaching plans, it has become clear that those outlines drawn up on the basis of Soviet blueprints have had the full support of the delegates, whereas those deviating from the Soviet example have given rise to serious dissension. The reason is simple. It is because Soviet outlines have come from scores of years of labor and have proved their superiority through practice. What reason is here for us to depart from Soviet blueprints?[17]

China's quest for Soviet-style education can be framed within the context of China's larger social, political, and economic reforms. The first Five-Year Plan, launched in 1953, was designed to serve the nation's goal to rapidly increase technological and engineering talent in China. But by the mid-1950s the bonds Mao had hoped to forge between China's communist government and the nation's intelligentsia had not formed to an extent Mao found satisfactory. "We (the CCP) can't get along without them," he said.

"Them" meant China's intellectuals, defined as persons with at least a high school education.[18] He was sure he could win them over—out of China's estimated five million "intellectuals," Mao speculated that only about 3 percent were actually hostile to Marxism.

In 1956 Mao initiated the Hundred Flowers campaign, during which those in the intellectual community were cordially invited to lend their voices of constructive criticism to the communist system.[19] The initial response to the invitation was not overwhelming. Some of China's intellectuals feared that "sticking one's neck out" in the figurative sense might in very real terms result in the loss of one's head. Repeated invitations finally convinced many of China's intellectuals to come forward and offer their ideas for improving the government, honestly and candidly, as Mao had asked. But instead of the "non-antagonistic contradiction" Mao was expecting, the party found itself bombarded with hostile criticisms, disparagements chiefly aimed at the government's decision to adopt Soviet-style education.

Mao had to re-assess. Evidently China's intellectuals were more unreceptive than he had initially thought. The Hundred Flowers initiative closed within five weeks of the deluge of criticism but its story was far from over. As the intellectuals had feared from the outset, their voices of disapproval soon elicited a backlash. Within a month after the campaign was dissolved, an anti-Rightist movement began, its purpose to rectify the thoughts of intellectuals and to chastise party members who had not behaved "properly." According to historian Ruth Hayhoe, during this campaign somewhere between 300,000 and 700,000 skilled workers were pronounced "rightist" and removed from their jobs. "The collective knowledge and wisdom of the whole generation of distinguished scholars nurtured within the Nationalist universities was to be lost for two decades . . . condemned to exile."[20]

THE GREAT LEAP

The decision to embark upon the Great Leap Forward rather than a second Five-Year Plan happened partly because of the party's recognition that further emulation of Stalinist industrial growth might not in fact be in China's best interest. What Mao decided to do instead was unprecedented in history. China would engage in a massive initiative of rural collectivization and reorganization of peasant energy, with de-centralization and zealous motivation as the new ruling paradigm. And rather than motivate peasants for this massive venture by offering material incentives, Mao would inspire them with ideology.

Mao Zedong inaugurated the Great Leap Forward in 1957 as an effort to bring the nation quickly into the forefront of economic development and the construction of thousands of steel plants across China became a central part of the plan. The job of rural society was to keep pace with the production of ample food for the country, along with sufficient surplus to export for sale—income that could help to further finance China's industrialization. The Communist revolution had already stripped landowners of their property and now millions of peasants were ordered to work in agricultural cooperatives to accomplish these goals.

"My parents were peasants who worked in the field," said Dali Yang, an assistant professor of political science at the University of Chicago. "We grew wheat in the area where I lived, and they were part of a production team . . . they would often bring up the topic of the Great Leap famine and how bad things were. . . . "[21]

Collective farming had been intended to improve conditions for everyone. Communal eating facilities, where peasants could consume all they wanted, were promised to be free of charge. But the utopian dream soon became a nightmare. When the Great Leap began, Mao had projected China would overtake Britain in production of steel and other products within fifteen years. But only a year later he radically revised the plan and demanded that the goal be accomplished much earlier, an order that plunged the country into even deeper debt as increasing amounts were allotted for China's industrial development. In 1958 government spending on heavy industry represented 56 percent of state capital investment, up from 38 percent in 1956.[22]

People had been mobilized by the millions, distributed across China to accomplish the goals of industrialization. Thousands of backyard furnaces for iron and steel were constructed and people worked together on massive building projects. In the winter of 1957, for example, millions of peasants had been gathered to build a large-scale water conservation works and local leaders competed to see whose community could create the most activity. But with the increasing focus on steel and iron production, agricultural tasks were being neglected as workers left the fields to work toward the development of industry. The rural communal mess halls that were supposed to supply food for free exhausted their grain reserves by 1959, and the famine had begun.

Some of the problems were out of anyone's hands. While 1958 had been a good year for crop harvests, the extremely poor weather of 1959 combined with overly demanding expectations and reports of mismanagement—a devastating mix of conditions.[23] Estimates vary about how many people died as a result of the famine—anywhere from 16 to 40 million before the experiment came to an end in 1961, depending on the source. By anyone's estimation the experiment was a disaster. In a last-ditch struggle to survive, farmers in nearly one-third of the rural communities ultimately decided to take matters into their own hands and abandoned the communes in favor of individual harvesting. Central control was slowly reduced and agricultural production gradually began to improve.

It may seem incongruous that at the same time rural Chinese were struggling to stay alive, education in China was expanding. Some of the growth was encouraged by a 1958 conference convened by the Central Committee of the CCP, the result a directive on education, which set forth three cardinal principles. First, education must serve proletarian politics. Second, it must be combined with productive labor. And third, it must be under the direction of the Communist Party.[24] The same document authorized the establishment of schools where studies alternated with employment (work-study schools). After that, work and education went hand in hand in China.

The revised draft of the "National Programme for the development of agriculture from 1956–1967" had been prepared by Mao himself and was adopted in 1957 by the party's Central Committee. It stated that educational establishments must be diversified in the countryside and that every effort would be made to provide education to the masses.

Between 1957 and 1960 the number of institutions of higher education in China grew from 229 to 1,289 and student enrollment climbed from 441,000 to 961,000. Part of the growth was due to a large-scale decentralization of education undertaken in 1958, during which the Ministry of Higher Education was abolished and many institutions were returned to provincial control. Locally supported institutions grew at a rapid pace, often offering less formal types of education. The excessively rapid growth of institutions and enrollments was not sustainable, however. By the early 1960s there arose serious issues concerning education quality and efficiency, problems compounded by those facing the nation at large.

In 1960 a document known as the Sixty Articles, which re-emphasized the importance of research and supported limiting the time students and teachers were expected to spend on "productive labor" and political work, was widely distributed. The Chinese government, still struggling to recover from the human and monetary losses of the Great Leap famine, reconsolidated its higher education system and by 1965 the number of universities had been reduced to 434, with a student population of 674,000. As the numbers declined, so did China's affection for the Soviet Union—a change of heart that would trigger an overall shift in national policy. Several of the Soviet programs that had been so quickly implemented at the beginning of the Mao era were now under scrutiny. Chinese education, in retrospect, was preparing for a minor renaissance, but it was one that would not fully manifest itself for another decade.

THE CULTURAL REVOLUTION

The year 1966 witnessed the outbreak of a national movement in china. The Cultural Revolution would reign for the next ten years, introducing changes, according to Hayhoe, "almost Biblical" in scope. Replacing the feudal-capitalistic values of the pro-Communist period with proletarian ones, using school as the transmitter of knowledge and values was now

China's aim. Rising to prominence was the so-called Gang of Four, a powerful group comprised of Mao Zedong's wife Jiang Qing (the leader of the four) and her associates Zhang Chunqiao, Yao Wenyuan, and Wang Hongwen. The gang effectively controlled many of the inner workings of the Chinese Communist Party through the latter stages of the Cultural Revolution and some still debate whether certain decisions were actually made by Mao or by the foursome.

The exact beginning of the Cultural Revolution is also questioned, but one incident that is known to have spurred it on was the display of a "big character" poster by Beijing University professor Nie Yuanzi and six other members of the philosophy department. With large letters the poster publicly accused the university's president Lu Ping, and several officials, of having bourgeois tendencies.[25]

Learning of the display, Mao Zedong decided it could be used to his party's advantage, and ordered the exhibit to be publicized—a fresh means of mobilizing support. Mao may have been fearful that the communist spirit was stagnating, that the bureaucrats of the CCP were beginning to behave like the imperialists of old. Concerned that powerful internal forces could constitute a threat, Mao began to purge not only intellectuals and "rightists" but some previously prominent members of the Communist Party.

Mao understood the power of things like "big character" posters—the emotional impact of communicating through art or poetry. The Confucian concept of music and imagery was in fact quite similar to that of the Communist Party's—that the arts could be devices for didactic change or the spread of ideals, and therefore should be under state control. During imperial times folk songs were sometimes banned if the lyrics spoke against Qing policy. In the mid-1800s Hong Xiuquan, leader of the Taiping Rebellion, had used songs to promote revolutionary propaganda and to rally troops. In 1903 singing was used as a form of student protest in Shanghai and around 1910 the Chinese government used "classroom songs," *xuetangge,* on a massive scale as a means of spreading desired social norms. Communists had been rewriting folks songs since the 1920s to use as vehicles for propaganda or information, a strategy especially effective among the rural population.[26]

In the 1930s so-called mass songs (*dazhong gequ*) gained popularity as a powerful protest medium among left-wing and nationalist groups in urban areas. After the founding of the People's Republic in 1949, songs as a form were put under the control of the CCP, reserved for the state to be used as weapons of "mass struggle"—lyrics designed to combine "revolutionary realism with revolutionary romanticism."[27] On the eve of the Cultural Revolution militant songs about class struggle and odes to the Communist Party and Mao Zedong were predominant themes. Mao would utilize music, art, and literature to inspire his growing legion of student "Red Guards."

THE RED GUARDS

Were they student fanatics ready to commit violence in the name of Mao Zedong? Or were they ill-fated heroes who sacrificed everything for the greater good? In a 1987 article, "I Was a Teenage Red Guard," Mo Bo described the movement from personal experience. "When the Cultural Revolution reached my school in 1967 I was 14," said Mo. "In the beginning, classes were interrupted from time to time; the teachers began to get worried . . . overnight, wall posters appeared everywhere . . . it was taken for granted the posters had been composed by the seniors . . . one depicted the eccentric geology teacher as a 'dirty bourgeois intellectual,' criticizing his 'yellow' diaries," Mo continued. "He was so eccentric that we all thought there must be something bourgeois about him." Following the example of the students in Beijing, Mo and his classmates formed an Organization of the Red Guards. "Everybody wanted to join. . . . "[28]

The students enjoyed having no classes and degrading the teachers, Mo readily confessed. Chairman Mao himself had told them that the "teacher takes the student as the enemy and uses examinations as weapons to attack the student."[29] Mao said this validated their actions. In 1966, in a meeting

Figure 6.1 Mao Zedong's student Red Guards, circa 1965.

with an estimated million Red Guards in Tiananmen Square, Mao put on a red armband to demonstrate his support, telling the students to attack the "Four Olds" of Chinese society—old customs, old culture, old habits, and old ideas.

In the past teachers had been intimidating, Mo recollected, but after the Red Guards assumed power in the school, "whenever a teacher came across a student they would lower their heads." Like most of his Red Guard friends, Mo "never did appreciate the beating-up of people business. The farthest we ever went was when the most unpopular teacher was made to kneel down and confess his crimes' to the students. One student hit the teacher's heels with a brick—I couldn't bear to look."[30]

Nobody understood Marxism, said Mo Bo. All they knew was that Mao understood it. The academic authorities in the fields of philosophy, history, literature, and art (but not science) had to be re-educated, Mao had declared, because they stood for an outdated ideology that was no longer good for China. "I think I believed this," said Mo. In time the organization became chaotic and much of Chinese society became involved, whether they were Red Guards or not. Some just "enjoyed being vandals." By then, he concluded, "nobody could tell who did what—let along for what reasons."[31]

It is speculated that the term "Red Guard" may have been coined by students at Tsinghua Middle School, who, instead of writing their real names of the "big character" posters, reportedly signed them "Red Guards." Now seeing themselves as personal warriors for Mao, the majority of this band of youths had been students before the outbreak of this era.

In August 1966 Mao granted the youthful rebels some exceptional privileges—the right to demonstrate, the right of assembly, and the right to publish their own tabloids for the purpose of public criticism of cadres at all levels. This heretofore unheard-of freedom to attack authority led to a flood of publications, including Red Guard songbooks, "little newspapers" (*xiaobao*), and illustrated informational booklets, distributed alongside Mao's "Little Red Books." Red Guard members and supporters would reportedly sing their songs in the streets, sometimes with the help of loudspeaker systems or local radio stations and lyrics were routinely printed in major newspapers such as the *People's Daily*. In addition to self-composed songs, students also composed *yuluge*—quotations from Mao Zedong set to music.

Many of the "guards" had signed on to the cause after attending one of the six massive youth rallies held in Beijing, gatherings organized by the People's Liberation Army and the Cultural Revolution Group. An estimated ten million youths attended these rallies and volunteered to become Red Guards—sentries who pledged to pit themselves against professors. The effort would have a paralyzing effect. College and university enrollments virtually halted for the next four years and graduate enrollments ended for an even longer time. Entrance examinations were discontinued, which meant that being accepted in an institution of higher learning was now primarily dependent on family status in the community, or connections to the

Communist Party. The Cultural Revolution was intended to dispense with the traditional model by which higher education was reserved for the few. But the effort had instead created a "new elite."[32]

Few in the next generation would have any hope for higher learning, and between 1967 and 1976 the number of postsecondary students in China dropped precipitously from 674,000 to 47,800.[33] In 1970 the government began letting certain universities reopen; however, the admission of students was often dependent on the applicants' political behavior, and procedures held inconsistent standards for peasants, workers, and soldiers. It was not until after the death of Mao Zedong, in 1976, that China's higher education system would resume its advance toward the Western model—a model experiencing its own period of transition.

In the 1960s and 1970s American higher education was immersed in a tide of social change resulting in a "generation gap" between old conservative and new liberal thinking. The postwar "baby boomers" had spawned a generation of new Americans who grew up in a golden age of prosperity and idealism—ideals that would be fundamentally altered during the Vietnam War. When China reopened its doors to Sino-American education exchange in the late 1970s, Chinese students coming to the United States would find a decidedly different college culture than earlier generations had encountered. Likewise, Chinese students traveling to U.S. institutions at the outset of the so-called third wave of enrollments—some of them former Red Guards—thought and acted quite differently from those who had come to America during the first and second waves of Chinese enrollments.

7   A Third Wave

> Education is a slow-moving but powerful force. It may not be fast enough or strong enough to save us from catastrophe, but it is the strongest force available for that purpose and its proper place, therefore, is not the periphery, but at the center of international relations.
>
> J. William Fulbright

Jimmy Carter was a young naval officer serving on an American submarine when he first visited China in 1949. Carter would turn twenty-five on October 1st that year, the same day the People's Republic of China was born. "I have always been proud that your birthday as a nation was on my birthday," he said in a speech at the Li Xiannian Library in Hong'an many years later. During his term as the thirty-ninth U.S. president (1977–1981), Carter was determined to repair the severed relationship between China and the United States. "I began to negotiate across the seas with my good friend, Deng Xiaoping," said Carter. "There were many problems we had to address . . . but he was a courageous and wise man. . . ."[1]

Deng Xiaoping had commanded the Second and Third Field Armies in China as they crossed the Changjiang and broke through the Guomindang line of defense, a victory that would mark the beginning of the collapse of the Nationalist government. On the eve of this ambitious operation, Deng had been made first secretary of the East China Bureau. It was in this capacity that Deng had also attended Mao Zedong's famous 1949 gathering in Tiananmen Square, where the chairman famously announced the birth of the People's Republic of China and closing of its doors to the West. Thirty years later Carter and Deng would meet face-to-face to negotiate the reopening of those doors. Their talks would become policy—a plan of action that would launch a new era of Sino-American education exchange, a "third wave" of Chinese student enrollments that continues today. At the time, neither man could have predicted the magnitude of China's extraordinary growth since that decision.

It is important to point out that, while Carter and Deng are often credited with spearheading the revival of Sino-American diplomatic relations, the process had actually been under way for some time and had enlisted the help of many. Among the earliest efforts toward reconciliation was the work of the Committee on Scholarly Communication with the People's Republic of China (CSCPRC).

THE COMMITTEE ON SCHOLARLY COMMUNICATION WITH THE PEOPLE'S REPUBLIC OF CHINA

The CSCPRC was begun when the Joint Committee on Contemporary China met to discuss the possibilities of reopening communications between American and Chinese scholars. The formation of the CSCPRC was motivated in part by scholars who, because of their professions, would be benefited by more access to China's culture and history. There were other motivations as well. China's scientific capability was becoming sophisticated, a point made clear by the 1962 detonation of its first atomic bomb. Scientists affiliated with the National Academy of Sciences looked for a means of convincing China to participate in the unofficial Pugwash Disarmament Conferences, meetings that would include the United States and the Soviet Union.[2]

Academic and scientific communities converged during the period from 1963 to 1966 and explored the possibilities of establishing a committee on China that would also include government representatives. Key figures joining the discussion were John Lindbeck, a professor of political science at Columbia University and chairman of the Joint Committee on Contemporary China, and Harrison Brown, foreign secretary of the National Academy of Sciences. This unique alliance soon grew to include social scientists, humanists, and natural scientists and as a team served to provide leverage for access to China.

The organizational structure for the CSCPRC was adopted in 1966 and the committee continued its work for the next three decades. Based at the National Academy of Sciences in Washington, DC, the American Council of Learned Societies in New York and the Social Science Research Council were included as equal sponsoring partners. Even in the midst of the Cultural Revolution, the CSCPRC made early attempts at communication. One such attempt was a letter that was hand-delivered by the committee's executive director Anne Keatley to the president of the Chinese Academy of Sciences, Guo Moruo, in 1971, in which the CSCPRC offered to initiate an exchange of scholars.[3]

NIXON, CARTER, DENG, AND THE RESUMPTION OF ACADEMIC EXCHANGE

President Richard Nixon's 1972 visit to China was a turning point in Sino-American academic relations, as it resulted in an agreement to initiate an exchange of academic delegations. A total of seventy-three such delegations were sent from both countries between 1972 and 1979. It was during these month-long visits that the American members of the delegations began to recognize the extent of the damage incurred by China's higher education as a result of the Cultural Revolution. It was clear that many of the Chinese visitors had little capacity for negotiating the sophisticated and complex learning environments they encountered in the U.S.—cutting-edge, open-discourse academic settings with which they were utterly unaccustomed. Beneficial results emerged from the delegations nevertheless. Among many examples was the book *Cancer in China*, an important contribution based on the country's striking epidemiological patterns of different kinds of cancer, demonstrating the significance of diet and location in studies.

Many contributed to the reopening of China's borders but according to a 2009 article in the *New York Times*, most Chinese believe that the credit ultimately belongs to Deng Xiaoping. No specific reforms were as important as his persistence in "further opening China's doors and encouraging its people to scour the world for new ideas in science, technology and management."[4] It is a claim difficult to dispute. One of Deng's first steps after he ascended to power in China was to promote talent. Deng had rushed to hold national entrance examinations and to reopen many universities that had been closed during the Cultural Revolution. His country's advance was his priority and Deng was willing to listen to new ideas. On many occasions he invited renowned scientists for talks and he would ask each one, "How can China catch up. . . . ?"

When Frank Press, President Jimmy Carter's science adviser, was dispatched on a diplomatic mission to China, Deng Xiaoping surprised him by proposing China send many more students and scholars to America than was first suggested. Not sure how to respond, Press placed a call to Washington, DC very late that night to advise the president of the unexpected proposal. Carter accepted Deng's offer immediately.

Secretary of State Cyrus Vance and national security adviser Zbigniew Brzezinski had also traveled to China on separate occasions in 1977 and 1978 to negotiate the possibilities of resuming diplomatic relations with the United States. Progress was made on October 1978 when the "Understanding on Educational Exchanges" was signed, an agreement that provided for the exchange of undergraduate students, graduate students, and visiting scholars to undertake study and research in China and the United States. It was during Brzezinski's visit that the United States announced its agreement to accept the three conditions set forth by China for the resumption of diplomatic relations—the severance of American diplomatic relations with Taiwan, abrogation of the mutual defense treaty between the United States and Taiwan, and the withdrawal of all U.S. forces from the island.[5] Leonard Woodcock, chief of the U.S. Liaison Office in China, was to conduct detailed negotiations with the Chinese side.

Then on January 31, 1979, Vice Premier Deng Xiaoping and Fang Yi, director of the State Science and Technology Commission, signed the "Agreement on Cooperation in Science and Technology," a landmark accord that provided an umbrella under which scientific, technological, and other educational exchanges could occur. The signing took place during

Deng Xiaoping's meeting with Jimmy Carter in Washington, DC, a goodwill visit Carter would record in his personal diary as "one of the delightful experiences of my Presidency," describing Deng as "smart, tough, intelligent, frank, courageous, personable, self-assured and friendly."[6] Within a few months of the signing, the first fifty Chinese students, "promising but poorly prepared," were sent to study in the United States. A consequence of the Mao era, unlike the "first wave" of Chinese enrollments to the United States, whose average age was about twelve, this time China had mostly scholars of an older generation to fill the first dispatches of students—some were in their forties.[7]

The United States soon authorized the granting of an unlimited number of academic visas to Chinese students and scholars who were accepted at American institutions of higher education. This was a fundamentally different arrangement than the Chinese had experienced in study-abroad programs with the Soviet Union, which demanded a strict numerical equality of "person-months."

After the signing of the agreements in 1979, the CSCPRC went to work to establish and provide single-year grants for individual research in China, which emphasized Chinese studies and the natural sciences. After 1979 the committee began administering the reciprocal Distinguished Scholar Exchange Program, a multinational, peer-reviewed competition. Within just a few years many and diverse exchange programs were added not just by the CSCPRC but also from a growing list of other organizations, public

Figure 7.1 Jimmy Carter and Deng Xiaoping 1979.

and private. Some offered multi-year grants and others offered collaborative research opportunities, and by the mid-1980s the many initiatives comprised a somewhat comprehensive framework for academic exchange.[8]

ECONOMICS AND EDUCATION REFORM

When China's imperial court first embarked upon its mission to secure Western science and technology through academic exchange, its motivations were to advance the economy and to secure sufficient information to build a suitable military. In the aftermath of the Mao era, China's study-abroad efforts remained narrowly aimed at the achievement of those same goals.

Chinese who had lived through Mao Zedong's repressive regime were hopeful that the collapse of many of his initiatives would improve China, as citizens began the hard work of building prosperity. To provide direction for its economic reforms, China dispatched delegates to Europe and America, and also East Asia, to learn how countries such as Japan, South Korea, and Singapore had been able to use market forces to allocate many of their resources, while also using industrial policy to provide administrative guidance. Chinese economists who were in favor of reform, Sun Yefang and Yu Guangyuan among them, paid visits to Yugoslavia and other Eastern European countries to study their methods. Then in late 1979 and early 1980 the Chinese Academy of Social Sciences invited Czech economist Ota Sik and exiled Polish economist Wlodzimierz Brus to hold seminars in China, lectures that drew large numbers of officials and scholars. "The descriptions of the reforms in Poland, Czechoslovakia, Hungary and elsewhere were eye-opening for the Chinese," wrote Wu Jinglian in 2011.[9] Both Brus and Sik advocated the theory of market socialism. According to this ideal, a certain degree of market forces are introduced to influence decisions and operations, within the framework of state ownership and the planned economy.

As it turned out, support for this theory was short-lived among Chinese economists and the lectures by Brus and Sik had an unexpected by-product. The analytical tools of the "modern economy" they endorsed were unfamiliar to the Chinese, and increasing speculation about China's ability to learn and apply these methods led many to instead sanction a return to more Westernized methods.

Between 1979 and early 1980 the Institute of Economic Research of the Chinese Academy of Social Services conducted three workshops, taught by respected foreign experts, most from developed countries. The workshops provided an opportunity for Chinese scholars in institutes of higher education and research institutions to learn the most recent achievements in modern economics, and allow them to observe China's system from the perspective of outsiders. In addition to the workshops, a number of scholars elected to study abroad or to do advanced research. Deng encouraged the government to begin sending thousands of China's brightest students to study economics in the United States, the United Kingdom, Europe, and Japan.

By the middle 1980s China had developed its own circle of economists who could be considered experts. In 1985 the World Bank organized and hosted a Sino-foreign cooperative research seminar on the Chinese economy, which published "China: Long-term Development Issues and Options." From this study the Overall Plan for the Reform of the Economic System was drafted. The plan basically stated that in a commodity economy, a complete market system constitutes the basis of economic mechanism. Enterprises determine their own activities autonomously based on their relationship in the market, and workers autonomously choose their occupations. The government then evolves from "mostly direct control to mostly indirect control."

In September 1985 another seminar was convened, this time on a Yangtze cruise ship in the Bashan. Called the "Bashan Steamship Conference," the meeting was organized by the World Bank, the State Economic Reform Commission, and the Development Research Center of the State Council, and its result was the adoption of the seventh Five-Year Plan, which was to be in effect through 1990.[10] The acquisition of knowledge to support the new plan was now a priority and the government would need to find creative ways to collaborate with American scientists and technologists. By 1992 the Fourteenth Party Congress set the goal of establishing a "socialist market economy," and at the Third Plenary Session in 1993, the "Decision on Several Issues Concerning Establishing a Socialist Market Economy" was formally adopted—a plan based on a much deeper understanding of the economy of developed nations. A critical function of the plan was to expand the introduction of foreign equipment and technology, an effort that has since dramatically increased the enrollment totals of Chinese students in American universities, a move that has also quickly narrowed the knowledge gap of earlier decades.

By the time China's goal for establishing a socialist market economy was fully adopted, progress in finding diverse scientific and academic collaborations was already well under way. Between 1978 and the mid-1980s the number of bilateral accords in science, technology, or education between Chinese and American government agencies grew from two to twenty-four and covered a broad range of areas—space technology, high-energy physics, environmental protection, earthquake studies, nuclear safety, transportation, statistics, and biomedical sciences. Accords included the Protocol on Cooperation in the Field of Atmospheric Science and Technology, signed by the Oceanographic and Atmospheric Administration in 1979. Others included the Protocol for Scientific and Technical Cooperation in the Earth Sciences, in cooperation with the U.S. Geological Survey (1980), and the Protocol for Scientific and Technical Cooperation in Earthquake Studies, a collaboration involving the U.S. Geological Survey and the National Science Foundation. Another was the Agreement on Cooperation in the Field of Management of Industrial Science and Technology, which partnered with the U.S. Department of Commerce. Cooperative efforts between the United States Department of Agriculture and the PRC remained productive until November that year, when the activities under the 1979 Understanding on Agricultural Exchange were suspended after China failed to import the amount of American grain the agreement had called for.

An especially innovative bilateral program was the 1979 "Cooperation in the Field of Management of Science and Technology," a collaborative effort of the United States Department of Commerce, China's State Economic Commission, State Science and Technology Commission, and China's Ministry of Education. Designed to find mechanisms for China's upgrading, some also viewed it as a way to train managers who would then be favorably disposed to work with American companies. The agreement was renewed in 1984 for a period of five years, and the result was the National Center for Industrial Science and Technology Management Development, established in Dalian City, China. More than 700 individuals received training in its first four classes. The State University of New York at Buffalo soon began offering a master's degree in business at the Dalian Center, with both governments agreeing to subsidize the program for its first five years with the provision of two million dollars.

Now that academic relations with China were proliferating beyond the programs formerly offered by the CSCPRC, involving direct university-to-university relations, the committee began providing consultant services to these emerging programs through a service called the U.S.-China Education Clearinghouse. Its quarterly publication, *The China Exchange News,* became an important mode of communication for administrators, faculty, and students. The committee also published resource materials that served as introductions to Chinese universities and research institutes.[11]

An important spin-off program from the CSCPRC was the Chinese University Development Project, another World Bank effort. Working with the National Academy of Science, the CSCPRC comprised the initial international advisory panel that advised both the World Bank and China's Ministry of Education. The Chinese University Development Project spearheaded multiple phases of World Bank support for higher education in China.[12] The CSCPRC's name later changed to the Committee on Scholarly Communication with China.

In the mid-1980s, the point at which many of these exchange initiatives were solidly underway, there were an estimated 1.1 million regular schools in China, 9.7 million teachers and 202.6 million full-time students—the largest school system in the world. In addition were 227,000 adult-education schools. Of the estimated 203 million total students in China, 134 million were enrolled in grades one through six. Only about two million were studying at the college level.[13] By the mid-1980s, China's goal of nine years of compulsory education (six primary and three junior-middle) had not been accomplished—as of October 1985 only about a third of China's regions had made primary educational universally available. Rudimentary training of faculty was part of the reason so few Chinese had access to a high level of study, a problem China openly acknowledged.

Chinese students studying the social sciences in the United States during the early part of the "third wave" were in a minority. In the academic year 1993–1994, only about 6.3 percent (2,796) of Chinese graduate students in the United States were enrolled in social-science degree programs, compared to 31.5 percent in physical and life science, 23.9 percent in engineering, 12 percent in math and computer science, and 8.7 percent in business.[14] The fields of study chosen by students during the earlier "second wave" of Chinese enrollments had been quite different. From 1905 until 1953, social sciences had been among the top fields of study for Chinese students in America, second only to engineering.

Much of the concentration on the sciences and technology in the 1980s was of course due to the government's focus on recovering the economy and military, and neither could be accomplished without expertise in those fields. Deng Xiaoping's program of "Four Modernizations" demanded the study of hard science and students were asked to study what was good for the government, and consequently for China. The 1980s and 1990s witnessed the development of many important and influential Sino-American educational programs—it was a period of academic growth that would have a profound effect on Chinese higher education in the upcoming century. While the large numbers and daunting features of China's educational system created political, pedagogical, and financial hurdles, they also produced circumstances that led to new discussions about fresh possibilities for student exchange.[15]

A THIRD WAVE OF EXCHANGE ORGANIZATIONS AND INITIATIVES

With the reopening of China's borders, the State Council of the People's Republic of China had approved the recommendation of the Ministry of Education and the Ministry of Foreign Affairs to establish the China Educational Association for International Exchange (CEAIE). Formally established in July 1981 and headquartered in Beijing, CEAIE became China's main not-for-profit organization in the business of conducting international educational exchanges, under the direct guidance of the Ministry of Education. In the early part of the new millennium its membership included about 150 institutions.

The CEAIE has served as the member institution or standing committee member of other national organizations including the Chinese People's Association for Friendship with Foreign Countries, China NGO (nongovernmental organization) Network for International Exchanges, and others. CEAIE is approved by the State Administration of Foreign Experts Affairs as having the authority to organize overseas training. In their years of service CEAIE has worked with more than one thousand partners associations and institutions in China, and has established working relationships with more than 170 educational organizations in more than fifty countries, including the United States. In 2006, CEAIE was granted special consultative status with the Economic and Social Council of the United Nations and in 2008 it became an NGO associated with the Department of Public Information of the United Nations. In 2009 CEAIE became the NGO in official relations with UNESCO.[16]

Like UNESCO and other American organizations, activities of the Institute of International Education (IIE) in China had slowed during the Mao era, but resurfaced after diplomatic and academic relations resumed. The Council for International Exchange of Scholars (CIES), the scholar division of the IIE, was an organization known for its expertise in conducting international exchange programs for scholars and university administrators, and it had helped administer the Fulbright Scholar Program since its inception, on behalf of the Department of State.

The national Program for Advanced Study and Research in China, administered by the CSCPRC, was part of the graduate study and research component of the Fulbright program. The Board of Foreign Scholars, which was comprised of educational and public leaders appointed by the president of the United States, handled program policy, supervised Fulbright exchanges, and was responsible for approving candidates. The United States Information Agency (USIA) administered the Fulbright program alongside the local supervision of the U.S. Embassy in Beijing.[17]

Adding to these administrative components was the CIES, which was contracted with the USIA to arrange publicity, process applications, and to make recommendations to the Board of Foreign Scholarships for sending Americans to universities in China as lecturers in the fields of American history, American literature, business management, economics, law, political science, and sociology.[18] Between 1980 and 1984 the CIES sent seventy-three American lecturers to twelve Chinese institutions, the majority to Beijing University and Shanghai Foreign Languages Institute. During the same period the council brought forty-five Chinese lecturers to America. Since then the program has expanded to include nearly fifty institutions throughout China, most of them under the jurisdiction of the Ministry of Education.

In 1985 the China-U.S. Educational Agreement formally incorporated the Fulbright program within its operational framework, under the guidance of the Chinese Ministry of Education. They would handle operational work such as selection, admission, and predeparture training of Chinese candidates, and reception of U.S. scholars was managed by the China Scholarship Council. Currently there are more than forty Chinese universities participating in the program.[19]

Another important organization that resurfaced after 1979 was the Council on International Educational Exchange (CIEE), originally founded as the Council on Student Travel in 1947. In 1979 China International

Travel Service authorized four CIEE China study tours. These tours were under the leadership of Chinese scholars and provided chiefly for undergraduate students who were selected from American colleges and universities. CIEE and Fudan University in Shanghai agreed to work together on the establishment of a China study program for U.S. college students, a program designed to include teaching by Chinese professors in English on Chinese culture, politics, language, business, and other subjects.

The CIEE began its first study-abroad program in 1980 for American students going to China and since then has hosted thousands of students at their study centers in Shanghai, Beijing, and Nanjing. The council also facilitates and operates ongoing relationships with secondary- and tertiary-level institutions and currently has a program of more than 65 schools, colleges, and universities supporting their Teach in China program. CIEE works with local Chinese representatives to actively recruit college and high school students each year to participate in cultural exchange programs, such as USA High School, Work and Travel USA, Global Leader Internship, and Hometown USA. Their efforts draw students from more than eighty colleges and universities across China. In 1993, under CIEE sponsorship, a six-semester-credit Chinese-language course, which offered additional elective courses, opened at National Changchi University of Taipei.

The Yale-China Association, like CIEE, had been rendered inactive in China after the communist takeover, but returned after the reopening of borders with new plans for education and exchange. In 1979, the Yale-China staff traveled back to Changsha to explore new academic-exchange opportunities with faculty and administrators at Hunan Medical College. The talks resulted in exchange agreements that led to the arrival of a number of Yale-China English teachers in late 1980, as well as exchanges of medical personnel between Hunan Medical College and Yale University. Later the same year, English instructors were also dispatched to Wuhan University and to Huazhong Normal University.

During the 1980s Yale-China's medical program brought around fifty personnel to the United States and sent about forty Americans to China for exchanges of medical expertise. Nearly one hundred Yale graduates took an active part in Yale-China's English teaching program in China during that period. By the 1990s the association had expanded its activities to include new areas, and soon language programs existed alongside new projects in environmental protection and pediatric cardiology. Creative arts affiliations were developed as well. One of many examples was a partnership facilitated between New Haven Long Wharf Theater and the Shanghai People's Art Theater, which resulted in a Chinese-language state production of Amy Tan's *The Joy Luck Club* in 1994. Also added were programs in American studies, legal education, public health, nursing, and service in the nonprofit sector for both Chinese and American students—all part of a vastly expanded Yale-China agenda.

Other organizations and programs that had been kept at bay during Mao's era likewise reclaimed their roles in education exchange after 1979. In December 1980 the National Science Foundation (NSF) inaugurated its program of Sino-American scientific cooperation by signing the U.S.-China Protocol on Cooperation in the Basic Sciences with the Chinese Academy of Sciences (CAS) and the Chinese Academy of Social Sciences (CASS). Activities under the protocol were managed by the U.S.-China Joint Working Group on Cooperation in Basic Sciences, comprised of Americans from NSF and Chinese from the CAS, the CASS, and the Ministry of Education. The program operated 43 cooperative research projects between 1980 and 1984, as well as 12 joint workshops and seminars.[20]

The National Association of Foreign Student Affairs (NAFSA), an organization that had grown to be an important component of education exchange since its founding in the 1940s, would also have renewed interest in China as the "third wave" gained momentum. In addition to providing services and resources for the many foreign student advisers working with the quickly expanding Chinese student populations, in 1993 NAFSA established the China Special Interest Group (SIG) to promote academic exchanges between China and the United States.

THE STUDENTS

When U.S.-China education exchange resumed after three decades of estrangement, Chinese students who arrived in America during the first years of the "third wave" had limited means of knowing what to expect. In 1978 traveling from Beijing to New York took about thirty hours. "A strange feeling overwhelms you. The whole world . . . has changed completely in the blink of an eye . . . only a few hours have passed [but] the true difference between China, a developing country, and America, a developed country, is as great as if you had time-traveled to a future century."[21]

"The U.S. was so attractive to me!" said one student. "I imagined it beautiful, different and full of opportunities. I had a dream of spending many years to study there."[22] A twenty-eight-year-old Chinese woman studying in America said that when she arrived in San Francisco it was a sunny day and white cumulus clouds were drifting in the sky. "I was thinking, Wow, even the clouds in America are whiter!"

Others had more traumatic initiations. Some students reported feeling isolated. "Even when you're surrounded by many friends, you still feel lonely. Something is missing. It's like you're wandering around . . . nobody truly knows who you are . . . my mind often travels back to my home city, my appetite craves for the dishes that my mom cooked for me. . . . "[23]

One doctoral student from Nanjing University arrived in 1986 with only 50 dollars in cash. When his adviser could not meet him at the airport, he was told he could take a taxi to the university, thirty miles away. "All the way I was watching the fare meter intensely and my heart was racing." When the meter reached $49 in desperation he asked to be let out. "My first impression?" he replied in an interview, was that "the digital display of that meter was leaping too fast."[24] For many Chinese students who arrived in the first years of the third wave, the biggest challenge had nothing to do with limited finances, academics, language, admission, passports, or adjusting to American life. For some the most vexing challenge would be the task of securing their work unit's permission to leave.

The social structure in China consisted of the government and the family, with the work unit serving as an intermediary for guidance. The government could be loved or hated and the family members could be scorned, but committing any offence against one's work unit was, at that time, unacceptable. It was the job of the work unit to dispense all social benefits. It managed births, carrying out China's one-child policy, as well as any benefits related to aging, illness, or death. "It decided what one ate and drank and where one disposed of waste; it issued pay, allocated housing and holiday goods, and admitted children to kindergarten."[25] And work units maintained a hidden dossier for each citizen.

If a prospective student gained admission to an American university and had received a financial guarantee, a letter of recommendation from the work unit had to be secured before the student could apply for a passport. The success of getting that letter depended to a large degree on whether the head of the unit was enlightened, or if the personal administrator was in a good mood that day. "You should never publicize your intention before you leave; deny it vehemently until you receive your passport. Even if you are already abroad, make sure that when you call China you say 'I haven't left yet.'"[26]

Adding to the aforementioned issues, some in this new generation of Chinese exchange students were laden with a further burden, one described by author Qian Ning, himself an exchange student in the 1980s, as a "dark shadow of history." He recounts the story of one of the first privately financed students to come to America, in 1981. After receiving his degree from a New York institution, the young man had become a successful investment banker in Boston and within a few years was able to purchase a fine home and an expensive car. "By any measure, he was leading the life of a typical middle-class American." But even after years in the United States, the man was plagued by paranoia. He showed alarm any time his doorbell was rung and often suspected he was being followed. "I'll get revenge for that" was a sentence he frequently spoke, referring to infringements both real and imagined. His actions and attitude, Qian Ning contended, were the result of his previous life in China—memories of police in the station in the Beijing district where his family had lived, "security cadres" of the public safety commission, and women on the local residence committee—uncomfortable reminders of repression and surveillance. "He could not forget his years during the Cultural Revolution before he came to

America."[27] Like many other Chinese families at the time, the man's parents were viewed with suspicion because of their scientific training in the United States. At one point they were imprisoned. The family was labeled as "bad" and for years the children were obliged to report to the police or the public safety commission to be lectured on discipline. They were not allowed to go outside their house during public celebrations, "not even to watch the fireworks." The man had been in America for ten years, but he had not shaken the experience.

The story is relevant because it is representative of the experience of many Chinese students who came to America just after China's borders reopened. A PhD candidate at the University of Michigan voiced his surprise at the intense hatred harbored by some mainland students. "I never would have thought they carried that much hate . . . some of these mainland students really hate—they gnash their teeth." For some the wounds would not heal quickly. Other students seemed to believe that once they left China, they could leave behind moral constraints. "They would do disgraceful things, shamelessly." Years of oppressive governmental regulation combined with deeply embedded Confucianism had woven a web of control through Chinese society. Even as early as elementary school, teachers would frighten the children by warning them to do well and obey the rules because they would someday be writing their own history—"don't let that history stain your dossier." From childhood on, people were penalized if they were thought to have committed political mistakes or if they conducted themselves somehow inappropriately. The highest imperative in life was "Don't ever make a mistake."[28]

Angry attitudes and paranoid behavior were by no means universal among Chinese students during the early years of the third wave—many more were models of decorum and scholarship and reminiscent of the first CEM students became popular and influential in the American classrooms they occupied. By the 1990s Chinese students were experiencing fewer restrictions in China, and adjustment to American life slowly became easier as well. One student reported, after his arrival in 1991, that it was "Really, nothing special," adding that he had "already seen a great deal of America in movies and magazines."[29]

ENGLISH-LANGUAGE TRAINING

In the early 1980s, because China had few "traditional" college-aged students qualified sufficiently to send to America, many midcareer specialists were sent to study science and engineering for one or two years. Because these scholars had attended Chinese universities when Russian was the preferred language, most had very little formal English training. Learning English sufficient to understand instruction in the classroom, and to survive daily life, was imperative.

Since its inception in 1964, the Test for English as a Foreign Language (TOEFL), a test of English proficiency for international students whose native language is not English, has been the most widely accepted English-language assessment and is now used in the admissions process in over 130 countries. The Chinese government agreed to an American proposal to establish TOEFL centers in China in December 1981 and the first tests were held in Beijing, Shanghai, and Guangzhou.[30] The number of TOEFL centers quickly expanded to eight cities and by 1987 there were twenty-nine examination sites in fifteen cities. The rate of expansion could not keep up with demand, however, in spite of the relatively high cost of the test. The fee that year was about $26—a sizable sum for many students.

Typically, American colleges require a TOEFL score of at least 500 for undergraduates and a minimum of 550 for graduate-level students. Modest improvement in PRC test scores on the TOEFL examination was evident in the first half of the decade—in the years from 1980 to July 1982 the mean score of PRC students was 473, compared to 491 in the period from July 1982 to June 1984. Chinese students' scores fell significantly behind the scores of international students in general, however.[31]

After 1989 as "study-abroad fever" (*liu xue re*) set in, Chinese students lined up to secure one of the limited number of tickets for the TOEFL.[32] *Tuofu,* the phonetic transliteration of TOEFL in Chinese, "became a household word with a Hong Kong flavor."[33] Would-be test takers stood in lines for hours, some organizing teams to take turns. Once one got in, the testing facilities were reportedly first-rate. Test-site colleges in Beijing, for example, opened their laboratories to the test takers. In America TOEFL facilities were less standardized and could range from a small lecture hall with a loud speaker and no headphones to a cutting-edge university auditorium.

CHEATING AND SPYING

Chinese students have come to American colleges and universities in record numbers since 1979, but an analysis of this phenomenon appearing in the *New York Times* reported that the overwhelming majority of these students cheat to gain admission. "Ninety percent of Chinese applicants submit false recommendations, 70 percent have other people write their personal essays, 50 percent have forged high school transcripts, and ten percent list academic awards and other achievements they did not receive," the article claimed.

This information was no revelation for American college-admissions personnel. "Chinese cheat, it's just the way they are, and accepting this is part of the cost of doing business in China." In too many cases admitting a student who can pay full tuition is the aim; gaining someone honest or qualified is not. "I was an English teacher at Guizhou University, the flagship of China's poorest province. When I assigned papers, they would often be cribbed from the internet (and when I say often, I mean 75 percent of the work submitted contained some sort of plagiarism, and about 10 percent was entirely cut-and-pasted from the web)." Some choose to view it as simply a manifestation of different accepted value systems.

A research report in 2010 by Zinch China, an online social networking and research business that matches Chinese students with colleges and scholarships, reported similar findings. Driven in part by aggressive agents and overzealous parents, 90 percent of recommendation letters are fabricated, 70 percent of essays are not written by the applicant, and half of high school transcripts are falsified. The report identified five basic categories of cheating: recommendation letters, essays, high school transcripts, financial aid applications, and awards.[34]

It is also well-known that the extent of misrepresentation can go far beyond college applications. According to the Federal Bureau of Investigation (FBI), America's universities have become infected with foreign spies posing as students and researchers, whose underlying mission is to secure technologies and government secrets to take back to their home countries. Reports of attempts by China and other East Asian countries to use academic channels to gather classified information increased eightfold between 2009 and 2010, according to Bloomberg. A case in point is Daniel J. Scheeres, who studied aerospace engineering and who took on a Chinese student to work with him at the University of Michigan. The student had listed her research background as connected with a civilian university and Scheeres did not suspect she had ties with the Chinese military. However as the student pressured him to reveal secrets about the research, it became apparent that her interests might not be merely of a civilian nature.[35]

Foreign intelligence services may also look to exploit American study-abroad programs as an opportunity to locate and turn American students. One example is Glenn Shriver, a former student at Grand Valley State University, who studied at East China Normal University in Shanghai. After graduation he was approached by Chinese intelligence service agents, who paid him more than $70,000 and sent him back to the United States, where he applied to work for the CIA. He admitted in 2011 that if accepted for the job he had planned to sell secrets to the Chinese. Shriver was apprehended and sentenced to four years in a federal prison. "Study abroad programs are an attractive target," said FBI counterintelligence director C. Frank Figliuzzi.

China, unlike its counterparts in other countries, deploys a freelance network that includes students, research, and false-front companies, according to David Major, president of the Center for Counterintelligence and Security Studies in Falls Church, Virginia. Many students in China are either forced to or volunteer to collect information, he said. Arizona State University president Michael Crow commented that the situation is "a little perplexing and overwhelming. We're in the business of trying to recruit more students from China. We are operating at a total openness mode, while we recognize there are people working beyond the rules to acquire information."[36]

THE INCIDENT AT TIANANMEN SQUARE

By all accounts, the Nobel Committee's decision to award the Peace Prize to Liu Xiaobo in 2010 was a tribute to his role in the 1989 democracy movement—a situation the Chinese government had spent twenty years trying to forget. Born in Changchun in northern China in 1955, Liu Xiaobo's story was not un-typical for his generation. As the son of a university professor, during the Cultural Revolution he had moved with his family to the protection of the Inner Mongolian countryside, where they remained from 1969 until 1973. After returning to his home region he spent two years in a rural commune in the province of Jilin, and then worked in construction.

When the Communist Party reinstated the national university entrance examination in 1977, Liu Xiaobo was admitted to the Chinese department of Jilin University, and graduated in 1982. In 1988 he was awarded a PhD from Beijing Normal University. He had not participated in the prodemocracy movement during the 1970s—his focus was literature and Western philosophy. By 1986 he had made a name for himself as a literary critic, and he created considerable controversy by writing an article condemning Chinese writers for their dependency on the Communist Party, criticizing their lack of ability to "think for themselves." The publication would cause him to be labeled the "black horse" of China's literary scene and his provocative ideas and seeming fearlessness in presenting his thoughts attracted the attention of the intelligentsia.[37] Soon he was lecturing in universities across China and in other countries as well. It was during his term as a visiting scholar at Columbia University in New York that the 1989 pro-democracy movement erupted in China.

Liu immediately returned to China and Tiananmen Square, where he launched a hunger strike with three of his comrades in protest of the repression imposed by the People's Liberation Army. The night before the massacre, Liu successfully negotiated a peaceful evacuation of Tiananmen Square with the army, and found refuge in a diplomatic compound. However, he could not tolerate being in a place of safety as his fellow citizens and students were being persecuted, so he left his apartment to return to the scene, and was arrested on June 6 and quickly labeled a "black hand" behind the movement. He spent the next twenty months in the Qincheng jail in Beijing.

His courageous efforts, in concert with the many other "revolutionaries," would have important results. On April 11, 1990, a Presidential Administrative Order was issued in response to the Tiananmen Square incident. It stated that Chinese students, visiting scholars, and other Chinese who had been in the United States between June 5, 1989, and April 11, 1990, would be permitted to remain until July 1, 1993. Simply put, if the president was unable to determine if Chinese students could return home without persecution from the government, then those students would be covered under this protection act. This meant they could choose instead to apply for a green card to become a permanent resident of the United States. In 1992 Bill Clinton assumed the American presidency and supported the act, and on June 30 the same year it became law.[38] In the first week, the four district offices of the Immigration and Naturalization Services received more than 40,000 green-card applications.

The passage of the act had been pushed by a student group led by the All-America Autonomous Federation of Chinese Students and Scholars. This "Green Card Party," which testified before the U.S. Congress and organized rallies to gain public support for China's human rights, was to a significant degree responsible for the act's retention.

The government of China protested the Protection Act, dismissing it as groundless. In 1992 many students had returned to China from the United States and they insisted none had received improper treatment. Their claim may have been largely true. According to a 1994 report from the Office of Human Rights and Humanitarian Affairs in the U.S. State Department, titled the "Memorandum on the State of the Nation and the Asylum Application," at least some of the students' claims in their plea for asylum had little credibility. The American consul general in Shanghai agreed with the report, saying that he had found no evidence of mistreatment of the returned students in China.

With or without the Protection Act, many Chinese would have managed to remain in the United States. According to Chinese government statistics, between 1978 and 1994 an estimated two hundred thousand students studied abroad and about one-third returned. Of those who traveled to America to study, less than 10 percent returned home to China.[39]

TO STAY OR GO?

Success stories of American-educated Chinese were a topic of increasing interest among China's newspapers and magazines during the 1980s and 1990s. Two themes were prevalent—the first being stories about Chinese who had made their way to the international lecterns. The second common theme centered on accounts of heroic students who, after graduating from an American university, decided to reject the high-salary job in the United States and return to the homeland instead.[40]

From the outset of the third wave, of deep concern for China was the low return rate of students who went to the United States and various attempts were made to circumvent that trend. In the mid-1980s He Dongchang, vice chairman of the State Educational Commission, traveled to Washington, DC, to sign a joint statement with his American counterpart, essentially a reaffirmation that state-sponsored students from China have an obligation to return home and utilize the degree for the benefit of China. After the 1989 Tiananmen Square incident and the resulting protection act, however, the wishes of the Chinese government were more or less ignored.

Studies have shown that Chinese students earning undergraduate degrees were more likely to remain in foreign countries after completing their programs than were visiting scholars. Between 1978 and 1991, for example, 65.2 percent of the visiting scholars returned to China (35,552 out of 54,526). Of the 18,898 state-sponsored degree candidates, only 14.1 percent went back to China after completing their studies. Another report disclosed that between 1978 and 1989 of the estimated 22,000 self-funded students from China, fewer than 1,000 returned.[41]

Part of the problem was the lingering suspicion of pending maltreatment of returned students due to any real or perceived anticommunist views. In 1992 Deng Xiaoping made his own appeal, declaring publicly that all Chinese citizens who elected to study abroad would be warmly welcomed back to their homeland regardless of their past political attitudes. Upon their return, he assured them they would be assigned "appropriate work."[42] Other efforts were made in the early 1990s to attract more American-educated Chinese back to the homeland, such as the Changjiang Scholar and the Chunhui Plan, both designed to recruit distinguished Chinese nationals working in foreign countries—precursors to Project 985 and other important initiatives to come.

It is important to note the uneven distribution of the returnees. A study conducted by David Lampton and his associates in the 1980s titled *A Relationship Restored* reported that of the total number of Chinese studying in the United States, the largest percentage came from Shanghai—about 37 percent of the self-sponsored students, those holding F-1, visas and about 19 percent of the J-1, state-sponsored students.[43] In 2002 *People's Daily* reported that about 50,000 of those students had returned to live and work in their native city of Shanghai—about one third of the total number of returnees.

Beijing and Jiangsu have also been the beneficiaries of large numbers of foreign-educated returnees. In 2001, about 110,000 students and scholars from Beijing had studied abroad and an estimated 40,000 had returned to work there. Other universities, especially those located in inland cities, received few returnees, a situation prompting efforts to recruit more foreign-educated Chinese to its remote regions, particularly the middle and western provinces. The Office of Returnee Affairs was established to handle these efforts and recruiters from the western provinces were also stationed in Beijing.[44]

A few years later another study was sponsored by the CSCPRC and supported by the USIA, titled *Chinese Students in America: Policies, Issues, and Numbers*. Part I of this study, based almost exclusively on Chinese articles and documents on the subject, looked at China's evolving policies with regard to sending students and scholars abroad for study, and Beijing's concerns about getting an appropriate level of return for the expenses involved. The second part of the study analyzed statistics on the flow of Chinese students and visiting scholars entering and leaving the United States since 1979, including their fields of study, sources of funding, and other characteristics. This study served to update the Lampton study, which looked at the exchanges from more of an American perspective.

Sino-American scholarly relations had by the mid-1990s become a "sophisticated, pluralistic collection of university, government agency and foundation programs with China."[45] China's efforts to recruit their own back to the homeland helped generate a massive collaborative effort—government, education, and industry—giving foreign-educated Chinese compelling reasons to return. The early programs started by the CSCPRC no longer needed an intermediary organization. By the mid-90s the Ford Foundation, the National Science Foundation, and other private groups had set up their own offices in China, reducing funding for the CSCPRC and the need for its services. In 1996 the president of the American Council of Learned Societies, Stanley Katz, announced that declining federal and private support would result in the closing of the CSCPRC's Washington, DC, office.

The closing was representative of the groundswell of change taking place in China. Since the 1990s China's academic and occupational landscape has been in a state of transformation that each year has attracted higher percentages of returnees to the front lines of its postmillennial rise to power—a "change of face" that will be discussed at length in the next chapter.

IMMIGRATION AND DOCUMENTATION

Since 1993, when the New York City World Trade Center was attacked, there was public outcry in the United States to overhaul and update the governmental systems that track international students within the United States. The bomber that detonated the bomb in 1993 had entered the country on a student visa. Questions soon arose over what appeared to be an inefficient paper trail for tracking foreign students and in 1996 a far more comprehensive system, the Illegal Immigration Reform and Immigrant Responsibility Act (IIRIRA), was initiated. Section 641 stipulated that a system to record information about international students in three visa categories (F, J, and M) should be implemented by January 1, 1998. (The F visa category is for students enrolled in a program of study in academic institutions; J is a category for exchange visitors or scholars; and the M visa is for students applying to a vocational or nonacademic institution.) These new requirements led to the creation of the Coordinated Interagency Partnership Regulating International Students (CIPRIS), which was implemented in 1997 and upheld until October 1999.

When terrorists attacked the World Trade Center in New York on September 11, 2001, killing thousands, it was soon discovered that some had been admitted to the United States on F1 student visas. President George Bush issued a Homeland Security directive in October calling for measures to end "abuse of student visas" and the prevention of "certain international groups" from receiving education in sensitive areas of study. The directive had come on the heels of the Patriot Act, which had already called for the full implementation of the IIRIRA. In 2002 an electronic tracking system, the Student and Exchange Visitor Information System (SEVIS), was implemented in an effort to reinforce national security—within it were additional and stringent visa requirements. Among the many changes was a stipulation that students could no longer enter the United States more than thirty days prior to the start of their program (it had previously been ninety days).[46]

Since the Immigration Act of 1924, international students in the United States had been classified as nonquota immigrants. But in view of the fact that students come to America for what is intended to be a temporary sojourn and not permanent residence, the Immigration Act of 1952 had reclassified students as nonimmigrant. The assumption was that intending immigrants could use student visas as a way of entering the country, and others might try to stay in the United States after the completion of study. Under SEVIS, the burden of proof was now on the applicant to establish his or her eligibility.[47]

Even though the new policies were set in force to help ensure compliance with immigration law and national security, the new SEVIS requirements also made the logistics of coming to America to study even more difficult, not just for students but for the institutions hosting them. The legislation had been rushed into existence in the wake of the September 11 attack, and any deviation from the detailed documentation could cause complications or delays. An associate director for public policy at NASFA accused the federal government of dismantling an industry "we spent 50 years establishing."[48] Many professionals in the field expressed concern that the new regulations could encourage international students to enroll in other countries, such as Australia or the United Kingdom. In 2003 NASFA recommended to the United States government that the SEVIS regulations should be updated to mirror the realities of the present day and that they remove any stipulations that did not make a genuine contribution to national security.

The new SEVIS requirements were cumbersome for most international students, but many Chinese found them especially so. In a *China Daily* article, a Chinese visiting scholar in Iowa explained that even now, many in China still depend on their work units for housing, health care, and even education. "My trips to Japan as a student and Thailand as a journalist didn't prepare me, either, as my Asian hosts took care of everything . . . when it came to the U.S., I've been caught in a kind of bureaucratic culture shock," the article continued. "Imagine my anxiety when it dawned on me that I had to pay the so-called SEVIS fee to get a J-1 visa."[49]

152 *A History of Higher Education Exchange*

THIRD WAVE ENROLLMENTS

In the census conducted for the 1978–1979 academic year, just before Deng Xiaoping's reopening of China's borders to Sino-American education exchange, IIE reported Taiwanese enrollments to be 17,560. Hong Kong had sent 9,900 the same year and there were fewer than 1,000 enrolled from the People's Republic of China. Within one year after Deng's announcement, enrollments from mainland China nearly tripled, to 2,770. By 1981 PRC enrollments had increased to 4,350.[50] The numbers of students from mainland China would quickly overtake Taiwanese enrollments and by 1985 there were approximately 14,000 students from the People's Republic of China in the United States.

Hong Kong and Taiwanese Enrollments

There has always existed a strong connection between Hong Kong and China's education exchange with the West, despite its small size and great distance from the Chinese capital.[51] The first dispatch of CEM students in 1872 included boys who had attended school there. Other prominent Chinese figures had also been schooled in Hong Kong, such as Sun Yat-sen, who studied at Hong Kong Medical College, and Nobel laureate Daniel Chee Tsui, who graduated from Hong Kong Pui Ching Middle School before going on to the University of Chicago. Hong Kong continually refined its role in education exchange in light of changes on the mainland, especially after 1979, when unprecedented numbers of Chinese students went to America for their degrees.

Hong Kong reaped some of the benefits of American-educated students, as many of the graduates were attracted to its professional ranks. Gaining substantial benefit were its universities, which actively recruited American-trained staff into its system. By capitalizing on its intimate knowledge of China, its international connections, and its communication infrastructure, Hong Kong transformed itself into a key center "not only for interpreting China's reform across cultures, but also for building mutual understanding between China and the rest of the world."[52] In this respect Hong Kong's universities took center stage. Increasing numbers of its professionals had roots on the mainland, studied in America, and then joined the professoriate in Hong Kong.

The "official" counts of how many mainland Chinese students have studied in the United States since the reopening of China's borders is rife with contradictions. According to Leo A. Orleans's (1988) book *Chinese Students in America: Policies, Issues and Numbers,* neither the Americans nor the Chinese could provide a precise census of enrollments in the first years of the third wave. In 1979, *China Education Almanac* reported a total of 1,750 Chinese students enrolled in United States higher education. In Orleans's book the number is reported as an estimated 2,700, a figure cited as emanating from the Xinhua News Agency. The Chinese government's official count was 1,277.[53] Some of the discrepancies are simply due to what was or was not included in each calculation; for example the government study did not include students who studied in the United States using private funds.

Lampton's study in *A Relationship Restored* (1986) agrees with Orleans's assessment that a count of Chinese enrollments in the early years of the third wave is difficult to precisely present. During the period 1979–1983, according to Lampton, 19,872 scholarly exchange visas were issued to mainland Chinese, of which 63 percent were J-1 category. The remaining 37 percent were F-1 student visas. However, when considering these figures one has to take into account other factors that skew the total—for example, some scholars went back to China during that period, only to return later and so were counted twice. Therefore Lampton concludes that "one can safely infer that the number of such persons [Chinese students and scholars] who have come to the United States during 1979–1983 is close to the 19,000 mark."[54]

According to IIE figures from its 1998/99 international student census, twenty years after the resumption of U.S.-China education exchange, there were 51,001 students from the People's Republic of China enrolled in U.S. higher education. Taiwan sent 30,855 and 9,665 were from Hong Kong, altogether a total of 91,951 Chinese students enrolled in America's classrooms. The next decade would witness enrollment increases even beyond the expectation of many forecasters. Only ten years later (2009/10) the totals had risen markedly—127,628 students from China, 26,685 from Taiwan, and 8,034 from Hong Kong—a total of 162,347. Those numbers would continue to climb in the next decade.

8 China's New Academic Face

For the first 150 years or so, Sino-American education trade was almost entirely one-way. Thousands of China's students were eager to earn degrees in prestigious U.S. universities, but few Americans were inclined to seek instruction from less-prestigious and far-less-developed Chinese institutions. Since the 1990s China has been on a course to change that. For more than two decades the Chinese government has dedicated ever-increasing sums toward the improvement of its system of higher education, and the changes are already quite remarkable.

Backed by expanding monetary support generated by a still-burgeoning economy, China's colleges and universities are fast becoming formidable contenders in the world's higher education market, as they attract increasingly greater shares of the world's international student enrollments. The lure of vastly upgraded institutions and the lessening of border restrictions for academics have proven irresistible for growing numbers of the world's students and scholars. In 2010, according to China's Ministry of Education, foreign enrollments had risen markedly, hitting a record high of 240,000 students—a striking contrast from sixty years prior when there were just twenty foreign university students in all of China.[1]

The postmillennial allure of China's "new academic face" for the world's students and scholars signifies a new era in Chinese educational history—keeping in mind that the formal establishment of a cohesive higher education system in China is in itself a fairly recent event. China's first modern (i.e., American-type) institution was Peiyang (Beiyang) University, which was established in 1895, not long after the end of the Sino-Japanese War. The devastating surrender to Japan had revitalized imperial interest in education reform and Qing leaders were moved to accept a proposal drawn up by Sheng Xuanhuai—a plan that pitched a long-range strategy intended to shore up China's strength and economic power through the development of its universities. Sanctioned by the emperor and with assistance from Charles Tenney, an American educator, Shang set in place the founding of the first "modern" university in China. The Peiyang Western Study School later became Peiyang University (today's Tianjin University), the first institution of higher education in China to fully adopt a Western system.

From the beginning, Peiyang operated according to an American model, teaching mainly Western learning in the areas of law, civil engineering, mining, metallurgy, and mechanics, using books and equipment purchased from the United States and Germany. Most of its early instructors had been recruited from the United States, graduates of Harvard, Stanford, and other high-ranking universities, effectively making Peiyang's first faculty competitive with many top-tier American institutions. In 1899 the university awarded its "First Imperially Written Diploma" to Wang Chonghui—a milestone for Chinese education. Wang would later become a judge to the international court. Other important graduates from Peiyang's early years include Liu Ruiheng, founder of the Chinese public health system, and Ma Yinchu, who was the first person in China to be awarded a PhD in economics. A half century after its founding Peiyang would merge with Hebei Technical College to become Tianjin University.

The historic opening of Peiying University was soon followed by the founding of Qiushi Academy, later named Zhejiang University, in 1897 and Peking University (Beijing University, known colloquially as Beida) a year after that. Nanjing University dates from 1902, when it was known as Sanjiang Normal School. Fudan University (whose name means "heavenly light shines day after day") had its start in 1905 and Harbin Institute of Technology opened in 1920. Many others followed and by 1949, when Mao Zedong and the Communist Party took control, there existed at least 200 institutions of higher education in mainland China. It was not until after the ascension of Deng Xiaoping that a uniform system of enrollments and operations was implemented. Among Deng's early decisions regarding education had been the resumption of a national examination system for college admissions and three such examinations were held between 1977 and the end of 1979. An estimated 18 million high school graduates participated and about 880,000 of them were accepted into China's colleges and universities.

Until this time China did not have a fully developed academic degree system in the modern sense, and only about 30 percent of its university faculty held postgraduate degrees. With the resumption of a formalized national college entrance examination, Chinese higher education began to upgrade its universities and China started to produce its own homegrown instructional staff. In the meantime, the reopening of China's educational borders in 1979 would allow students and scholars to pursue degrees in the West—mostly in the United States—to fill the temporary void of qualified educators.

Another change that served to advance college enrollments in China happened in 1993 when the Central Committee of the Chinese Communist Party and the State Council jointly issued the Program for Education Reform that once again allowed private universities. New colleges could now be founded by nongovernment entities—a major alteration in a higher education system that had previously been under the control of the central government. This move would expand enrollments over the next several years. According to a report issued by China's Ministry of Education, in 1990 less than 4 percent of citizens aged 18–23 were enrolled in Chinese higher education institutions, compared to 22 percent in 2005.[2]

In 1995, two years after the inclusion of private universities, China's Project 211 was announced. Designed for university building, this project afforded special funding for a select group of 100 institutions to help improve their overall performance. Then in 1998, the Ministry of Education launched a follow-up program called Project 985, which narrowed the focus to nine elite Chinese universities—the so-called C9 League—with the intention of making them top-ranking in the world by the early twenty-first century. The 985 effort was expanded in 2004 to include additional institutions and it was during this time that many of the remaining Soviet-style subject colleges were combined into comprehensive institutions that more resembled American universities.

CHINA'S IVY LEAGUE

The Celestial Kingdom has since ancient times considered itself supreme among nations and for millennia the people of China have been unwilling to accept the notion that they could be anything less. Wars, rebellions, economic disruptions, governmental upheavals, and a string of natural disasters over the centuries have sometimes enfeebled China, but rarely for long. China has historically rebounded to successfully address its weaknesses and the academic arena has been no exception.

On May 4, 1998, on the hundredth anniversary of the founding of Peking University, President Jiang Zemin proclaimed with great pride that "in order to realize modernization [China] will build several universities into world class." The following year nine Chinese universities were each given one billion yuan (about $162 million—some received more) to build new facilities and to generally improve. These chosen few, the C9 League, were to become China's elite institutions of higher education for the twenty-first century, slated to be competitive with the finest universities in the United States or Western Europe. While they lack the sports teams that initially linked America's eight elite colleges (Harvard, Yale, Brown, Cornell, Princeton, Dartmouth, Columbia, and the University of Pennsylvania), this group of nine aspires to become China's own "Ivy League."

According to Education Ministry spokeswoman Xu Mei, the effort is an "attempt that is conducive to the country's construction of high-quality colleges, cultivation of top-notch innovative talents and enhanced cooperation and exchanges between Chinese universities and their foreign counterparts."[3] On the C9 list are some of China's oldest and most respected institutions, among them Tsinghua University, the "indemnity college."

Tsinghua had already enjoyed a long and prestigious history and at its centennial celebration in 2011 Yale's president Richard C. Levin hailed the university's many accomplishments. In its first century Tsinghua played an integral role in the development of China and many of its 170,000 graduates became leaders in their fields. "The first two Chinese to be awarded the Nobel Prize, Chen Ning Yang and T. D. Lee, were both educated at Tsinghua. Professor Qian Xuesan, Professor Zhu Guangya, and Professor Qian Sangiang . . . have made important contributions to China's scientific development," continued Levin. "We at Yale are especially proud of our role in your early history. Four of the first five presidents of Tsinghua studied at Yale."[4]

Tsinghua has earned more state science and technology awards than any other Chinese university, and has been at the forefront of forging partnerships with institutions in the United States—collaborations that have included MIT, Johns Hopkins, the University of Michigan, and Columbia, to name a few. Tsinghua has also implemented successful collaborations with industry leaders such as Toyota, Boeing, and United Technologies to form joint research centers with at least thirty companies. Today around 3,200 Tsinghua students go abroad annually and each year its campus in China hosts more than 800 visiting students and scholars.

Other members of the C9 League include Beijing (Peking)[5] University, Zhejiang University in Hangzhou, the Harbin Institute of Technology, Fudan University, Shanghai Jiao Tong University, Nanjing University, the University of Science and Technology of China, Xi'an Jiaotong University, and a military school in Hefei. Cooperative agreements among the schools feature flexible student programs, close collaboration on the training of postgraduates, and the establishment of a system which allows students to earn credits by attending classes at the member universities—important steps in the C9 plan.

But there have been challenges. China hopes to produce world-class research institutions in an environment where open inquiry and access to information remains severely limited—conditions generally inhospitable to true scientific study. Some question China's ability to effectively balance governmental constraints with academic freedom. "To form a league is merely a formality . . . what is important is the spirit of chasing academic freedom, which Chinese universities lack," commented a faculty member at China University of Political Science and Law. "If the nine universities can do some creation in academic freedom, it values much more than mutual recognition of academic marks. . . . "[6]

Just as the newly forged C9 League was beginning to consider these and other issues, in 2001 China gained admission to the World Trade Organization. It was an association that would impact China's quest for international enrollments by providing opportunities for exchanges with many more countries. But even as Westernization and internationalization of its academic system moved forward, as late as 2005 China's higher education was still heavily under the influence of the Soviet model. In 2008 Premier

Wen Jaibao chaired an executive committee that drafted an education development plan designed to reflect a balance of interests and influences of each model—Western, Soviet, and Chinese—a bold and pragmatic decision with a vision to the future.

In 2012, in a work report delivered to the National People's Congress, Wen announced that the government expenditure would begin allotting no less than 4 percent of the gross national product toward the advancement of higher education and academic exchange. China's minister of finance Xie Xuren assured that the logistics of the budgeted disbursement would be accomplished that same year—a boost in funding that held the promise of even more academic expansion and a decision that would further advance the attractiveness of China's universities to the world.

Among China's motivations for marketing its universities to foreign students has been the goal of promoting its influence and manifesting its philosophy through "soft power." The idea is hardly a new one. Teddy Roosevelt upheld an almost identical rationale a century earlier when he supported Sino-American education exchange, with the full intention that American ideology (and Christianity) would discreetly permeate China as a result. "Many men who have received their early training at one of the American schools or colleges in China are now mightily influencing the industrial, political and moral life of their land," said Roosevelt.[7]

In the twenty-first century U.S.-China higher education exchange is not the one-way path it was in Roosevelt's time. Since the turn of the new millennium China has attracted steadily increasing numbers of students from the United States who are drawn to its rich and ancient history, and to the opportunities emerging from its economic rise. The number of Americans studying in China grew 30 percent between 2001 and 2007 and by 2012, according to IIE's Open Doors report, about 15,000 Americans were enrolled in China's colleges and universities. A *New York Times* article quoted Allan E. Goodman, who stated that interest in China "is growing dramatically . . . people used to go to China to study the history and language, and many still do, but with China looming so large in all our futures, there's been a real shift, and more students go for an understanding of what's happening economically and politically."[8]

To support this trend, in 2005 Joe Lieberman and Lamar Alexander introduced the United States–China Cultural Engagement Act, authorizing $1.3 billion in federal funds to provide for Chinese-language instruction in American schools. The funds also increased consular activity supporting American commercial ventures and provided for physical and virtual exchanges between the two countries.

Although traditional study-abroad locations still attracted the most Americans in 2008, by 2012 China had become the fifth most popular destination, after Great Britain, Italy, Spain, and France. "I think it will be a challenge," said one eighteen-year-old California student when asked about her decision to study full-time in China (most Americans go to China for a semester), "but I'm really excited to be pursuing something I'm passionate about."[9] Rajika Bhandari, the Institute of International Education's deputy vice president for research and evaluation, explained that "U.S. students are increasingly aware of the need to obtain more practical skills, foreign language skills and cultural experiences that . . . help them be more competitive. . . ."[10]

In the second decade of the new millennium, there are still about ten times more Chinese students coming to the United States for educational programs than Americans going to China, and about 600 times more Chinese studying English than there are Americans study Mandarin. But those gaps are narrowing. By the year 2020 China plans to be hosting at least a half million foreign students in its universities, including a substantial population of Americans.[11]

THE 100,000 STRONG INITIATIVE

Student exchanges with China, said Michelle Obama in a speech at Howard University, "are a key component of this administration's foreign policy agenda," echoing the president's stated aim of substantially increasing the number of Americans studying in China.[12] It is a goal tempered with worries about its achievability, however. Persuading large numbers of American students to go to China to study, especially if they are from groups that rarely go overseas (such as minority and community college students, as the president hopes for) will necessitate considerable change, including an expansion of foreign-study programs and of curricular offerings in Chinese language, culture, and politics on American campuses. Such changes will take time to implement. There is also the question of whether or not China actually has the capacity to host this expansion in American enrollments. IIE president Goodman commented that while the initiative was a bold venture, "it's realizable,"[13] although he later cautioned that his comment was not without some reservation.

President Barack Obama first introduced the 100,000 Strong Initiative in 2009 and Secretary of State Hillary Clinton officially launched its operation in Beijing in 2010. The initiative, intended in part to prepare the next generation of American experts on China, drew enthusiastic support from the Chinese government and the Chinese Ministry of Education, and through the China Scholarship Council, quickly committed 10,000 "Bridge Scholarships" for American students to study in China's institutions. Offered under the U.S.-China Consultation on People-to-People Exchange (CPE), the scholarships were made available to students with schools accepting credit transfer from their institution's Chinese partner university.

"China would like to provide positive assistance to the U.S. initiative to send 100,000 students to study in China over the next four years," said State Councilor Liu Yangdong to Secretary Clinton.[14] The two countries could benefit from exploring new ways for cultural exchange, she added, and in support of the initiative China would increase the number of government-funded scholarships for Chinese who want to pursue doctorates in the United States.

"It is an attempt to implement China's 10-year national education outline and an important part of the country's diplomatic work to show Chinese culture to the global community," said Zhang Xiuqin, director-general of the ministry's Department of International Cooperation and Exchange. "The country's booming economic development, stable social environment and cultural charm have contributed to the increasing number of international students, of which 93 percent are self-funding this year. . . . "[15] The plan to which Zhang referred was the National Outline for Medium and Long-Term Education Reform and Development (2010–2020), which includes strategies for expanding international cooperation and higher learning exchange. By 2012 American students were eligible for CPE scholarships in forty Chinese universities.

The 100,000 Strong Initiative is to complement successful study-abroad and language-study programs already in force through the State Department's Bureau of Educational and Cultural Affairs, the Department of Education, and the Department of Defense. The initiative seeks to rely fully on private-sector philanthropic support to direct funds to existing U.S.-China educational-exchange programs that look to expand.

Figure 8.1 Secretary of State Hillary Clinton and American exchange students during the U.S.-China Consultations on People-to-People Exchange in Beijing, 2012. Courtesy of the U.S. Department of State.

As with most Sino-American collaborations, these expansion efforts have not been without complication and one obstacle made its appearance early on, in the admissions process. When the 100,000 Strong Initiative was first launched, the taking of SAT examinations was still prohibited in mainland China—a relic of a time when it was less open to Western procedures. Other American-based tests had long been permitted, such as the Advance Placement examinations that allowed high school students to earn college credit; however, students wanting to take the college-entrance SAT exams had to go to Hong Kong (unlike Mainland China, the former British colony was allowed to administer SAT examinations) or perhaps to South Korea. Other testing centers existed in Taiwan, Macao, and other locations. A twenty-year-old Chinese student, in a 2011 *Business Week* interview, summed it up simply. Traveling all the way to another country just to take the SAT was "a hassle."[16]

Officials had mixed feelings about the SAT policy, according to Tom Melcher of *Zinch China,* an online social network in the business of matching Chinese students with U.S. colleges and scholarships. It could be politically invasive to have the SAT "blasted on all the walls of the high schools."[17] The need for efficiency won out, and after an effective campaign for policy change the nonprofit College Board, which owns the PSAT, SAT, and Advanced Placement tests, began offering the PSAT in China in 2012. Within mainland China, however, the SAT was at that point still only administered within schools for dependents of foreign personnel, known as international schools—institutions authorized to enroll students holding passports from foreign countries.

In spite of these and other complications, the 100,000 Strong Initiative has already served to spawn other programs and policies supporting the expansion of Sino-American academic exchange. In 2011 the Institute of International Education announced that ten United States institutions would participate in the International Academic Partnerships Program (IAPP), a project funded by the Department of Education's Fund for the Improvement of Postsecondary Education (FIPSE) and managed by IIE's Center for International Partnerships in Higher Education.[18] The ten campuses selected to participate include Greenville Technical College, Jacksonville State University, Lake Washington Technical College, Marymount Manhattan College, Saginaw Valley State University, Southern Methodist University, State University of New York at Fredonia, College of New Jersey, University of Southern Indiana, and Utah Valley University. In addition to developing plans for educational partnerships with China, the IIE also established a "toolkit" of best practices for international collegiate partnerships.

The IAPP initiative was one of several sponsored by the Institute of International Education in its effort to support President Obama's 100,000 Strong project. IIE also announced the relaunching of the Freeman Awards for Study in Asia (Freeman-Asia), a venture supported with a substantial grant of $2 million from the Freeman Foundation. The institute also published the IIE Passport Study Abroad in China, a special edition in its series of study-abroad directories, which lists 350 programs open to American graduate and undergraduate students offered by the two governments, third party providers, private foundations, and U.S. higher education institutions.

EAST-WEST ACADEMIC PARTNERSHIPS

Since the opening years of the new millennium, students and scholars in the United States are increasingly interested in China. Much of the attraction has been driven by a decade or so of nonstop American media coverage of China's exploding economic power, its hosting of the Olympics, incidences concerning Tibet and the Dalai Lama, Yao Ming's famous career as the center for the Houston Rockets, and a host of other China-related headlines. Colleges across America have experienced a surge of interest in programs relating to the Chinese. A case in point is the Inter-University Program for Chinese Language Studies, a consortium of thirteen American universities whose applicants skyrocketed during the first millennial decade, according to program director Tom Gold, a professor at the University of California. When he assumed the position in 2000, said Gold, the program accepted about 97 percent of the students who applied, but by 2008 they were only accepting one in three. [19]

Other American institutions have been hard-pressed to keep up with their students' interest in China. At Syracuse University one China program proved insufficient to meet student demand and in 2006 it started a Beijing program in collaboration with Tsinghua University. Another of many more examples, the State University of New York at Oswego went from one small exchange docket in Beijing to seven partner destinations throughout China, supplemented by two faculty-led short-term programs, one on business and another on Chinese culture.

As China has gone about the business of building its own Ivy League, more and more American institutions have brought their campuses to China. This fairly sudden abundance of good-quality institutions in China—both Chinese and American—is not only attracting greater numbers of students from the United States but is also keeping more Chinese students home. And with expanding occupational opportunities in China, higher percentages of American-educated Chinese students are opting to return home after graduation.

Among the most well-developed and extensive American university collaborations with China have been those established with Johns Hopkins. The Johns Hopkins University–Nanjing University Center for Chinese and American Studies was established even before China's millennial push for domestic academic opportunities. Begun in 1986, the center was the creation of its president Steven Muller and Nanjing University's president

Kuang Yaming.[20] Here, midcareer professionals from China and the West could live and study together in one of a variety of fields, including law, journalism, government, or business, an experience designed to deepen their understanding of each other's cultures and to expand their academic backgrounds in topics relating to international relations. In 2006, responding to burgeoning interest in China, the center underwent a $21 million campus expansion and introduced a new two-year Master of Arts in International Studies program. At the time the Hopkins–Nanjing Center was the only joint academic program to offer a master's degree fully accredited in China and the United States. Today an estimated two thousand Center graduates are working in diplomacy, business, academia, journalism, government, finance, and nonprofit organizations in China and America.

Other American operations in China include Duke's campus in Kunshan, Harvard's Senior Executive Program in Shanghai, and Auburn University's facility in Danyang. In 2010 the University of Chicago opened a research center in Beijing, quickly followed by Stanford's center, and in 2012 officials broke ground on the construction site for Wenzhou-Kean University in Zhejiang Province.

Especially notable was an agreement signed with New York University to set up a campus in Shanghai in collaboration with a Chinese institution—China's first Sino-American university.[21] New York University Shanghai (NYU Shanghai) scheduled its opening for 2013, with the expectation that about 51 percent of enrollments would come from the Chinese mainland, while 49 percent would be international students. Student applicants for NYU Shanghai are required to demonstrate the same talent required of them by top universities around the world, said NYU president John Sexton. The syllabi and curricula of NYU Shanghai are constructed to follow the example of the world's leading universities, featuring "all-around" education, English lectures, and small classes to encourage open discussion. By 2012 about 200 faculty members of NYU and about 100 scholars worldwide expressed interest in joining NYU Shanghai.

Many other East-West collaborations have either already been established or are in the development process. In 2000 Liaoning Normal University (LNU) and Missouri State University (MSU) created the LNU-MSU College of International Business in Dalian, China. University of Maryland's Robert H. Smith School of Business opened in Beijing and Shanghai. Ohio University has set up operations in Hong Kong and University of Dayton has a campus in Shanghai. In 2009 Yale University partnered with Tsinghua in international healthcare management as part of Goldman Sachs' 10,000 Women Initiative, a program designed to train 500 female students from rural China. And the list of Sino-American higher education partnerships continues to grow.

"We will also emphasize a multilateral approach that will build up the network of education exchanges," said Shen Yang, deputy director-general of the department of international cooperation and exchanges in the

Ministry of Education.[22] Credit transfer agreements and mutual recognition of academic credentials (now signed with at least thirty-four countries) have been an important part of realizing the plan.

But as Sino-American academic collaborations have quickly risen, so have the subtle complications and United States institutions "should prepare for interesting times" when dealing with local Chinese authorities, cautioned an article in *Forbes*. China's most recent five-year plan lists educational development as a key objective, and for that reason local partners and provincial governments are generally very eager to cooperate and will often go out of their way to be accommodating, the article continued. "That said, dealing with the government will be unlike any experience most universities have had before. They will need to have representatives on the ground in China with strong local cultural know-how, shrewd negotiating skills, and keen business sense, to navigate the labyrinths of bureaus, approvals and special permits. . . . "[23]

In tandem with the logistical challenges has been the task of finding sufficient faculty to fill the growing number of positions in Chinese institutions. The economic downturn in the United States, combined with these new opportunities, has tempted a rising number of academics to pack their bags for an extended term in China. As Western universities continue to suffer from budget cuts, academics looking for opportunities farther afield are discovering that the Chinese are welcoming foreign professors with open arms.

Individual Chinese universities have been busy recruiting Western academics for some time, but more recently the Chinese government has further enticed foreigners with new opportunities that offer a range of incentives. In 2011 the Thousand Foreign Experts program was announced, an effort designed to attract up to one thousand foreign academics and entrepreneurs to China over a period of ten years. An extension of the 2008 Thousand Talent initiative, this new program instantly attracted hundreds of applicants from the United States, Japan, Germany, and a host of other countries, according to a report by Xinhua, China's official news agency.[24]

Li Jun, an assistant professor at the Department of International Education and Lifelong Learning at the Hong Kong Institute of Education, said China needs to continue to attract more foreign academics to help lift its international competitiveness. "They can use that to recruit students and to get recognition from the public," said Li, adding that the presence of top foreign academics has helped Chinese universities attract more research funding and made it easier for them to connect with the international academic community at large. "Their papers will be written in English . . . in terms of international recognition of scholars that will be a big help for the universities."[25]

Alex Katsomitros, a research analyst at the Observatory on Borderless Higher Education in London, said Chinese institutions should be most interested in attracting academics who specialized in the so-called stem subjects—science, technology, engineering, and mathematics—which lift economic growth through innovation and are seen as "politically neutral." The social sciences and humanities academics are understandably less willing to move to China, he added.

CONCERNS AND CRITICISMS

Not everyone regards the transformation of Chinese higher education over the past two decades, nor the rapidly expanding number of Sino-American collaborations, as entirely good things. In a 2012 article in *The Chronicle of Higher Education,* University of Michigan professor and associate director of the UM-Peking University Joint Institute, Brian Coppola, along with associate dean for global education Yong Zhao, warned that the education systems in China and the United States seem to be heading in opposite directions—both aimed squarely at what the other system is trying to give up. In America, the implementation of programs such as No Child Left Behind and Race to the Top have combined with increasing calls for more standardization and accountability. U.S. institutions are now embracing the sort of regimented, uniform, standards-based, test-driven education that has weighed down China's education system for centuries. What we are witnessing now, they contend, is nothing less than a reversal of ideals. Just as China is actively embracing the traditional values of American education and its penchant for encouraging creativity, individuality, innovation, and nonconformity, the United States seems to be moving away from those historic archetypes. "China is beginning to understand what our [America's] real strength has always been. By embracing a broadly divergent array of knowledge and experience, we bring diverse and unexpected perspectives to any problem or situation, allowing us to adapt rapidly to change. By not standardizing anything, we end up being to handle everything."[26]

Obstacles still stand in the way of comprehensive educational reform in China as it tries to distance itself from a long history of inflexible, standards-based education. "By recognizing and finding value in the core principles of a true liberal-arts education, China is seeking to avoid the inherent problems that have accompanied its traditional approach to education—problems that the United States is already in danger of adopting."[27] The United States is beginning to see evidence of an increase in something the Chinese call *gaofen dineng*—a term for the condition of a schooled population that exhibits "high scores with low ability."

The correlation between high standardized-test scores and low understanding has been well-documented by a number of respected researchers in the United States—studies that seem to have been misplaced by educators and politicians now supporting a more standardized and centralized approach. "In their [China's] enthusiasm to . . . emulate our strengths, our

Asian colleagues are holding a compellingly interesting mirror up to us, reflecting exactly those things that have given us a pre-eminent position for so long."[28]

Philosophical and political divides permeate East-West educational ventures. The Johns Hopkins University–Nanjing University Center for Chinese and American Studies labors under this reality. While America has academic freedom, which allows open discussion in classrooms, "we know that in China that is not true," said Carolyn Townsley, director of the Hopkins-Nanjing Center in Washington, DC, in an interview about the teaching of sensitive subjects, such as Tibet or the Tiananmen Square incident. "We are not trying to be instigators . . . the mission of the center is to build better relations with the Chinese, so we're not going to stir that up."[29] New York University promised that their Shanghai campus will have unblocked Internet use, even though no one outside the Chinese government actually claims to have completely unrestricted access. Content ranging from Facebook, Twitter, some Western newspapers, and even basic scholarly sources are regularly unavailable, even to those with the ability to circumnavigate the Great Firewall, China's censorship network. "NYU, Duke, and other foreign universities planning to operate in China realize that respecting Chinese laws also means respecting limitations of their academic and intellectual freedom," commented Cheng Li, a China expert at the Brookings Institution. "The idea that Duke and NYU could maintain comparable academic freedom in China is self-deceiving . . . [and] completely out of touch with reality."[30]

An example of China' handling of intellectual-freedom issues is the case of the "Xinjiang 13," a group of American university scholars that encountered considerable backlash. The group's offense was the coauthoring of *Xingiang: China's Muslim Borderland,* a book published in 2004. The "Xinjiang 13," a name the authors gave themselves, were subsequently denied permission to enter China, prohibited from flying on a Chinese airline, and pressured to publicly express pro-China views. In order to appease officials and return to China, two of the authors offered written statements in which they disavowed support for the independence movement in Xinjiang Province. "People who are engaged in perfectly legitimate scholarly pursuits can have their careers stymied if not destroyed," said Tim Reiser, foreign-policy adviser to United States Senator Patrick Leahy. The colleges that employed the Xinjiang scholars, reportedly reluctant to press Chinese authorities about the individual cases, took no collective action.

Dru Gladney, an anthropology professor at Pomona College in California and one of the "Xinjiang 13" authors, expressed disappointment with their inaction, lamenting that colleges are "so eager to jump on the China bandwagon, they put financial interests ahead of academic freedom." Already some of America's most prominent Chinese scholars are banned in Beijing, among them Perry Link, professor emeritus at Princeton University, who has not been able to enter China since 1995. Link's offense was smuggling a dissident astrophysicist into the U.S. embassy in Beijing for protection during the 1989 Tiananmen Square uprising. He had also helped edit the "Tiananmen Papers," a collection of leaked internal documents released in 2002. Columbia University Professor Andrew Nathan is another on China's blacklist, as well as Robert Barnett, who, after ignoring two warnings from Chinese officials that his comments should "lean more" in China's direction, encountered roadblocks when applying for visas in 2008 and 2009.[31]

Concerns have been expressed by China's former premier.[32] At a lecture in 2011 at Tsinghua University, 82-year-old Zhu Rongji, premier from 1998 to 2003 and the founding dean of Tsinghua University's school of economics and management, dismissed the Outline of China's National Plan for Medium and Long-term Education Reform and Development (2010–2020) as "empty talk." Criticisms of government policy from such a prominent figure are extremely rare in China. Among his concerns has been the rapid expansion of college and university enrollments, which increased sixfold between 1998 and 2011. Intended to stimulate the economy, Zhu said, the effort had instead led to rampant academic plagiarism, declining academic morality, and rising unemployment of university graduates. Zhu also lamented the lack of sufficient state support for education in rural China. Zhu's comments were not published by official media, although they were circulated on the blog site Sina Weibo.

Some analysts believe the comments point to emerging ideological rifts within the Chinese leadership regarding the direction of Chinese higher education in the next decade. Others, such as Hong Kong University of Science and Technology professor Ding Xueliang, think that criticism such as Zhu's will have little impact on policy. "Currently, if you want to make more meaningful reforms, you will face objections or obstacles posed by university bureaucrats since the reforms are likely to take away their control of resources. The bureaucrats like to limit any freedom left to university presidents, faculty or deans," Ding told *University World News*. Unlike in the economic realm, where many state-owned entities have undergone far-reaching reforms to break away from bureaucratic control, in some respects the higher education sector remains "old-fashioned," Ding said, pervasive in their quest to remain the same. Also the same is the central government's resolve to avoid a repeat of the 1989 student-led Tiananmen Square incident. "Preceding the protests were waves of student activism on campus, interactions between professors and students, and visits by overseas academics. All this is still well-remembered by the Chinese government."[33] In China remembering the past is a critical component for guiding the future.

THE CONFUCIUS INSTITUTES

The Chinese inclination to learn from the stories of the past and to persevere for the future was the subject of an article in a 2006 issue of *China*

Daily. The article recounted a folk story about an old Chinese man who wanted to move two mountains that were too near his house, as their presence made his passage to town long and difficult.[34] His neighbors scoffed at the idea. "You are foolish. You are too old and weak to level a small hill, let alone two big mountains." But the old man replied, "I have sons, and my sons have sons. I will have endless progeny, but the mountains won't grow any higher."

The story, *yugong yishan,* is well known to Chinese children, much like *The Little Engine That Could* is a bedtime standard for young Americans. Both are intended to instill the value of persistence and patience when trying to accomplish a monumental task. "I think I can! I think I can!" was a voice of encouragement in the American version, extolling the virtues of simply not giving up. The inspirational anecdote had been included in Mao Zedong's "Little Red Book" during the Cultural Revolution.

After telling the *yugong yishan* tale to a group of dinner guests, the host asked what they thought. Two Germans at the table wondered why the old Chinese man in the story had insisted that the only means of solving the problem was to move the mountain by hand, even if the task took generations to achieve. "You don't understand what the story is about," said one of the Chinese guests.

The writer of the article, an American, related to the group how he thought his own countrymen might respond to such a situation. The American would, rather than just remove the mountains, figure out a way to use them or better still make money from their use, he suggested. The Germans offered other options, including the idea of simply leaving the mountains where they were and building the house somewhere more convenient. What the party finally agreed upon at the end of the evening was that the intercultural sharing of ideas and stories from folklore could benefit everyone. "Whether it was the centuries of persistence of the Chinese, or the practicality of the Germans, or the innovation of the Americans, these traits were now coming together today at a rapid pace to enrich all of us."[35]

China is now in the business of exporting these age-old stories and philosophies around the world through its Confucius Institutes. Since 2004 more than sixty American colleges and universities have accepted tens of millions of dollars from a Chinese government–affiliated body known as the Hanban, for the purpose of establishing Confucius Institutes on their campuses. Hanban, an acronym for the officials at the Office of Chinese Language Council International, states in its bylaws that the Confucius Institutes are governed by principles of "mutual respect, friendly negotiations, and mutual benefit." The agenda is subtle but absolute in its intention. In President Hu Jintao's 2007 address to the seventeenth Communist Party congress, he said China must "enhance culture as part of the soft power of our country."[36]

China has been careful not to encourage the Confucius Institutes to act "as overt purveyors of the party's political viewpoints" and in fact little evidence suggests they are doing so. What is important, Hanban officials say, is that the world is given a "correct" understanding of China. The promotion of Confucianism or Confucian ideals is not the aim. Instead, party officials use Confucius in a more symbolic way—a sort of Father Christmas symbol of "avuncular Chineseness rather than as the proponent of a philosophical outlook."[37]

Among the first U.S. institutions in the United States to partner with Hanban was the University of Maryland, which initiated its Confucius Institute in 2004, not long after the first program had been established in Seoul. Stanford and Columbia and dozens of others have also welcomed Confucius Institutes to their campuses. However, not all offers of funding have been well received by American institutions—the University of Pennsylvania and Dickinson State College in North Dakota are among those which have flatly declined the proposition.

Since 2004 the Confucius Institutes have opened more than 350 outposts around the world, to mixed reviews. From a proponents' point of view, the institutes provide a chance for American students to learn about China from the Chinese themselves, with programs designed not just for colleges but also for public schools in the surrounding community. Some see the institutes as a godsend, offering not just Beijing-trained and Chinese-financed language teachers and materials, but also funds to cover a director's salary and a program of public events. "When you set up a Confucius Institute you get a ready-made partner," according to the executive director of the Confucius Institute at the London School of Economics.

Universities that agree to host Confucius Institutes are expected to provide premises and also a faculty member to serve as administrator. In return, Hanban provides the school $100,000 annually (figures vary depending on the institution) as well as visiting instructors, teaching materials, and an open invitation to apply for even more. American higher education administrators worry, however, that "such largess" may come with too many strings attached. The danger, should their university sign the agreement and collect the funds, is the very real possibility of self-imposed censorship in order to comply with Chinese Communist Party ideals. This was the potential risk that the University of Pennsylvania's East Asian Studies faculty cited as most concerning when the members voted unanimously to reject a Confucius Institute. Freedom of speech, a basic constitutional right for which many Americans had fought and died, in their view should not be sacrificed on any level in exchange for money from China.

In the wake of the recent recession, which rendered so many American universities desperate for funds, refusing such an offer in an effort to protect academic freedom might be considered nothing less than an act of patriotism. Others contend that quiet compliance with the Confucian Institute's agenda, even with the constraints on their college's academic freedom, is offset by the benefits of the cultural knowledge and interaction that the institutes bring with them. Sometimes economic concerns take precedent. Yesterday's American universities, which have historically been fortresses for the protection of freedom of academic speech and research, have in recent years been in dire need of funds and, as University of Pennsylvania history professor Arthur Waldon explained, "the Chinese have a lot of money."

Once a university commits to having a Confucius Institute on campus, it takes on a second set of opinions and authority that is answerable to the Chinese Communist Party and that is not subject to American scholarly review. Aside from the Confucian Institute's lengthy list of proscribed subjects is another—a roster of topics that are forbidden. Strictly off limits is any discussion of the Dalai Lama, Tibet, Taiwan, the 1989 Tiananmen Square incident, or China's military buildup, to name just a few.

According to Stanford University dean Richard Saller, Hanban's negotiations can be aggressive and overt. Stanford was offered $4 million to open a Confucius Institute on its campus and endow a professorship, on the condition that the professor would never discuss Tibet. Stanford refused due to objections among its faculty and administration, but they were finally convinced to accept the money anyway, which they used to endow a chair in classical Chinese poetry. Columbia University, on the other hand, accepted the money on the spot and implemented its Confucius Institute with little controversy among its faculty or administration.

A covert approach is not uncommon. A tenured historian at the University of Chicago, who had signed a petition protesting the opening of a Confucius Institute there, reported that even though he was a member of the board of the university's East Asian study center, he was never informed of the university's acceptance of the institute until the day it opened.

A few American campuses that host Confucius Institutes have reported incidences of job discrimination resulting from its presence. Reminiscent of the McCarthy era, to be identified as a critic of the institute can end careers, charged an untenured American faculty member in a recent article. His department received a lot of money from its Confucius Institute, he claimed, which was under the direction of a senior faculty member who also happened to be a voting member on his tenure case. The pressure to comply with Chinese-mandated restrictions, he claimed, was underlying but powerful.

Complaints such as these have been isolated, however Confucius Institutes have raised some legal concerns. A recent policy directive sent by the State Department to universities that sponsor Confucius Institutes suggests that the language and cultural centers will have to change how they operate, or risk "falling afoul" of American visa laws. The memorandum, first released in a 2012 article in *The Chronicle of Higher Education*, stated that Confucius Institute instructors teaching in America's K–12 schools on university-sponsored visas were in violation of regulations governing J-1 visas and that they should leave the country at the end of the academic year. A preliminary review by the State Department had determined that institute members teaching in Confucius Classrooms (the elementary, middle school, junior high, and high school components of Confucius Institute) must obtain American K–12 accreditation in order to continue to serve as teachers at those levels.[38] After nearly a decade of overlooking these concerns it was uncertain when or how the State Department intended to implement the changes—decisions that would directly affect the qualifications and placement of about 600 educators.

The memorandum did not spell out how the centers could be accredited nor did it offer a time frame, although stand-alone and university-based language components can be accredited through the Accrediting Council for Continuing Education and Training or the Commission on English Language Program Accreditation—a process of securing approval that can exceed one year. Because foreign professors and students at the university level are prohibited from teaching in American elementary and secondary schools, the teachers would have to reapply for the correct visa and then return to the United States, a process that would additionally require finding a new sponsor.

The policy memorandum generated considerable alarm on many American campuses and in China. Wang Yongli, an official with Hanban, told *The Chronicle* that any action to remove the teachers could harm Sino-American exchanges, as the teachers had come to the United States in the spirit of friendship. About a week after the memorandum was released in *The Chronicle* (the situation also made headlines in China), the U.S. State Department seemed to back down.[39] Its chief spokeswoman Victoria Nuland said in a news briefing that department officials were going to "do our best to fix this" without forcing anyone to leave, and an investigation would be conducted, she added. The news was a relief to the many universities that host Confucius Institutes; they wondered how they could continue providing Chinese-language instruction, one of the chief missions of many of the centers, without sufficient teachers.

One reason the visa issue finally came to light, generating the subsequent memorandum, was a growing number of alerts from American teachers and other educators who expressed concern about the content of some of the Confucius Institutes' teaching materials. A closer investigation into the instructional methods revealed not only the visa issue, but raised questions about the accuracy and intent of some of the information being presented in American classrooms by the Chinese teachers from the Confucius Institutes.

One example of the "teaching tools" in question was an educational website constructed by the Confucius Institute called "The War to Resist U.S. Aggression and Aid Korea." The webpage, which appeared in the "Kids" section of the site used for teaching Chinese history in American classrooms, explained that during the Korean War China had triumphantly "crushed the imperialists' (America's) aggressive ambitions and enhanced China's international prestige"—a viewpoint closely hewn to the Chinese Communist Party's official narrative. The video went on to explain that the United States had manipulated the United Nations Security Council to pass a resolution to organize a United Nations Command, consisting mainly of U.S. troops and intended to expand the aggression against Korea. The United States military then tried to seize the entire peninsula, the video explained to the children. The lesson continued by affirming that the Americans also bombed Chinese villages near the Chinese-Korean border, and only then did China enter the conflict as "volunteers." The image of a victorious Chairman Mao crosses the video screen with a caption stating that the Chinese "made the decision to resist the United States, aid Korea and protect our mother land." China's volunteers defeated the United Nations forces beyond the 38th Parallel, successfully turning the war around and winning an environment of relative stability for the construction of New China.

"That's strictly propaganda," said Frank Cohee of the Korean War Veterans Association. "I was there when the Chinese came in." Ted Barker, a founder of the Korean War Project, said that the video contents were blatantly propagandistic and did not follow the facts as recorded by thousands of participants and historians. The page was instantly purged by Hanban, deleted a day after Christopher Hughes, a professor at the London School of Economics, forwarded the discovered link to a group of colleagues who had met to discuss Confucius Institute teaching materials.

The now-deleted video is just one of a series of lessons describing Chinese history in terms that closely resemble official Communist Party positions on the subject—the sort of "reconstructed" facts taught regularly in schools across China. Associate professor of Asian studies at the University of Manitoba, Terence Russell, characterized the materials as "scary," adding that they are not appropriate for America's schools. "This material clearly does not meet even the most basic criteria for 'neutrality' . . . the nationalistic chest-thumping is deafening throughout," Russell added. June Teufel Dreyer, professor at the University of Miami, provided an analysis of some of the videos created by the Confucius Institute on the Korean and the Sino-Japanese Wars, saying that many are "outrageous distortions" of what actually happened. Her conclusion was that the videos sought to create the image of a blameless, heroic China "fighting valiantly for the good and true . . . they just happen to distort history badly in the process."[40]

Even in light of the criticisms, many of the Confucius Institutes' language and cultural programs have been extremely well received both on campuses and in the communities, and it can be successfully argued that learning has been significantly advanced through their efforts, in spite of its sometimes propagandistic tactics. The many Chinese teachers who visit and instruct in American schools are for the most part capable and devoted educators, genuinely interested in sharing the richness of China's history. Few who have witnessed their work would discount its value. In the second decade of the millennium, the advance of Confucius Institutes is showing no sign of slowing down, as they partner with ever-increasing numbers of

American colleges and universities—institutions that believe they can effectively balance the monetary and manpower advantages against the sacrifice of full and free expression in the classroom.

ENROLLMENTS

At the close of the first decade of the new millennium, America's population of international students had reached 700,000 and Chinese enrollments approached 160,000. The People's Republic of China was by then the leading sender of students and scholars to America, with India following close behind. And the United States was sending record numbers of students to China. Taken from IIE's Open Doors reports, enrollment figures between 1999 and 2011 display those trends:

	# of Students From China	% Change from Previous Year	# of U.S. Study Abroad Students Going to China
2010/11	157,558	23.5%	14,596
2009/10	127,628	29.9%	13,910
2008/09	98,235	21.1%	13,674
2007/08	81,127	19.8%	13,188
2006/07	67,723	8.2%	11,064
2005/06	62,582	0.1%	8,830
2004/05	62,523	1.2%	6,391
2003/04	61,765	-4.6%	4,737
2002/03	64,757	2.4%	2,493
2001/02	63,211	5.5%	3,911
2000/01	59,939	10.0%	2,942
1999/00	54,466	6.8%	2,949

Most professionals in the business of forecasting international student-enrollment numbers agree that this general trend will continue as we approach 2030, although Chinese enrollments in the United States are predicted to slow, partly due to China's changing demographics and because of its upgraded domestic facilities. American enrollments in China, however, show no evidence of impending decline.

9   Leaning Toward Mid-Century

As we approach 2030, the target year for many current forecasts, what is the status of U.S.-China higher education exchange and what will be its future? Based on a review of recent studies and predictions from respected economists, educators, and an assortment of other experts, an overview of current trends, predictions, and recommendations for the future of academic exchange is offered in this final chapter.

Recent actions by the Chinese are serving to drive these predictions. A 2013 article in the *New York Times* reported that China is committed to making a 250-billion-dollar-per-year investment in what economists call human capital. Reminiscent of when the United States helped build a white-collar middle class in the late 1940s and 1950s by using the G.I. Bill to education millions of war veterans, the Chinese are providing substantial subsidies to educate tens of millions of young citizens as they relocate from farms to urban China. The goal, said the article, is to alter the currently accepted norm, in which a very small number of elite oversee vast armies of semitrained workers and laborers. China wants to "move up the development curve" by fostering a far more broadly educated public.[1]

CURRENT AND TRENDING STATISTICS

Today China and India combined make up about 25 percent of the world's postsecondary student population and for the past several years the United States has hosted more Chinese students than any other foreign population.[2] However, India may overtake China as the fastest growing market for undergraduates studying abroad as early as 2015, according to some statisticians. Rahul Choudaha, an international education specialist, reports that the Chinese population in the 15- to 19-year age bracket is projected to decline by around 17 percent by 2015, which translates to about 18 million fewer college-going citizens. India, by contrast, is expected to increase its college-age population by five million (five percent) in the same period.[3] Choudaha pointed out that the offspring of Indians who started working in "new-age" industries such as information technology in the 1990s will be graduating from 2015 onward, a generation with parents who have more spending power for their children's education.

The deceleration of Chinese mobility was the topic of a British Council report released in late 2012, which predicted China will be sending a total of 585,000 undergraduate and graduate students abroad annually by 2020, just 17,000 more than it sent in 2012. The author of the report, Janet Ilieva, said their research predicts a slowdown in tertiary enrollments globally, mostly due to the demographic changes going on now. The global mobility rate has remained unchanged at two percent for a number of years. In addition to demographic changes, China's slowdown is driven by its vastly improved domestic-education standard and still-growing prosperity, both disincentives to study abroad.

Demand for greater diversity of foreign student populations in American colleges and universities will also be a factor, alongside new efforts to restore credibility to the admissions process, added Ilieva, " . . . the potential threat to the integrity of the admissions process due to fraudulent agent behavior may lead universities to consider ways of becoming less dependent on Chinese students."[4]

In the 2012/13 academic year, according to IIE's *Open Doors* census, China was still the top sender of students to the United States with enrollments approaching 200,000—up 23.1 percent from the previous year. The majority of Chinese students in the United States that year were studying at the graduate level (45.6 percent graduate, 38.4 percent undergraduate, 9.5 percent in Optional Practical Training, and 6.5 percent listed as "other").

As with all previous generations the preponderance of Chinese students and scholars still seek out top-tier American universities (preferably Ivy League) over less prestigious four-year institutions or community colleges, which are in most cases selected only when less-than-optimal grades, insufficient English-language skills, or limited funding disallow other choices. The institutions in the United States hosting the greatest numbers of Chinese students (beginning with the largest enrollments) are the University of Southern California, the University of Illinois, New York University, Purdue University, Columbia University, the University of California Los Angeles, Northwestern University, the University of Michigan, Michigan State University, and Ohio State University. By state, California and New York's higher education institutions attract the greatest number of Chinese and of foreign students in general, at both graduate and undergraduate levels.

In the past most Chinese have come to America for graduate-level training, but for the past few years undergraduate enrollments are on the rise, not just from China but from other top-sending countries as well. It is a new trend that is "likely to be a game changer," according to IIE's Allan E. Goodman. Undergraduates stay in the country longer, and they also have more impact on campus culture, both inside and outside the classroom. Recruiters are flooding China looking for new undergraduates, according to the deputy director of college counseling at Beijing National Day School, "trying to find a nugget . . . trying to strike a vein."[5]

Victor Johnson, senior adviser for public policy for NAFSA, praised the Obama administration for setting student recruitment and study-abroad goals in China, even though it did not put money behind the effort, noting that the setting of any national objective is a step forward in itself. Organizations such as World Educational Services and the College Board have offered recent predictions about what demand for American degrees will look like over the next few years. Both regard China as a viable market for the near future. Clay Hensley, director of international strategy and relations at the College Board, pointed out that the value of speaking English, combined with the advantage of making connections in the United States and the fact that the Chinese economy is still so robust, creates "the perfect storm."

Nonetheless, some colleges report they are reaching a saturation point with China. Some now look to diversify, an effort that appears to be gathering momentum. Fordham University, to provide one example, where 40 percent of its international freshmen hailed from China in 2012, is laying new groundwork in countries like the Philippines, Indonesia, Vietnam, and parts of Latin America. "We want a balance of students from around the world, for both economic reasons and cultural reasons," said Fordham's associate director of international student admissions.[6]

AMERICAN STUDENTS AND SCHOLARS IN CHINA

According to IIE's most recent census figures, China is now the fifth most popular country for Americans studying abroad. The number of United States citizens studying in China has been increasing around 5 percent for each of the last few years, and enrollments are projected to continue to rise through the second decade of the millennium.

In 2012 the Ministry of Education reported a total of 23,292 Americans studying in China with financial support from a bilateral government program, an increase of 18.4 percent over the previous year. Zhang Xiuqin, head of the international affairs department of the ministry, remarked at a press conference that China and the United States have made considerable progress in such exchanges under the China-U.S. High Level Consultation on People-to-People Exchange program launched in 2010. Even greater avenues of exchange are expected to emerge from the rapidly growing attractiveness of online learning.

MOOC AND THE ONLINE LEARNING EXPLOSION

The year 2012 was transformative in education, according to Chris Proulx, president and CEO of eCornell. "Between the introduction of the MOOC and the explosive growth in the number of online offerings, all eyes were on higher education." Since 2012 increasing numbers of students have been able to learn from leading faculty at elite institutions through online educational sources, an opportunity now reaching far beyond the traditional classroom. The time is coming, continued Proulx, when professors will be "collaborating across universities to collectively create and distribute for-credit curriculum for an online semester."[7]

The expansion will not be measured only in terms of enrollments. In fact, enrollments in for-profit ventures were down in 2013 and some companies, among them the University of Phoenix, saw the closing of some of their facilities. The growth, according to Proulx, will be especially robust in top-tier universities, where online activity has nearly doubled over the past two years. A big part of this current and projected growth is attributed to massive open online courses, or MOOCs.

What is a MOOC? Traditional online courses in higher education charge tuition, earn college credit, and limit enrollment to a "standard" size class. MOOC courses do not carry credit, are free of charge, and classes can be massive—anyone with Internet access may enroll. MOOC classes are necessarily unique in their instructional design because of the vast numbers of students, a situation that restricts or even eliminates student-teacher interaction. Very different from its antecedent "open courseware," MOOC offers full courses, complete with lectures.

According to the *New York Times,* the "big three" of the MOOC world include edX, a nonprofit start-up from Harvard and the Massachusetts Institute of Technology, which was set up as an experiment in 2011. By the end of 2012 edX had enrolled more than 370,000 in its first courses. "That's nothing," the article continued. Coursera, founded just a year before, has now reached more than 1.7 million. It is a trend growing "faster than Facebook."[8]

Another of MOOC's big three is Udacity, a company formed by David Stavens and his colleagues Sebastian Thrun and Michael Sokolsky after more than 150,000 students signed up for Dr. Thrun's "Introduction to Artificial Intelligence" course. "We were three guys in Sebastian's living room and now we have 40 employees full time."[9] Anant Agarwal, president of edX, is calling 2012 the "year of disruption," adding that it is a long way from being over.

Elite universities are affiliating with Coursera at a furious pace. It now offers courses from thirty-three of the biggest names in postsecondary education, a list that includes Princeton, Brown, Columbia, and Duke. And as more courses are offered free to anyone with an Internet connection, some of these respected professors are developing an almost cultlike following abroad, especially in China. The chief attraction of MOOC in China is that these open online courses offer an inside glimpse into places like America's exclusive Ivy League, free of charge.

The enormous popularity of American open online courses is already beginning to influence Chinese higher education, as greater numbers of students sign up for free programs in subjects such as economics, chemistry, and engineering. There are many questions surrounding the future of the MOOC model, however, such as the costs of sustaining courses over time, and whether or not they will someday count for credit—and if so how can they be packaged into a degree or certificate program? Higher education's buzzwords for the next couple of years may be "hybrid program," commented Chris Proulx.

The potential for the MOOC model to alter how the world's students learn and how they earn degrees in the future is enormous. Combined with existing online academic programs, the advance of new cyber-classrooms may soon enable students to earn college degrees from universities around the world, without traveling anywhere. This phenomenon of online learning and world connectivity holds the potential to forever and dramatically alter how professors instruct, where and how students learn, and how traditional brick-and-mortar institutions of higher education will operate in the future.

THE OBAMA ADMINISTRATION AND EDUCATION EXCHANGE

President Barak Obama's reelection virtually guarantees active governmental support for the expansion of U.S.-China academic collaboration through the end of his term—in particular a continuation of the 100,000 Strong Initiative and its goal of enrolling that number of American students in Chinese colleges and universities by 2014. Since its implementation the initiative has attracted the attention of academics, but more recently it is generating interest among a broader population. With encouragement from the Obama administration, people with public forums, such as entertainers and other popular figures, are being recruited to help promote the effort and further its introduction to potential students.

For example on July 29, 2011, Secretary of State Hillary Rodham Clinton met with Grammy Award–winning musician will.i.am of the Black Eyed Peas. In the meeting Clinton talked about the significance of building cultural and educational ties between the United States and China and the importance of furthering the goals of President Obama's 100,000 Strong Initiative—especially for America's underserved communities. In support of Obama's vision, will.i.am agreed to direct a concert in Beijing that would celebrate U.S.-China educational and cultural exchanges. "Kids from underserved communities rarely have the opportunity to study and travel abroad, and we want to change that," he told the secretary of State.[10] The concert was organized by Americans Promoting Study Abroad, a nonprofit group, and also featured John Legend and the Bucky Johnson band. Scheduled for December, funds raised from the event were earmarked for the support of study-abroad programs in China for American students.

In 2012 Secretary Clinton and Chinese State Councilor Liu Yandong hailed the future of intercultural engagement during the third annual U.S.-

China Consultation on People-to-People Exchange (CPE), an organization that works to enhance Sino-American ties in the areas of education, culture, sports, science and technology, and women's issues. At the closing of the session Clinton announced to the group several new private-sector pledges now in place to further support the 100,000 Strong Initiative.

Since its inception the initiative had received pledges totaling more than $15 million and the Chinese government contributed an estimated 20,000 scholarships for Americans to study in China. The new donations, said Clinton, will add $1 million in seed money from the Ford Foundation for the purpose of setting up a private nonprofit to promote and perpetuate the goals of the initiative. Another donation is from GlamourPin, a Web-based commerce platform for Chinese consumers, which has agreed to contribute by providing a royalty of one percent of all sales. The Bank of China donated $315,000, she continued, Microsoft pledged $100,000 and Motorola Mobility Foundation added another $400,000. These donations are designated for the support of study-abroad opportunities for underserved high school students, through Americans Promoting Study Abroad, the Chicago Public School System, One World Now!, and also the D.C. Center for Global Education and Leadership. Deloitte and Hilton Worldwide have also each committed $100,000.

In addition to recent efforts to expand ties between American high schools and their counterparts in Jiangsu Province, the 100,000 Strong Initiative recently called upon presidents of public and private historically black colleges and universities (HBCUs) to double the number of students they send to China for study-abroad programs. The Thurgood Marshall College Fund, under the umbrella of the 100,000 Strong Initiative, is working to create scholarships that will provide funding.

The IIE and China's Hanban have also agreed to work together on new scholarships to provide more opportunities for American study abroad in China. These scholarships are intended to enable 60–70 American students who are pursuing MA or PhD degrees in the United States to spend two or three semesters in a host university in China for advanced language training, coursework, and research related to the study of modern and contemporary China. China's new president Xi Jinping reportedly supports these efforts, as well as the continuation of the Obama administration's 100,000 Strong Initiative—although his overall perspective on China's higher education policies is still somewhat unrevealed. Xi's views and his decisions over the next few years could serve to advance the current direction of Sino-American academic exchange. Or they may substantially alter its future course.

REDDER THAN RED

Had there not been the long waiting list to get into a juvenile center in Beijing in 1968, Xi Jinping's life might have turned out very differently.

Born in 1953, the son of a revolutionary war hero, Xi was raised in a life of relative privilege. As a child his days were spent in a compound, playing and studying with the children of other senior leaders. He and most of his childhood playmates, the so-called princelings, now hold powerful positions in China's business community and in its government.

Like many families of that time, Xi's had been targeted during the turmoil of the Cultural Revolution. The young Xi was reportedly beaten by a group of student Red Guards and he narrowly avoided detention in the juvenile center when he dared to talk back to them. He joined the Communist Party in 1974. At the end of the Cultural Revolution in 1979, Xi and his family were "rehabilitated," after which he enrolled at Tsinghua University to study chemical engineering and Marxist theory. In part because he was already an active member of the party, and possibly with the help of some personal connections, Xi's first job after graduation was as an assistant to the minister of defense, an award indicating his favor by insiders. In the aftermath of the Cultural Revolution, said a neighbor, Xi had chosen to survive by "becoming redder than red."[11]

After being appointed to a local government post in Hebei Province near Beijing, he went on to serve in Fujian in 1985 and by 1999 he was governor. In March 2013 Xi Jinping, ethnic Han, native of Fuping, took the reigns as China's new leader.

Since his ascension to power Xi has made the fight against official corruption, a growing source of discontent in China, among his first missions. Not correcting the problem could lead to the "collapse of the Party and the downfall of the state," he warned. The Chinese should learn from the experience of other countries, where corruption has played a big role in conflicts over lengthy periods, leading to the overthrow of the political power, Xi commented in a 2013 CNN interview. He was assumedly referring to the events of recent years in Libya, Egypt, Syria, and other authoritarian regimes that have been upended in the wake of the Arab Spring.

Xi is also facing considerable pressure for other changes, not just within the party but from the intelligentsia and the emerging middle class—changes relating to the censorship of information. Incidences of unrest over such restrictions have been increasing in recent years—one example, the 2012 protest over the censorship of a pro-reform newspaper, *Southern Weekly*. The newspaper had apparently released an editorial calling for "constitutionalism," a piece that was quickly recalled and rewritten by a government censor. Outrage spread from the local workers to the Internet, and protest against the censorship won the support of bloggers and an assortment of celebrities. A subsequent demonstration in Guangzhou attracted hundreds.

Around the same time as the *Southern Weekly* controversy, a group of seventy-two mainstream intellectuals produced a "Proposal for Consensus on Reform" that calls for a fresh adherence to the Chinese constitution, which nominally guarantees free speech and assembly to China's citizens.

An article in *The Economist* was quick to point out that the authors of this proposal are not dissidents but established and respected scholars from leading universities.[12]

According to a 2013 article in the *Washington Post*, while the Communist Party has in the past ignored such petitions, the dangers of continuing to do so are increasing. Academics and others warn that without systematic reform, the current escalation of popular discontent over the issue of freedom of expression and information could lead to "turmoil and chaos." Alongside China's extraordinary economic successes, the view that censorship should be less restrictive seems to have become pervasive among its citizens, particularly its youth.[13]

Publications in China recently balked at running an editorial supplied by the Communist Party's propaganda office in Beijing, a piece bluntly declaring that a free press in China is impossible. The issue of a free press, and by extension academic freedom, is not showing any signs of going away. But even in light of what appears to be increasing public disenchantment over the Chinese government's restrictions on speech and information, there have been recent reports of an additional tightening of Internet controls, new constraints that Xi himself may have encouraged. Such reports heighten concerns for America's university collaborations in China, all of which depend on an environment of open inquiry and information if they are to produce anything resembling true research. These roadblocks to scientific discovery and open learning in China may present a growing dilemma for students deciding whether or not to attend a Chinese-based institution, even if it sports an American Ivy League name on its face. Xi Jinping's college-age daughter Mingze, the new "princess" of China—by all accounts as bright and studious as she is pretty—has recently been residing in Massachusetts, working toward her degree from Harvard.

ECONOMY-DRIVEN EDUCATION

China's economic future now hinges on reconciling its educational goals to match the challenges and opportunities fast approaching, according to recent research in both economic and academic sectors. In 2011 the International Economic Association (IEA) held its 16th Triennial World Congress in Beijing. The conference was called in the aftermath of the economic crisis, the consequences of which had "cast shadows over the global economic landscape."[14] Significant changes in economic structure, mechanisms, and institutions were taking place globally, making it an especially appropriate time for economists to gather and present their analyses—as well as their prescriptions for the future of economic policy. Around 400 papers were presented at the conference, and the committee organized five lectures, four plenary panels, and twenty-two sessions on various topics, inviting around ninety leading scholars to participate. The congress met at historic Tsinghua University, which was celebrating its centenary.

The rise of industrialized China is a transformative event in the history of world economy, the group concluded, but it appears that China may be facing a turning point—a new transition after thirty years of successfully transforming a command economy to a market economy.

This transition may be understood within a new conceptual and analytical framework, according to conference reports—one that "unifies development economics and demography in a long-term perspective."[15] This current stage of development, according to the group, is now about to end, and improvements in the quality of human resources rather than an expansion of their quantity are imperative if China is to continue to advance. "This transition to the phase of human capital-based development is the key for China to sustain per capita income growth, albeit slower than in the past three decades, to avoid a stall referred to as the 'middle-income trap.'"[16]

As is well-recognized, these changes are soon to be complicated by another—a phase of "post-demographic transition" characterized by an aging population. The combination will result in an increase in the dependency ratio of the population of China, concluded the congress. To deal with the changes, Chinese economic policies and its educational systems, at all levels, must be adapted accordingly if China is to have sufficient and suitable applicants to fill the jobs it is now creating.

LITTLE EMPERORS

Citing the topic's sensitivity, three publishers refused to print Jame Liang's book, *Too Many People in China?*—a book whose thesis is that the demographic changes brought about by the one-child policy will now challenge China's goal of moving from being the "factory of the world" to a more entrepreneurial economy.

Put in place in 1979, the one-child policy, according to China's National Population and Family Planning Commission, averted a surge in births that would have added an estimated 400 million Chinese to a population that already exceeded 1.3 billion. It is a claim that was for a long time widely supported, but in more recent years it has been questioned. "The belief is that the Chinese people like to have many children" and it is doomed by a population explosion if this tendency is not controlled, said Wang Feng, senior fellow and director at the Brookings-Tsinghua Center for Public Policy at Tsinghua University.[17] These attitudes date to the period immediately following the Cultural Revolution when the country suffered food shortages and food rationing, he explained. In the mid-1960s Chinese couples had an average of about six children, compared to 1.5 children in 2013. By 2030, demographers predict China's population will peak at about 1.4 billion.

According to World Bank estimates, until now China has enjoyed what economists call the "demographic dividend"—a growing labor force contributing about 0.9 percent to annual economic growth. That dividend will begin to disappear as the working-age population peaks and then starts to shrink, perhaps dropping as much as 20 percent over the next few years, according to the United Nations Department of Economic and Social Affairs. While it took the United States and Europe about a century to become "aging societies," in China it has taken fewer than forty years. "For the first time," reported Philip O'Keefe, human development director at World Bank in Beijing, "we are seeing a country getting old before it has gotten rich."[18]

China's one-child policy may be somewhat of a misnomer, as there are numerous exceptions to the rule. For example, rural couples whose first child is female may have a second, and parents who are both only children may also have two offspring. Some estimates report that only around one-third of China's population is still under strict one-child regulation. However, in spite of the relaxation of the policy since 1979 it remains a topic of controversy in China—in part due to its "dark side" of forced abortions. Media has in recent years brought far more attention to the issue, for example, the case of a 22-year-old woman from Shanxi Province who was reportedly forced by government officials to endure an abortion when she was seven months pregnant. A photograph of the woman with her dead baby on a hospital bed went viral on Weibo (China's Twitter), sparking a new wave of public outcry.

One effect of the one-child policy has been the development of new generations of so-called little emperors—a term referring to an only child of doting parents. Dependent on just one offspring to lead the family toward a prosperous future, China's millions of only children are frequently described as overindulged and spoiled, with every family resource slated for their education and future success.

China's girls have benefited from the policy and, as only children, have to some degree become "little emperors" themselves—although they still lag far behind males in overall enrollments and professional success. In earlier times most daughters would not have been groomed for higher education, but now parental expectations formerly reserved for boys are also distributed to girls. Since the implementation of the one-child policy, female enrollments in China's higher education institutions, as well as in their participation in study-abroad programs, have increased significantly.

Researchers agree that the aging of China's population combined with a lowered birth rate is altering its future workforce. Complicating the problem further is a burgeoning number of Chinese children receiving subpar education—together a set of circumstances that may require changes in China's educational system as a whole. As China continues to work toward modernizing its economy, according to some experts, its rising population of impoverished "migrant children" could be a deterrent to the nation's ability to develop the workforce it will need for a successful future.

Based on information from *The Hechinger Report*, a publication of Teachers College at Columbia University, a 2012 article in *Time World* described the private schools in southern China that have taken on the task of educating some of the country's most disadvantaged students. These children, so-called migrant students, earned that designation due to their parents' decision to move from the countryside into the city without official approval. Chinese law prohibits citizens from relocating without governmental permission, a policy aimed at keeping China's population evenly distributed.[19] Nonetheless, in recent decades hundreds of millions have fled rural areas without obtaining permission, hoping to find work. Because of their status as unofficial migrants, municipal governments have often been unwilling or unable to provide public services such as health care or education.

To help educate this growing population of migrant children, many non-profit agencies, nongovernmental organizations, and private citizens have worked to set up thousands of schools, most at the elementary level. These private schools are typically understaffed and their teachers are oftentimes less than fully qualified, a consequence of shoestring budgets. At the Dexin School, for example, as with most of these private efforts , facilities are meager and volunteers are essential for their existence—qualified or not:

> With dirt streaking their faces and clothes, children shout and run around a concrete courtyard that doubles as a playground at the Dexin School. Minutes later, they squirm in their seats after being corralled into classrooms with bars on the windows. Their voices can be heard disrupting their English class as American volunteers try to get them to repeat phrases like "You are beautiful."[20]

Researchers warn that the subpar education being loosely administered to such a large population of young citizens will affect China's productivity in the long run. According to Matthew Boswell, a project manager for Stanford University's Rural Education Action Project (an organization formed to help reduce China's growing rural-urban academic achievement gap), it is an "enormous and growing problem" requiring the immediate attention of China's national authorities. In agreement with the conclusions drawn by the World Bank's gathering of economic experts, in order for China to maintain superpower status, "its workforce needs to be more literate and better educated."[21]

The achievement gap between the migrant children and the students enrolled in China's public schools is concerning. Only a few years ago, in 2010, the world was stunned as Shanghai's fifteen-years olds beat their peers around the world on international assessments in reading, math, and science. Americans of the same age finished in the bottom half of the countries examined. (It should be noted that the Chinese scores were generated from public schools and did not include migrant students. In America all children are provided public school education and assessment scores are comprehensive.) Studies have shown that, even though migrant students in private city schools outperformed students who still resided in poor rural areas, they were academically inferior to those attending urban public schools. For educators who are invested in helping migrant students succeed, the slow progress can be discouraging. As one teacher put it, "If it weren't for this school, maybe some kids would just pick up food on the street or become beggars. . . . "[22]

China's public schools clearly have the ability to turn out highly capable students; however, if China fails to offer a similar level of academic training for all of its youth, it could result in millions becoming virtually unemployable as adults. "I can't think of other problems that have such far-reaching impacts on society," commented Henan Cheng of Loyola University in Chicago, a researcher who has studied migrant education in Kunming in Yunnan Province.[23] Figures vary, but some nonprofits estimate that there are more than 225 million migrants now living in Chinese cities, about 10 percent of them children. Authorities on population growth warn that China should brace for as many as 350 million migrants by 2050.

China has already taken important steps to curb the problem. As early as 2006 the government began allowing migrant children to enroll in some public schools and many of the private schools now qualify for subsidies to help with their expenses. However, the process of enrolling in public schools can reportedly be daunting. Students are required to obtain as many as seven official certificates in some cities, documenting things like birthplace, before they can attend. And while education is provided for their city-born peers for free, migrant students may be required to pay tuition as high as 1,000 yuan per semester (about $150)—a sizable fee for most families of migrant children. Adding to the impediments have been frequent incidences of behavioral problems among the migrant children, a common by-product of poverty and hardship.

Some progress is being reported, however. In Kunming, for example, the local government has been able to increase migrant access to its schools over the years, and today around half of its migrant students are able to attend the public schools—although they are often segregated from the urban children or sent to the least prestigious facilities. The rest, if they go to school at all, still attend schools like the one in Dexin.

CHINA 2030

According to the Pew Research Center's 2012 survey on global attitudes, as economic and geopolitical competition has grown between the United States and China, Americans and Chinese have progressively hardened their views of each other. Chinese assessments regarding relations with the United States have become significantly more negative over the last two years especially, and China's level of confidence in the Obama administration has reportedly dropped as well. A Pew global-attitudes survey conducted in 2011 found that in fifteen out of twenty-two nations, the general opinion is that China will replace the United States as the world's leading superpower.

When the American public was asked whether they viewed China as a partner, competitor or enemy, the responses were 16 percent, 66 percent, and 15 percent, respectively. Asked whether China can be trusted, 68 percent responded "not too much" or "not at all." The top concern of Americans, according to Pew's survey, is the debt held by the Chinese.[24] It is within this environment of competition and growing mistrust, as China seeks to improve its own educational system to best confront economic issues, information restrictions and demographic changes, that U.S.-China education exchange will exist for the foreseeable future.

Many of the plans recently put forth by China's Ministry of Education, strategies to improve the country's system of education from its kindergartens to its universities, are now underway. The Outline of China's National Plan for Medium and Long-Term Education Reform and Development (2010–2020) took two years to draw up before it was officially adopted, and underwent about forty revisions.[25]

The plan sets a series of goals to be achieved by 2020, including the universalizing of preschool education, improving nine-year compulsory education, and raising the senior high school gross enrollment rate to 90 percent. In higher education, among other things the plan calls for the creation of world-class universities, as well as improved teaching and research and greater freedom for institutions of higher learning to set their academic goals. It also seeks to revise China's entrance examination system and to achieve a 40 percent enrollment rate in higher education.[26] The United Nations Educational, Scientific and Cultural Organization (UNESCO) and the World Bank have both commended the plan as farsighted and ambitious.

The plan also aims to attract more world-class scholars and researchers to work in China, to import more and better teaching materials and texts, and to establish 250 additional Confucius Institutes in eighty countries. It endorses the sending of greater numbers of Chinese students to study abroad, and also sets the goal of attracting a half million international students to its own colleges and universities by 2020—a figure that, if accomplished, will make China the world's top educational destination. More scholarships will be offered, expanded language programs will be supported, and many more courses are to be taught in English, according to the plan.

A 2011 report developed by China's Ministry of Finance and the World, the Development Research Center of the State Council, and the World Bank, is titled *China 2030: Building a Modern, Harmonious, and Creative High-Income Society*. In sum, the publication recommends China approach midcentury by building upon its considerable strengths—high savings, increasing numbers of skilled professionals, and the potential for further urbanization. China should capitalize on external opportunities, including continued globalization, the growth of other emerging economies, and the promise of new technologies. Moreover, China will need to address some significant challenges, including its aging society, rising inequality, and a growing environmental deficit.

The report goes on to propose six basic strategies for China's future development. First, it suggests the rethinking of the role of the state and the private sector to build competition. Second, it encourages the adoption of an open innovation system with links to global research and development networks, and third, China should look to green development as a new avenue of growth. Fourth, equality of opportunity and social protection should be provided for everyone, and fifth, the fiscal system should be strengthened along with the improvement of fiscal sustainability. Lastly, China should ensure as an international stakeholder that it continues its integration with global markets.[27] These efforts must be approached within an environment of greater transparency, combined with an ongoing effort to lessen fraudulence, a plan to heighten China's credibility in the eyes of the rest of the world.

TRUTHINESS

"I'm no fan of dictionaries or reference books, that's elitist . . . I don't trust books, they're all facts and no heart . . . who is Britannica to tell me the Panama Canal was finished in 1914?" Stephen Colbert, a popular American political satirist, used humor in his newscast to suggest that some of the country's critical decisions may have been the result of taking license with the facts in order to advance a particular viewpoint—using as an example George Bush's stated beliefs about Iraq prior to its invasion. The "truthiness" of something, according to Colbert, is what feels right, without regard to evidence, intellectual examination, or facts—perhaps better described as "truth by consensus"—a charge often levied against open-access informational sites such as Wikipedia. Colbert, tongue partly-in-cheek, hailed the idea. Anyone can read the news to you, he told his television audience. "I promise to *feel* the news *at* you."[28]

Both China and America have exercised "truthiness" in their dealings with each other, both in the diplomatic arena and in educational exchange. One could cite possibly questionable motivations of some early Christian missionaries in China, or Teddy Roosevelt's underlying quest for "soft power" after the Boxer Rebellion, or the attempt of today's Confucius Institutes to accomplish a similar result. Was Teddy Roosevelt's incentive to allot the Boxer Indemnity remission to China for scholarships strictly an act of diplomatic goodwill and fair play? Not entirely. His motivations included the promotion of his own Christian philosophy and an expectation that academic interaction would encourage the Chinese to think more

"American," thus making diplomatic dealings with the Celestial Kingdom lean more in favor of the United States. And in fact diplomatic relations did improve for a time. Have the Chinese used exchange-student spies to uncover confidential technology to further benefit China? Evidence reveals that it has, and China's economy and ability to defend itself have likely benefited. Do initiatives like the Confucius Institutes willingly present history through a Chinese lens? Of course, but by doing so they also provide a different viewpoint, one held by millions of Chinese. Do Chinese students bend the truth when applying for admission to American universities? It is well known that many do—but once they get in, most work very hard and succeed in earning their degrees.

Further, has knowledge been significantly advanced in America's classrooms through the personal interactions, intercultural education, and language training emanating from education exchange with China? Thousands of teachers say it has. And have treasured relationships and lifelong bonds been generated between citizens of the two countries through these academic exchanges? Such friendships are countless. Truthiness can sometimes yield positive results.

EPILOG: A CAUTIONARY TALE

Today a bronze statue of Yung Wing, the "runaway" who was the first Chinese ever to graduate from an American university and the driving force behind Sino-American exchange, is on permanent display at Yale University's Betts House on Prospect Street. Its unveiling took place on the 150th anniversary of his graduation, accompanied by an impressive photographic exhibition that was prepared in his honor by the people of Zhuhai, Yung's hometown.

The young man who dreamed of finding a way to provide his countrymen the same academic benefits he enjoyed in the United States turned his aspirations into a lifelong quest. "I was determined that the rising generation of China should enjoy the same educational advantages that I had enjoyed; that through western education China might be regenerated, become enlightened and powerful. To accomplish that became the guiding light of my ambition." After seemingly endless failures, Yung succeeded in convincing the Qing imperial court to send its first dispatch of thirty Chinese boys to America to study, initiating an educational collaboration that continues today. In 1872, Yung Wing could not possibly have foreseen the reach of his mission.

As we move toward midcentury, professionals who are in the business of working with U.S.-China academic exchange will face both old and new challenges—rapidly changing economic conditions, educational reforms to meet those conditions, demographic shifts, governmental and political divides, and difficult choices involving money and freedom—all within a world of technology and interconnectivity beyond anyone's predictions. Battles have been won but others loom ahead.

Yung Wing's vision for higher learning exchange was only realized after extraordinary perseverance and personal sacrifice, achieved in unexplored territory, amid a clash of politics and cultures—difficult conditions that in some respects are not so far removed from the complex challenges facing Sino-American education exchange today. A self-described dreamer, Yung Wing held fast to the belief that it is simply impossible for anything truly worthwhile to be accomplished without one. But he held no illusions about reality.

Appendix A

TIMELINE

1784	The first representatives of the United States went to China aboard the *Empress of China* to establish diplomatic recognition and trade
1810s	The opium trade begins
1830	The first American Protestant missionaries arrive in China
1839	The outbreak of the Opium Wars
1842	The signing of the Treaty of Nanjing
1847	The coolie trade begins in the West
1850–64	Taiping Rebellion
1860	Qing court begins Self-Strengthening programs
1854	Yung Wing becomes the first Chinese to graduate from an American university
1858	Treaty of Tianjin (Tientsin) signed
1862	Anson Burlingame becomes Chinese representative; first U.S. legation established in China
1868	Burlingame-Seward Treaty
1872	Chinese Educational Mission sends its first 30 students to America
1881	Chinese Educational Mission students recalled to China
1882	Chinese Exclusion Act
1898	Hundred Days Reform movement
1900	The Boxer Rebellion
1901	Boxer Protocol signed
1902, 1904	The Geary Act is expanded and extended, further restricting Chinese immigration
1904	Imperial examination system abolished
1905–1906	Anti-American boycotts in China
1908	Remittance of the Boxer Indemnity
1909	First Indemnity Scholarship students dispatched to America; second wave of Chinese enrollments in the U.S. begins

Appendix A

1911	Tsinghua College opens; Chinese Students' Alliance created
1919	On May 4 students march in Beijing in protest of the Treaty of Versailles
1920–21	John Dewey lectures in China
1922	Anti-missionary movement in China
1924	Second part of Boxer Indemnity remission used to establish the China Foundation for the Promotion of Education and Culture; National Origins Act is passed
1925	Death of Sun-Yat-sen; his son Chiang Kai-shek would succeed him to lead the Nationalist Party.
1927	Nationalist capital established in Nanjing
1928	United States formally recognizes the new Nationalist government; Tsinghua becomes a university
1945–49	Civil war in China between the Guomindang and the Communists
1949	People's Republic of China founded under Mao Zedong; Nationalists flee to Taiwan to establish the Republic of China
1950	The Korean War begins
1952	China begins restructuring education systems to reflect the Soviet model
1956	Hundred Flowers Movement
1965	U.S. Immigration and Naturalization Act passed
1966	Mao Zedong's Cultural Revolution begins
1972	Ping-pong diplomacy; President Richard Nixon visits China
1976	Mao Zedong dies
1979	Deng Xiaoping and Jimmy Carter sign trade agreement; Taiwan Relations Act passed; third wave of Chinese enrollments in the U.S. begins
1984	President Ronald Reagan visits China
1988	China surpasses Taiwan as leading sender of students to the U.S.
1989	June 4th incident at Tiananmen Square initiates hiatus in U.S.-China relations
1992	U.S.-China relations reopen when President George H. W. Bush and Chinese Premier Li Peng met on the sidelines of a U.N. conference
1992	Protection Act becomes law under Bill Clinton's administration
1995	China announces Project 211
1996	Illegal Immigration Reform and Immigrant Responsibility Act (IIRIRA) initiated
1998	China begins Project 985 and C9 League
1999	China becomes leading sender of students to the United States

2002	Student and Exchange Visitor Information System implemented
2004	Confucius Institutes begin operation
2005	U.S.-China Cultural Engagement Act introduced
2009	President Obama introduces the 100,000 Strong Initiative
2010	U.S. Secretary of State Hillary Clinton launches 100,000 Strong Initiative in Beijing
2010	China's National Outline for Medium and Long-Term Education Reform is implemented (2010–2020)
2011	China's Thousand Foreign Experts program begins
2012	Introduction of massive open online courses
2013	New York University Shanghai, China's first Sino-American university opens
2013	Xi Jinping becomes China's president

Appendix B

CONFUCIUS INSTITUTES IN THE UNITED STATES

Alfred University
Arizona State University
Bryant University
Chicago Public Schools
Cleveland State University
Columbia University
Community College of Denver
Emory University
George Mason University
Georgia State University
Indiana University
Kennesaw State University
Kentucky University
Miami Dade College
Miami University, Ohio
Michigan State University
New Mexico State University
North Carolina State University
Pace University
Pennsylvania State University
Pfeiffer University
Portland State University
Presbyterian College
Purdue University
Rutgers University
San Diego State University
San Francisco State University
Stanford University
State of Washington
Texas A&M University

Troy University
University of Akron
University of Alaska, Anchorage
University of Arizona
University of California, Los Angeles
University of Chicago
University of Central Arkansas
University of Delaware
University of Hawaii
University of Iowa
University of Kansas
University of Maryland
University of Massachusetts
University of Memphis
University of Michigan
University of Minnesota
University of Montana
University of Nebraska–Lincoln
University of New York
University of Oklahoma
University of Pittsburgh
University of Rhode Island
University of South Carolina
University of South Florida
University of Texas at Dallas
University of Texas at San Antonio
University of Toledo
University of Utah
University of Wisconsin–Platteville
Valparaiso University
Wayne State University
Webster University
West Kentucky University
Western Michigan University
Xavier University

Appendix C

WONG KAI KAH'S LETTER TO MRS. BARTLETT, 1882

Shanghai, China
January 28, 1882

My dear Mrs. Bartlett,

I feel well and strong enough now to write you a letter, though it may not be very interesting. I was prostrated with Shanghai fever for five weeks, and on my sick bed I often thought of writing to you, but the hand that could not lift a quill was not fit to pen a letter. I wonder whether you really wish to know our misfortunes ever since we stepped on the shores of our generous and native land. You will be astonished to learn the shabby and mean treatment we received at the hands of our paternal government. Perhaps you are already informed through some other source, but at any rate I will recount to you everything that has been done for our good(?).

The first sight of Shanghai we steamed up to the wharf in a steam launch as our "Japan" had to stop at Woo Sung, since it could not pass the sand bars at low tide--thrilled us thinking what a joyous welcome was waiting for us, and what a sea of familiar faces would soon surround us, and our country would soon extend her arms to embrace us in maternal kindness! But alas! Vain thoughts! The tall spires grew taller, the indistinct buildings grew more distinct, and we grew wilder and more enthusiastic over our imaginary reception, while the launch glided over the placid and yellow waters of the Yang Tze until it touched the wharf, with a sudden jar, which awoke us from our Utopian dreams. True, a sea of faces was looking down on us, but no friendly recognition, no kindly smile greeted our forlorn band. Crowds of coolies wheel-barrows and jinrickshaw men were shouting, gesticulating, and quarreling for business. One solitary man cam aboard to receive us--our postal manager--to whom we telegraphed from Japan. But the postal manager, Mr. Luk is a fool of the first class, he has not even the average brain of a Chinaman. Instead of employing carriages or boats to convey us to our destined place, the Chinese Harbor Master's office, he packed us on wheel-barrows which have but one wheel and progress very slowly. And thus we were exposed to the gaping and jeering crowd who followed us and mocked our clothing, which was badly cut, and sewed together by the Chinese tailors, in San Francisco, and ill suited to the fashions of the dandyish and fast Shanghaiese. Some of the wheel-barrows had no pass to go through the French concession, and many of us had to get down and walk, carrying our bags in our hands, an almost inexcusable act of debasing oneself in the eyes of the so-called Chinese gentleman. After walking through the French settlement we entered the Chinese territory, and if you ever wish to find a paradise, and the infernal regions placed side by side, you had better come here; the filth and fifty-seven different kinds of foul smells, and the muddy uneven slippery walk made of stones fairly sickened us. We trudged on cursing our fate, our cool reception, our stupid manager, and last, but not the least, our Chinese shoes which pinched our feet, and cramped our toes; until we came to the Harbor Master's house, a spacious building facing the river, comparatively clean and well ventilated. After roll and a substantial supper, not elaborately prepared, we were dispatched with a detachment of Chinese marines acting as a guard over us to prevent our escaping from the grasp of our paternal government (?) to the "Knowledge Wishing Institution" inside of the city behind the court of the Shanghai Taotai. Your Western imagination is too sublime to conceive a place so vile as this so-called institution; you may have read about Turkish prisons or Andersonville Horrors, but compared with this they must have been enviable places. I will test the power of my pen by attempting to describe the "jail" where we were confined after our glorious venture, and if I fail then you may understand how terribly horrible the place is. The "Knowledge Wishing Institution" has not been used for over ten years and superstition had given birth to ghosts and goblins which are said to have taken the abode to themselves and have displayed fantastic and awful shapes to the eyes of horrified Celestials; for ten long years its doors were closed, its ceilings were not touched by a brush, nor its floors by a broom; ten years saw the stone pavements turning green with mould, the wooden frames of the windows and doors rotting in the damp atmosphere. An unwholesome breath of damp air greeting us as we entered its folding doors caused us to think the shadowy beings pitied our miserable plight; the night was advancing, and we could see a sort of vapory smoke rising from the brick floor, and our clothes soon became moist, and a drowsy influence seemed to over-power us, but that was kept at bay by the fierce indignation which burned in every heart; long and terrible were the imprecations poured forth upon the heads of our managers and upon him who caused our premature return. But like dogs baying at the moon, we were wasting our breath, and staring vacantly at the cobwebed walls, we finally sought our downy couches; first our hands came in cntact with something wet, which we found to be our covering, and mattress and then we felt something hard which was the board placed across two benchs; this primative arrangement was dignified with the name of bed constructed specially for our accomodation. But sleep, like death puts an end to all the evils and griefs and while the body is in the blessed arms of Morpheus extreme suffering of the present often leads our mind to the happy times of the past and to mingle over again with joy and mirth of bygone days. And those, I imagine, who were able to close their eyes must have wandered once more to their happy homes far across the sea, where tender hands guarded and guided them to the path of Righteousness and true manhood, where loving voices taught them first the words of our Lord's Prayer, and where kindly smiles were ever ready to greet them; they must have visited once more our dear Alma Mater, and have their ears ring again with the familiar tunes of "Amici" and "Auld Lang Syne."

Grey morn and chilly wind brought us from our happy wanderings to stern reality again and the day wore away in vain hope of getting release from our confinement. It was doubly unfortunate

-3-

for us inbeing shut up just the time when the feast of the moon took place. There were many of us whose fathers, relatives and friends were awaiting us with wines and banquets in full preparation and longed to gaze upon and sit by the sides of their dear ones who had been so long away on the other hemisphere across the big, big sea. But such pleasures were denied them, we were to receive no liberty until we had our "Kewtous" to the Shanghai Taotai. Accordingly, after four days's groaning and complaining we were summoned to hold audience with the highest official in Shanghai. In three bodies were we mustered with enough guards to keep a regiment in quiet subjection; we commenced our journey in the midst of crowds of spectators whose comments were far from being flattering, and marched through piles of dirt and filth which commanded the entrances of Taotai Yamen. Now a huge edifice time-worn and wormeaten met our sight; rusty swords broken blunderbusses ancient cannons, opium-struck soldiers and servants presented a strange appearance to our unsophisticated eyes which were accustomed to Barbaric splender and not to eastern dilapidation and culpable megligence. Alas, the Taotai who gets ten or fifteen thousands of tales, equivalent to $20,000 or $25,000 for his legal income besides presents from those who court his favor, cannot keep his official residence and the outer court in repairs.

After much waiting and unnecessary delay we were at last ushered in to the presence of his Excellency and we prostrated ourselves before his majestic presence; he however returned our salute and motioned us to stand out each according to his division in which he went to America. After he inquired of us our different accomplishments and the courses we pursued the "great Man" dismissed us allowing us to depart from the "Prison" at 10 a.m. and returning at 4 p.m. much to the dislike of the boys. Two days afterward I boarded the English mail "Rosetta" and accompanied Mr. Yung Wei Chun to Hongkong.

Skirting along the bold and rocky shores of the Chinese Sea we saw scenery equal to any our eyes ever met. White clouds floating above the brow of dark hills covered the autumnal skies while the waters were deep green; here and there were clustered groups of fishing boats sheltering themselves under over hanging rocks and wild hawks every now and then made a dart for some of the funny tribe. A storm arose, the skirt of a severe typhoon caught us, and for two days we were rather unsightly looking things. Poor Tsceuck was very seasick and was in the arms of Morpheus almost all the time and could take in nothing except fruits. Hongkong is an English colony situated on the side of a bleak hill and has steps to go from one street to another. It is clean and well kept and has a garrison of English soldiers. A beautiful harbor lies in front of the city and is studded with men-of-war of all nations.

After staying three weeks at Hongkong I took my departure for Swatow 178 miles away from the English colony on board of a coast steamer. The journey lasted 24 hours and the fare was $25.00, 1st class European. It was early Sunday morning that I stepped on the soil of Swatow where my father and family are staying. Now my parents knew nothing of my arrival--the postal arrangements in China being so imperfect that my letters sent a week before went on the same steamer as I did and I was obliged to find out my father's residence, a very hard task indeed in a community where no one can be understood or no one can understand their dialect, my

Appendix C 199

father being the Linguist in the Swatow Customs a prominent position both officially and commercially; but in Swatow the case becomes different a stranger can no more understand the "Swatowians" than you can Arabic without learning it. They pronounce my name "Wong" "Kong and it was through the kindness of Mr. Campbell an English Merchant there that I could make the man at the Custom house understand what I wanted, a rather curious episode to see a foreigner playing a part of an interpreter to two Chinese. After the door keeper at the Customs conversed a few minutes with Mr. Campbell he called one of his men and told him to take me to my father's house. Before parting with Mr. Campbell I was rather taken a-back when I was informed by him that the door keeper of the Customs asked whether it was Wong the "boy" at the Customs or Linguist Wong the great man that I was seeking for. The idea of connecting me with the waiting boy was rather startling; maybe it was the verdant and puzzled look I wore roused the uncalled for in the door keepers breast. Being brought to the doors of a colossal building I was told that within lived the dear ones from whom I had been separated for nine long years nor did "Open Seasame" unbar the pounderous gates but the united efforts of four fists at last brought the sleeping servants to the threshold though it was already half past ten. The servant was cross being waked up so un-ceremoniously and taking me for one of those poor devils who ever seek favors from those who are better off than themselves he forbade me going any further than his own domain. I understood him to say something about my father's not being up until nine and that his hour of seeing visitors not until ten. I was desperate to think that within a stone throw lay peacefully sleeping my dear parents, brother and sister and yet I was to be kept back by a servant. I called into play all my linguistic powers and the deaf and dumb signs but the invariable reply from him was a shake of his head. Having failed in every other experiment I suddenly remembered that all the world over, savage or civilized, young or old, address their parents pa and ma and I tried that dodge; a gleam of light shot across his face and he looked at me closely to see that he was not imposed upon. That was a happy thought however for I was the perfect image of my sister. His manner suddenly changed and he was one of the politest creatures I ever saw; he grasped my bags and ushered me upstairs. The servants were waked up one by one and there were many to be waked up. My mother dressed in a hurry to come out though she thought I was my cousin until she saw me; tears were in her eyes as she saw my face which she had longed to see for ten long years; then my father came out to receive me and who can describe his joy as he looked into my face and smiled. Ah! there is no joy as the joy of parents who find their son restored to them in good health after the absence of ten long years. We sons may forget our parents as we are carried away on the wings of pleasure but not so with them, every thought reminds them of their dear ones far away and days seem years to them as they long to see us, waiting with strained eyes and out stretched necks. My sister made her appearance soon after and it seemed that I saw my own image in her. My father's house is a large one containing about 15 bedrooms and 3 parlors and two pluviums surrounded by three walls. But joy is short lived when one serves the Chinese government. For one day and a half I enjoyed all that a son could enjoy after he had wandered away from home so long and then jumping on board another Steamer I returned to Hongkong promising my parents that I should probably come back in a month or two on a leave of absence.

    My greatest disappointment on reaching Shanghai later was to find that a large portion of my friends had departed for Tientsin.

among them were Sheu Chi and Yang Tsang. Tun Yen was still in Shanghai getting ready to start for the same place with four others. Alas! friends whom I had associated with so long were separated from me without the chance of saying goodbye and we know not when we shall see them again. How like a dream all these things are happening, I expect someday to awake from it! Yang Tsang is now in Canton enjoying his leave of abscence with his family. Tun Yen is in Tientsin teaching the telegraph school boys the rudiments of English language. Sheu Chi is an assistant translator of the Taotai in Tientsin. They receive 12 and ten taels respectively. Yang Tsang expects to go to the Ka Ping mines so his salary is not determined. The rest of the boys are distributed in various places to finish (?) their education not according to their predilections or the course they had been pursuing in America but more in accordance with the wishes of the Chinese Officials whose ignorance and stupidity render them unfit to judge in such matters. Several boys intending to take law as their profession were carted to the Naval Academy where they have a chance to become Captains and Admirals (?) of the future navy of China! Let a Nelson command the Chinese navy and she will not be able to overcome the canoes of the Fijii Islanders. The entire military force of a province combined with a naval force for the Coast defense could not for months capture one piratical band composed at the most of 200 men though the leader had put to death one captain of a gunboat, beheaded several military mandarins with the red buttons and burned several villages. Poor Hong Yen is now pining away in the Imperial Chinese Naval Academy, high sounding in name but in reality a dungeon. Sixteen were sent to Foo Chow where they too are now studying in the Naval Academy. Several are now in the Torpedo school in Tientsin harbor. Four are in the Shanghai arsenal studying under Soo Vung.

We are waiting for the arrival of Mr. Yung Wing to whom we look for our liberation from such outrageous treatment by our government. Our confidence in Mr. Wing still remains unshaken though his long delay in coming made some doubt his power in influencing the Viceroy. We are only mortals, we have not the patience of Job. We are like the shoots of young trees transplanted from the rich soil and luxurient climate to the arid desert of ignorance and superstition. We are not flourishing but withering away slowly though perceptibly. We draw down on us the pity of many interested and sensible foreigners. They are powerless though they can do a good deal by writing for the papers.

I have called several times on Mr. and Mrs. Brown and they have been very kind to me. It is so pleasant to find some friends who can appreciate you and your education and your ambition. Their little girl Louisa is very pretty and smart. She is fond only of the Chinese way of cooking.

Your family will ever inspire me with love and kind remembrances and if ever chance brings me to America I shall first seek your family which has made me what I am.

I am now in the Foreign office at Shanghai with Chung Mun Yew and Lu Kwok Shui. We receive 10 taels each and board ourselves. The arsenal boys get 5 taels a month and have to feed themselves. Our government is so generous and yet so well versed in political economy that it barely keeps us above the point of starvation. Whether we are liable to be frozen to death or not they care nothing about that, that is our own look out. Whether our families are in danger of being starved and frozen, that is still further from the minds of the government. Such is the progressive policy of China so civilized under foreign influence. She deserves no pity, she needs a good thrashing and a thorough washing before she is fit to govern her millions.

There is a great danger of the students slipping back into their old way and habits. Some have shown symptoms of degenerating into their country-men's mode and manner of living but the majority seem to present an adamantine firmness against all the complications and the deadening effects of officialism.

But everything depends on Mr. Wing. I hope he will do a great deal both for the good of China and for our benefit. A certain article of the North China Daily News says that the best thing for us is to be sent abroad as China is not ready for us.

You will please write soon. Mom Yew sends his best regards so also Kwok Shiu. With my best love to all,

I am your loving boy,

(Signed) Wong Kai Kah

Notes

NOTES TO CHAPTER 1

1. John King Fairbank, *China, A New History* (Cambridge, MA: The Belknap Press of Harvard University, 2006): 92–93.
2. Joseph Needham, *Science and Civilization in China, Volume 1*, Introductory Orientation (Cambridge University Press, 1954).
3. Thaddeus T'ui-Chieh Hang, "Why Chinese Civilization Has Not Discovered Modern Sciences," *Cultural Heritage and Contemporary Change,* Series III, Asia (vol. 9, 1995): 123–130.
4. Ibid.
5. From the Foreword of Fu Xi, *The I Ching or Book of Changes* (Princeton University Press, 1967), contributed by Carl Jung.
6. Thaddeus T'ui-Chieh Hang, "Why Chinese Civilization," 123–130.
7. Ibid.
8. Tina Stiefel, *The Intellectual Revolution of Twelfth Century Europe* (New York: St. Martin's Press, 1985): 44–45.
9. Allen G. Debus, *The French Paracelsians* (Cambridge University Press, 1991).
10. Thaddeus T'ui-Chieh Hang, "Why Chinese Civilization," 123–130.
11. Frederick Rudolph, *The American College and University* (Athens and London: University of Georgia Press, 1990): 4.
12. Ibid., 5. Also see Samuel Eliot Morison, *The Founding of Harvard College* (Cambridge, MA: Harvard University Press, 1935).
13. Ibid.
14. New England's First Fruits, 1640. *Collections of the Massachusetts Historical Society,* 1792, Volume 1, pp. 242–248. These writings, which celebrated the early American colonial colleges, were an anonymous tract originally published in London in 1643.
15. Christopher J. Lucas, *American Higher Education* (New York: St. Martin's Press, 1994): 100.
16. Ibid., 103
17. Rudolph, *The American College and University,* 23–43.
18. Ibid., 21.
19. Ibid., 22.
20. Richard Hofstadter and Wilson Smith, eds. *American Higher Education: A Documentary History* (Chicago: Chicago University Press, 1961).
21. Rudolph, *The American College and University,* 68–85.
22. Barbara L. Narendra, "Benjamin Silliman and the Peabody Museum" (*Discovery* 14, 1979): 13–29. Also see Frederick Rudolph, *The American College and University,* 222.

23. The practice of slavery in the United States has historically been attributed almost exclusively to the South, an accusation promoted before the advent of the Civil War, in part to rally public opinion in support of using military force for its annexation. While fewer in number, there existed many African slaves in northern states. When Silliman studied at Yale, there were an estimated 5,000 slaves in Connecticut alone.
24. Rudolph, *The American College and University*, 223.
25. A. Hunter Dupree, *Asa Gray, 1810–1888* (Cambridge: Belknap Press of Harvard University, 1959).
26. Rudolph, *The American College and University*, 225.
27. Samuel Elliot Morison, *Three Centuries of Harvard 1636–1936* (Cambridge: Harvard University Press, 1936): 230–231. See also Teresa Brawner Bevis and Christopher J. Lucas, *International Students in American Colleges and Universities: A History* (New York: Palgrave Macmillan, 2007): 31–40.
28. Rudolph, *The American College and University*, 125–127.
29. Lucas, American Higher Education, 120.
30. Rudolph, *The American College and University*, 86–109.
31. Anna Galicich, *The German Americans* (New York: Chelsea House, 1989). Also see Theodore Huebener, *The Germans in America* (Philadelphia: Chilton Co., 1962).
32. Rudolph, *The American College and University*, 373–393. Also see John S. Brubacher and Willis Rudy, *Higher Education in Transition: A History of American Colleges and Universities, 1636–1976*, 3rd edition (York: Harper & Row, 1976): 131–136.
33. Rudolph, *The American College and University*, 48.
34. Ibid., 44–67. Also see Roger L. Geiger, "The Era of Multipurpose Colleges in American Higher Education, 1850–1890" (*History of Higher Education Annual*, vol. 15, 1995): 56. A formal census was released after the Civil War which reported 563 colleges and universities in 1869, in "120 Years of American Education: A Statistical Report" (Table 172, Government Printing Office, Washington, D.C., 1998).
35. Paul H. Mattingly, "The Political Culture of America's Antebellum Colleges" (*History of Higher Education Annual*, vol. 17, 1997): 73–95.
36. Rudolph, *The American College and University*, 44–67.
37. Ibid.
38. Rudolph, *The American College and University*, 307–328.
39. Y. C. Wang, *Chinese Intellectuals and the West, 1872–1949* (Chapel Hill: University of North Carolina Press, 1966).
40. T. K. Chu, "150 Years of Chinese Students in America" (*Harvard China Review* Spring 2004): 8.
41. Wang, *Chinese Intellectuals*, vii.
42. Bertrand Russell, *The Problem of China* (Rockville, MD: Arc Manor, 2007): 18.
43. Y. C. Wang, *Chinese Intellectuals*, 3.
44. Ibid.
45. Ibid., 4.
46. Ibid., 5.
47. Ibid., 6.
48. Ibid., 12–16.
49. Ibid.
50. Itty Chan, "Women of China: From the Three Obediences to Half-the-Sky" (*Journal of Research and Development in Education*, vol. 10, no. 4, 1977): 38–52.
51. Rosanne Lin, "Talents Oppressed," in *China Daily*, April 18, 2002.

52. Li Yu-ning, editor, *Chinese Women through Chinese Eyes* (Armonk and London: M. E. Sharpe, Inc., 1992), in Chapter 1, "Women's Place in History" by Hu Shi.
53. Ibid., 1.
54. Ibid., 3.
55. Katrina Gulliver, "Sophia Chen Zen and Westernized Chinese Feminism", *Journal of Chinese Overseas* (4.2 2008): 258–274.
56. Rosanne Lin, "Talents Oppressed," in *China Daily*, April 18, 2002.
57. From *Asia for Educators*, "Two Hundred Years of U.S. Trade with China, 1784–1984" (Columbia University website, http://afe.easia.columbia.edu/special/china_1750_us.htm, accessed November 1, 2012).
58. J. R. Haddad, *The Romance of China: Excursion and China in United States Cultures, 1776–1976*. Program by the American Historical Association and Columbia University Press. http://www.gutenberg.org, accessed November 1, 2012.
59. Carl Seaburg and Stanley Patterson, *Merchant Prince of Boston, Colonel T.H. Perkins, 1764–1854* (Cambridge: Harvard University Press, 1971): 56.
60. J. R. Haddad, *The Romance of China*.
61. Mills, Brothers, and Co. *Auction Catalog*, June 5, 1832 reprint of New York auction items (Boston: Childs Gallery, 1968).
62. Walter Barrett, *The Old Merchants of New York City* (New York: Carleton, 1863): 40.
63. Ibid. The chests contained 130–160 pounds of opium.
64. William De Bary and Richard Lufrano, *Sources of Chinese Tradition: From 1600 Through the Twentieth Century* (New York: Columbia University Press, 2000): 201–204; also see Lin Zexu's letter to Britain's Queen Victoria to protest the opium trade, in T. Walter Wallbank and Alastair M. Taylor, *Civilizations Past and Present*, 1992. Some historians question whether Queen Victoria ever received or read the letter.
65. Stuart Creighton Miller, "The American Trader's Image, 1785–1840," chapter in *The Unwelcome Immigrant: The American Image of the Chinese, 1785–1882* (Berkeley: University of California Press, 1969).
66. *The New York Daily Advertiser*, October 20, 1834.
67. *New-York Commercial Advertiser*, October 18, 1834.
68. Advertisements were placed in the *New-York Commercial Advertiser*, *New York Sun*, *The New-York Daily Advertiser*, and the *New York Evening Post* from November 6, 1834 through the end of the month.
69. Honorable Caleb Cushing, "China and the Chinese," (*New York Herald*, November 1, vol. XI, no. 281, 1845): 1.
70. T. K. Chu, "150 Years", 9.
71. John Nevius, *China and the Chinese* (Philadelphia: Presbyterian Board of Publication, 1882): 354–361.
72. Ibid.
73. Arthur H. Smith, *Chinese Characteristics* (New York: Fleming H. Revell Company, 1894, originally published in Shanghai, 1890): 316–330.

NOTES TO CHAPTER 2

1. Yung Wing, *My Life in China and America*. (New York: Henry Holt and Company, 1909): 6.
2. Ibid., 4.
3. Ibid., 9–10.
4. Ibid.

5. Thomas E. LaFargue, *China's First Hundred*. (Pullman, Washington: Washington State University Press, 1987): 18. The Morrison school had been established in memory of Robert Morrison, the first Protestant missionary to work in China.
6. Yung Wing, *My Life*, 11.
7. Ibid., 21.
8. Ibid., 22.
9. Thomas LaFargue, *China's First Hundred*, 21.
10. Yung Wing, *My Life*, 37.
11. *The New York Times* (June 21, 1854): 2.
12. Yung Wing, *My Life*, 39.
13. From The Yung Wing Project website: http://ywproject.x10.mx/index.htm, accessed July 12, 2012.
14. Teresa B. Bevis and Christopher J. Lucas, *International Students in American Colleges and Universities: A History* (New York: Palgrave Macmillan, 2007): 40.
15. Ibid., 60–61.
16. Yung Wing, *My Life*, 40.
17. Yung Wing, *My Life*. Also see F. L. Hawks Pott, "China's Method of Revising Her Educational System," *Annals of the American Academy of Political and Social Science* (vol. 39, January 1912): 83–86.
18. Shunshin Chin, *The Taiping Rebellion*. Armonk, New York: East Gate Book, 2001. Also see Jonathan D. Spence, *God's Chinese Son: The Taiping Heavenly Kingdom of Hong Xiuquan* (New York: W.W. Norton and Company, 1996).
19. Ibid.
20. Excerpted from the basic document of the Taiping Kingdom, called "The Land System of the Heavenly Kingdom," published in 1853. From Franz Michael, *The Taiping Rebellion: History and Documents, vol. 2, Documents and Comments* (Seattle: University of Washington Press, 1971): 313–315, 319–320.
21. LaFargue, *China's First Hundred*, 24–25.
22. Philip A. Kuhn, *Rebellion and Its Enemies in Late Imperial China* (Cambridge: Harvard University Press, 1970): 185–186.
23. Kiyoshi K. Kawakami, "The Life Story of Dr. Yung Wing," the *New York Times* (Saturday Review of Books, March 12, 1910): BR4.
24. Y. C. Wang, *Chinese Intellectuals and the West* (Chapel Hill: North Carolina University Press, 1966), 41.
25. From the Yale University website: http://www.yale.edu/cusy/imperialstudents.htm, accessed July 12, 2012.
26. Y. C. Wang, 41.
27. Dalong Li, "The Central Kingdom and the Realm Under Heaven Coming to Mean the Same: The Process of the Formation of Territory in Ancient China," *Frontiers of History in China* (vol. 3, no. 3, 2008): 323–352.
28. From Chinese Educational Mission Connections website: CEMconnections.org, accessed July 12, 2012.
29. Jonathan D. Spence, *The Search for Modern China* (New York and London: W.W. Norton, 1999): 145–160. Also see Jack Gray, *Rebellions and Revolutions: China from the 1800s to the 1980s* (Oxford: Oxford University Press, 1990): 39–92.
30. Stacey Bieler, *Patriots or Traitors?* (Armonk, NY: M.E. Sharpe, 2004): 3–4. Also see Earl Swisher, *China's Management of the American Barbarians: A Study of Sino-American Relations* (New Haven: Yale University Press, 1951): 153–158.

31. Y. C. Wang, *Chinese Intellectuals*, 42.
32. Yung Wing, *My Life*, 136.
33. Yung Wing, *My Life*, 136–150. Also see Edmund H. Worthy, Jr., "Yung Wing in America," *The Pacific Historical Review* (vol. 34, no. 3, August): 265–287.
34. Yung Wing, *My Life*, 140.
35. John Fryer, "Chinese Education—Past, Present and Future" (*Current Chinese Readings* XVIII 1897): 381–382. Also see Thomas LaFargue, *China's First Hundred*, 29.
36. Yung Wing, *My Life*, 157.
37. T. K. Chu, "150 Years of Chinese Students in America," *Harvard China Review* (Spring 2004): 19. Also see Charles J. McClain, *In Search of Equality: The Chinese Struggle against Discrimination in Nineteenth-Century America* (Berkeley: University of California Press, 1994).
38. T. K. Chu, *150 Years*, 19.
39. T. K. Chu, *150 Years*, 16. Also see Frederick Wells Williams, *Anson Burlingame and the First Chinese Mission to Foreign Powers* (New York: Charles Scribner's Sons, 1912): 149–150.
40. T. K. Chu, *150 Years*, 16.
41. Ibid.
42. Ibid.
43. Shih-Shan Henry Tsai, *The Chinese Experience in America* (Bloomington: Indiana University Press, 1986).
44. Suping Lu, "Chinese Exclusion Acts: A Brief History of United States Legislation Aimed at Chinese Immigrants," *Readex,* a division of NewsBank, Inc. (April 2008, vol. 3, no. 2). Available from website: www.readex.com, accessed October 1, 2012.
45. Paul H. Clyde, *United States Policy toward China: Diplomatic and Public Documents* (Durham, NC: Duke University Press, 1940): 85.
46. Yung Wing, *My Life*, 159–164.
47. Yung Wing, *My Life*, 168.
48. LaFargue, *China's First Hundred*, 27.
49. Yung Wing, *My Life*, 175.
50. The ages of the boys differ depending on what method of calculation is used. In China the age changed with the turning of the calendar year, not on the actual date of birth, as in America. Therefore if a boy was 11 years old by Chinese calculation, he might be 10 using the American method.
51. Ibid.
52. John King Fairbank, "Patterns behind the Tientsin Massacre," *Harvard Journal of Asiatic Studies* (Vol. 20, No. 3–4, December 1957): 480–511. Also see the *New York Times,* "The Tien-Tsin Massacre," September 17, 1870.
53. Yung Wing, *My Life*, 180.
54. China's "pony express" was in operation as early as the 13th century and is mentioned in Marco Polo's writings, where he describes "horse changing stations" located every 25 miles across China. The system was not for public use, but was a system of transferring official imperial correspondence.
55. LaFargue, *China's First Hundred*, 32.
56. Yung Wing, *My Life*, 181.
57. Edward J. M. Rhodes, "In the Shadow of Yung Wing," *Pacific Historical Review* (vol. 74, no. 1, February 2005): 19–58. Also see Yung Wing, *My Life*, 183.
58. Y. C. Wang, *Chinese Intellectuals*, 43.
59. Ibid.

60. Ibid., 44.
61. Ibid., 43.
62. LaFargue, *China's First Hundred*, 33.
63. LaFargue, *China's First Hundred*, 33–34. Also see Yung Wing, *My Life*, 188.
64. Yung Wing, *My Life*, 187. Also see "The Chinese Educational Mission," the *New York Times*, August 18, 1873.
65. Judith Ann Schiff, "When East Meets West," *Yale Alumni Magazine* (November/December 2004).

NOTES TO CHAPTER 3

1. The *New York Times*, August 18, 1873.
2. In the early 1870s the Shanghai daotai was Shen Bingcheng, followed by Feng Junguang.
3. Thomas LaFargue, *China's First Hundred* (Pullman, Washington: Washington State University Press): 37; also see Edward J. M. Rhodes, "In the Shadow of Yung Wing, *Pacific Historical Review*, February 2005, vol. 74, no. 1, 19–58.
4. By 1872 the Pacific Mail Steamship Company was making two trips each month between San Francisco and Hong Kong, via Yokohama, and also had a branch service between Yokohama and Shanghai
5. LaFargue, 37.
6. Yung Wing, *My Life in China and America*. New York: Henry Holt and Company, 1909, 202.
7. Ibid., 188.
8. Thomas LaFargue, 38.
9. Ibid., 39.
10. Ibid., 35.
11. Ibid., 38–39.
12. Yung Wing, 191–192. Yung Wing would later hold substantial stock in Gatling's company.
13. In *Harper's Weekly*, August 31, 1867, issue, 246–247. Also see John Draper, "The Heathen Chinese," in *Harper's Weekly*, March 29, 1879, 246.
14. Yung Wing, 192.
15. Ibid., 193–195.
16. *The American Missionary*, vol. 32, no. 11, November 1878, 321.
17. LaFargue, 53.
18. William Lyon Phelps, *Chinese Schoolmates*. New York: Oxford University Press, 1939, 83–86.
19. Judith Ann Schiff, "When East Meets West," *Yale Alumni Magazine*, November/December 2004; also available on the Yale Alumni Magazine website: www.yalealumnimagazine.com. Accessed July 12, 2012.
20. Available at: http://www.yale.edu/cusy/imperialstudents.htm. Accessed July 12, 2012.
21. William Lyon Phelps, *Chinese Schoolmates* (New York: Oxford university Press, 1939): 83–86. Also see T. K. Chu, "150 Years of Chinese Students in America," *Harvard China Review*, Spring 2004, 11.
22. Steve Courtney, "Rising Power in the East: Joe Twichell, Mark Twain and the Chinese Educational Mission, 1872–81." Available at www.ahcc.org. Accessed July 12, 2012.
23. LaFargue, 189. Also see Anita Marchant, "Yung Wing and the Chinese Educational Commission in Hartford," unpublished manuscript (master of arts dissertation, Trinity College, 1999).

24. Timothy Kao, "Yung Wing and Young Chinese Students in America (1872–1881), from The Chinese Students Memorial Society website: www.120students.org. Accessed July 12, 2012. Also see Yung Wing, 190–196.
25. Yung Wing, 199.
26. Ibid., 200.
27. Ibid.
28. Ibid., 201.
29. Ibid., 205.
30. Ibid.
31. Ibid., 207–209.
32. Yung Wing, 208.
33. In *Harper's Weekly*, "A Breach of National Faith," March 9, 1879, 182.
34. Roger Daniels. *Asian America* (Seattle: University of Washington Press, 1988): 52.
35. John Draper, "The Heathen Chinee," *Harper's Weekly*, March 29, 1879, 246–247.
36. William Wei, "The Chinese-American Experience: An Introduction," available from *HarpWeek*, Immigrant and Ethnic America, http://immigrants.com. Accessed July 12, 2012.
37. From the *New York Times*, "China's Backward Step: The Recall of the Students in This Country,". September 2, 1881, 5. Also see Stacey Bieler, *Patriots or Traitors* (Armonk, NY: M. E. Sharpe, 2004): 8–9; Thomas LaFargue, 47–52; and from the *New York Times*, "China's Educational Mission; Why the Scheme Is Abandoned—An Illiberal Spirit Predominant," July 16, 1881, 5.
38. Yung Wing, 211–215. Also see LaFargue, pp. 49–51; and in an inset titled "Yung Wing and the Chinese Education Mission," in *Yale's 2007 Endowment*.
39. Yung Wing, 213–214.
40. *Hartford Daily Courant*, August 9, 1881, 2.
41. *Hartford Daily Courant*, September 27, 1881, 2.
42. Qian Ning, *Chinese Students Encounter America* (Seattle and London: University of Washington Press): xi.
43. Ibid.
44. From *The New York Times*, December 1, 1879.
45. LaFargue, 53.
46. Rhodes, 176.
47. Rhodes, 177.
48. Rhodes, 179.
49. Rhodes, 184.
50. Ibid., 56.
51. Yung Wing, 217.
52. Yung Wing, 218.
53. Yung Wing, 222.
54. The *New York Times*, October 16, 1910.
55. LaFargue, 55–56, 67–114. Also see Y. C. Wang, *Chinese Intellectuals and the West* (Chapel Hill: University of North Carolina Press, 1966): 88–90.
56. Ibid., 76.
57. Ibid., 73–81.
58. Ibid., 75.
59. Ibid., 77.
60. T. K. Chu, 20.
61. Rhodes, 28–29.
62. Wang, 465–470.

63. Rhodes, 88–92.
64. Ibid, 106.
65. *The Hartford Courant*, April 25, 1907, 15.
66. *The Yale Banner*, Volume 35, 1878–79, 59.
67. LaFargue, p. 90. Also see *Far Eastern Review*, November 1911, 193.
68. Ibid., 93.
69. A list of all CEM students and their occupations is available from online from Chinese Educational Mission Connections at www.cemconnections.org. Also see LaFargue, 173–176.
70. *The Yale Banner*, 1878, vol. 35, 69.
71. Former CEM student Yung Kwai wrote about Luk's return to America in "Recollections of the CEM."
72. There was another Sheffield graduate, Zeng Pu, but he is typically not included in the official count because he had been dismissed from the program. See Rhodes, Chapter 9, for an account of the story.
73. LaFargue, 141.
74. *Decatur Morning Review*, 1891.5.3, 10.
75. "Asked to Resign," *San Francisco Call*, 1894.6.14, 10.
76. Kenneth Cott, "Mexican Diplomacy and the Chinese Issue, 1876–1910," *Hispanic American Historical Review* 67.1 (February 1987): 69.
77. "Disgraceful Race Riots in Vancouver," *Evening Chronicle*, 1907.9.10, 1.
78. "Chinese Make Strong Protest," *San Francisco Chronicle*, 1906.4.30.
79. Ibid. 90–91.
80. *Yale Banner*, 1879–80, 60.
81. Rhodes, 145.
82. Joseph A. Reaves, 2002. *Taking in a Game: A History of Baseball in Asia* (University of Nebraska Press): 24–27.
83. Rhodes, 187.
84. The *New York Times*, "Sir Chentung's Successor," April 24, 1907 issue.
85. Also see Gilbert Reid, "Graduates of Our Colleges in High Posts in China," the *New York Times*, October 16, 1910, Sunday Edition, SM12.
86. Chinese Educational Mission Connections, www.cemconnections.org. Accessed July 12, 2012. Also see Gilbert Reid, SM12.
87. Qian, Gang and Hu Jingcao, *Liumei Youtong: Chinese Educational Mission Students* (Shanghai: Wenhui Publishing, 1985).
88. Ibid. Also see *Who's Who of American Returned Students*. Beijing: Tsing Hua College, 1917. Reprinted by Chinese Materials Center, Inc., San Francisco, 1978.
89. Later disillusioned with some of the tactics of the new government, Hoy renounced his participation and returned to Hong Kong.

NOTES TO CHAPTER 4

1. Theodore Roosevelt, *The Awakening of China* (New York: Board of Foreign Missions of the Reformed Church of America, 1908).
2. Robert Barde, "An Alleged Wife," *The U.S. National Archives and Records Administration* (Spring 2004, vol. 36, no. 1).
3. John King Fairbank and Merle Goldman, *China, A New History* (Cambridge, MA: Belknap Press of Harvard University Press, 2006): 226–227; also see Robert Barde, "An Alleged Wife," *The U.S. National Archives and Records Administration* (Spring 2004, vol. 36, no. 1).
4. Y. C. Wang, Chinese Intellectuals and the West (Chapel Hill: University of North Carolina Press, 1966): 78.

5. Fairbank, 226.
6. Ibid., 228; also see Young Tsu Wong, "Revisionism Reconsidered: Kang Youwei and the Reform Movement of 1898," *The Journal of Asian Studies* (vol. 51, no. 3, August 1992): 513–544.
7. Ibid., 229.
8. Ibid., 230–231.
9. Ibid.
10. Stacey Beiler, *"Patriots or Traitors"* (Armonk, NY: M.E. Sharpe, 2004): 30.
11. Howard Beale, *Theodore Roosevelt and the Rise of America to World Power* (Baltimore: Johns Hopkins University Press, 1956): 189.
12. George Keenan, in *American Diplomacy, 1900–1950* (Chicago: University of Chicago Press, 1951): 21–37.
13. The *New York Times,* June 23, 1907.
14. T. K Chu, "150 Years of Chinese Students in America," *Harvard China Review* (Spring 2004): 14.
15. Ibid., 12–13.
16. Ibid.
17. Robert McElroy, Tsinghua, A Monument of Friendship, *The Chinese Students' Monthly,* vol. 8, no. 2, December 1922.
18. The complete record may be found in House Document, No. 1275, of the Second Session of the Sixtieth Congress.
19. Arthur Smith, *China and America Today* (New York: Fleming H. Revell Company, 1907): 165.
20. Theodore Roosevelt, *The Awakening of China*.
21. Qian Ning, *Chinese Students Encounter America* (Seattle and London: University of Washington Press, 2002): xv.
22. Edward J. M. Rhoads, *Stepping Forth into the World* (Hong Kong University Press, 2011): 209.
23. Sarah Conger, *Letters from China* (Chicago: A.C. McClurg & Co., 1909): 373.
24. Berthold Laufer, "Modern Chinese Collections in Historical Light: With Especial Reference to the American Museum's Collection Representative of Chinese Culture a Decade Ago," *American Museum Journal* 12 (April 1912): 137.
25. Beiler, 66.
26. Ibid., 82–83.
27. Ibid., 65.
28. Y. C. Wang, *Chinese Intellectuals and the West* (Chapel Hill: University of North Carolina Press, 1966): 111; also see "Government Education," April 1920, pp. 189–190.
29. Ibid.
30. Yale-China Association website: www.yalechina.org/stories. Accessed April 27, 2012.
31. Ibid.
32. Ibid.
33. Soren Rottman, "A Portrait of Sophie Zhu, Long-Time Friend of Yale-China, Yale-China: http://www.yalechina.org/articles/pdf/Sophie%20Zhu%20Article.pdf, accessed July 12, 2012.
34. Nancy E. Chapman, *The Yale-China Association: A Centennial History* (Chinese University Press, 2001).
35. Beiler, 67. In 1917 a total of 159 Chinese women were studying in the United States, supported by their families or by provincial or indemnity scholarships.

36. T. K. Chu, 15.
37. Beiler, 202–203.
38. Ibid., 205–206.
39. Rosanne Lin, "Talents Oppressed," *Shanghai Star*, April 18, 2002.
40. Yeili Ye, *Seeking Modernity in China's Name: Chinese Students in the United States* (Stanford, CA: Stanford University Press, 2001).
41. Morris Bishop. *A History of Cornell*. Ithaca, New York (Cornell University Press, 1962): 403.
42. Beiler, 171–189.
43. Ibid.
44. Ibid.
45. Ibid., 187–197.
46. Seymour C. Y. Cheng, "A Plea for Justice," *Chinese Student Monthly* (June 1927): 35–36; editorial, "Correct Information about China," *Chinese Student Monthly* (February 1919): 220–221.
47. American Council Institute of Pacific Relations, Vol. III-7, April 6, 1934, 1.
48. Beiler, 79.
49. Fairbank, 279–280.
50. Center on Chinese Education, Teachers College Columbia University. Available from website: http://www.tc.columbia.edu/centers/coce. Accessed February 8, 2012.
51. Ibid.

NOTES TO CHAPTER 5

1. Baoyan Cheng, "U.S.-China Educational Exchange: State, Society and Intercultural Relations" (review), *China Review International* (vol. 16, no. 4, 2009): 536–541.
2. Jessica Ching Sze Wang, *John Dewey in China*, SUNY Series in Chinese Philosophy and Culture (Albany: State University of New York Press, 2007): 13–30.
3. Youzhong Sun, "The Trans-Pacific Experience of John Dewey," *The Japanese Journal of American Studies* (no. 18 2007). Also see Barry Keenan, *The Dewey Experiment in China: Educational Reform and Political Power in the Early Republic* (Cambridge, MA, and London: Harvard University Press, 1977).
4. Liu Yu-sheng, *The Crisis of Chinese Consciousness* (Madison: University of Wisconsin Press, 1979): 11
5. Christopher Cosans, *Owen's Ape and Darwin's Bulldog* (Bloomington: Indiana University Press, 2009).
6. Youzhong Sun, "The Trans-Pacific Experience of John Dewey," *The Japanese Journal of American Studies* (no. 18, 2007).
7. Zhou Hongyu and Chen Jingrong, *Paul Monroe and Education of Modern China*, Chinese University of Hong Kong, *Educational Journal* (vol. 35, no. 1, 2007): 1–38.
8. The *New York Times*, September 11, 1921, "To Show China How to Run Her Schools."
9. Zhou Hongyu and Chen Jingrong, 1–38.
10. Paul Monroe, *China: A Nation in Evolution* (The Chatauqua Press, 1927).
11. Chiang Yung-chen, "Chinese Students in America in the Early Twentieth Century," *Chinese Studies in History* (vol. 36, no. 3, Spring 2003): 38–62.
12. Ibid.
13. Y. C. Wang, *Chinese Intellectuals and the West* (Chapel Hill: University of North Carolina Press, 1966),.

14. Chiang Yung-chen, 53.
15. Ibid., 40.
16. Nathaniel Peffer, "The Returned Students," *The Chinese Students' Monthly* 18 (April 6, 1922): 4.
17. Stacey Beiler, *Patriots or Traitors?* (Armonk, NY: M.E. Sharpe, 2004): 79–80.
18. Ibid, 204.
19. John N. Thomas, *Asian Scholars and American Politics* (University of Washington Press, 1974).
20. Nancy E. Chapman and Jessica C. Plumb, *The Yale-China Association: A Centennial History* (The Chinese University Press 2001). Also see the Yale-China Association website: http://www.yalechina.org/history/stories. Accessed May 30, 2012.
21. Teresa Brawner Bevis and Christopher J. Lucas, *International Students in American Colleges and Universities: A History* (New York: Palgrave Macmillan, 2007): 6.
22. Kennon H. Nakamura and Matthew C. Weed, "U.S. Public Diplomacy: Background and Current Issues," December 18, 2009, Congressional Research Service, www.crs.gov. Accessed June 7, 2012.
23. David M. Lampton, *A Relationship Restored* (Washington, DC, National Academy Press): 66–68.

NOTES TO CHAPTER 6

1. Douglas Stiffler, "Resistance to the Sovietization of Higher Education in China," in *Universities Under Dictatorship,* John Connelly and Michael Grüttner, eds. (University Park: Pennsylvania University, 2005): 213–245.
2. Ruth Hayhoe, *China's Universities 1895–1995: A Century of Cultural Conflict* (New York: Garland Publishing, 1996): 45.
3. Stiffler, 219.
4. Committee on Educational Interchange Policy, "Chinese Students in the United States, 1848–55, A Study in Government Policy," 1956.
5. Zhai Qiang, "China and the Geneva Conference of 1954," *The China Quarterly Number 129,* March 1992, 103–122.
6. Ibid.
7. Ellen Schrecker, *The Age of McCarthyism* (Boston: St. Martin's Press, 1994): 70–72.
8. Raymond B. Allen, "Communists Should Not Teach in American Colleges" (Educational Forum, 1949, vol. 13, no. 4).
9. Nancy E. Chapman and Jessica C. Plumb, *The Yale-China Association: A Centennial History* (The Chinese University Press, 2001).
10. Ibid.
11. Ibid.
12. Reclus, Elisee, "Formosa." *The earth and its inhabitants: Asia.* Volume II, *East Asia: Chinese Empire, Corea and Japan.* Edited by A. H. Keane (New York: D. Appleton, 1884).
13. Institute of International Education, *Open Doors Report 1950/51,* 10.
14. Masahito Aoki and Jinglian Wu, *The Chinese Economy: A New Transition* (New York: Palgrave Macmillan, 2011): 14
15. Ibid.
16. John Fairbank and Merle Goldman, *China: A New History* (Cambridge: Belknap Press, 2006): 362.
17. Arthur H. Steiner, "The Curriculum in Chinese Socialist Education," *Pacific Affairs,* September 1958.

18. Fairbank, 364.
19. Ibid.
20. Hayhoe, 92.
21. Dali Yang, *Calamity and Reform in China: State, Rural Society and Institutional Change since the Great Leap Famine* (Stanford University Press, 1988).
22. William Harms, "China's Great Leap Forward," *The University of Chicago Chronicle,* March 14, 1996, vol. 15, no. 13.
23. Fairbank, 373, 410.
24. Ibid., 372.
25. "Big character" posters were large, wall-mounted posters that used oversized Chinese characters as a means of propaganda, protest, and popular communication. Produced since imperial times, the practice increased after 1911 when the Chinese population was more literate.
26. Isabel F. K. Wong, "Geming Gequ: Songs for the Education of the Masses," in *Popular Chinese Literature and Performing Arts in the People's Republic of China 1949–1979.*
27. For an analysis of Soviet influences on Maoist theories of art, see Igor Golomshtok, *Totalitarian Art in the Soviet Union, the Third Reich, Fascist Italy and the People's Republic of China* (London: Collins-Harvill, 1990).
28. Mo Bo, "I Was a Teenage Red Guard," *New Internationalist,* April 1987, no. 170.
29. Ibid.
30. Ibid.
31. Ibid.
32. Fairbank, 383–405.
33. Susan Porter Robinson, "Higher Education in China: The Next Superpower is Coming of Age," American Council on Education. Also see Philip G. Altbach and Toru Umakoshi, *Asian Universities* (Johns Hopkins University Press, 2004).

NOTES TO CHAPTER 7

1. Excerpted from Jimmy Carter's speech at the Li Xiannian Library in Hong'an, China, January 14, 2009.
2. Mary Brown Bullock, "Mission Accomplished: The Influence of the CSCPRC on Educational Relations with China," Cheng Li, ed., *Bridging Minds Across the Pacific* (Lanham, MD: Lexington Books, 2005): 49–68.
3. Ibid.
4. Ezra F. Vogel, "But Deng Is the Leader to Celebrate," the *New York Times,* October 2009.
5. Ministry of Foreign Affairs of the People's Republic of China, 2001, "The Establishment of Sino-U.S. Diplomatic Relations and Vice Premier Deng Xiaoping's Visit to the United States," www.fmprc.gov.cn. Accessed April 27, 2012.
6. Ezra F. Vogel, *Deng Xiaoping and the Transformation of China* (Cambridge, MA: Belknap Press of Harvard University Press, 2011).
7. T. K. Chu, "150 Years of Chinese Students in America" (*Harvard China Review,* Spring 2004): 8
8. David Lampton, *A Relationship Restored* (National Academy Press, 1986): 70–72.
9. Masahiko Aoki and Jinglian Wu, 2011, *The Chinese Economy: A New Transition* (New York: Palgrave Macmillan, 2011): 14–17.

10. "Stoking the Furnace," in *The Economist*, March 3, 2012. Available from: http://www.economist.com/node/21548972.
11. Bullock, 60–61.
12. Ibid. Also see the *Evaluation Report: Chinese University Development Project* (1986) for a report on the first phase of the endeavor.
13. Bullock, 49–68.
14. Shiping Zheng, "Sino-U.S. Educational Exchanges and International Relations Studies in China," in Cheng Li, ed., *Bridging Minds across the Pacific* (Lanham, MD: Lexington Books, 2005): 134; also see IIE's *Open Doors 1994–1995 Report on Educational Exchange*, 52–53.
15. Linda A. Reed, "Education in the People's Republic of China and U.S.-China Educational Exchanges," 1988 NAFSA National Association for Foreign Student Affairs, Washington, DC.
16. From the CEAIE website http://en.ceaie.edu.cn. Accessed February 8, 2012.
17. Lampton, 66–67.
18. Ibid; also see *CIES Annual Report 1983*, 18.
19. From the Office of Educational Affairs of the Embassy of P.R. China in USA, www.sino-education.org. Accessed May 30, 2011.
20. David Lampton, 69.
21. Qian Ning, 63.
22. Dongziao Zin, *Crossing Borders* (University Press of America, 2009): 91.
23. Dongziao Zin, 105.
24. Qian Ning, 64.
25. Qian Ning, 44.
26. Qian Ning, 45.
27. Ibid.
28. Qian Ning, 172–173
29. Qian Ning, 64.
30. Qian Ning, 35.
31. Qian Ning, 127.
32. Beiler, 357.
33. Qian Ning, 35.
34. Jason Ma, "College Apps Cheating Scandal Is a Learning Moment for China," in *Forbes* Online, www.forbes.com. Accessed February 13, 2012.
35. Daniel Golden, "American Universities Infected by Foreign Spies," *Bloomberg,* April 8, 2012.
36. Ibid.
37. Jean-Philippe Beja, "Liu Xiaobo: Living in Truth and Paying the Price," December 10, 2010, from Amnesty International website: takeaction@amnestyusa.org.
38. Qian Ning, 197.
39. Ibid.
40. Qian Ning, 102.
41. Cheng Li, "Coming Home to Teach,", in Cheng Li, ed., *Bridging Minds across the Pacific* (Lanham, MD: Lexington Books, 2005): 78–79.
42. Ibid., p. 79; also see Xin Fuliang, "The Basic Line of Thinking in Shanghai's Efforts to Attract Overseas Chinese Intellect," *Chinese Education and Society* (vol. 34, no. 3, May/June 2001): 65–77.
43. Cheng Li, 90; also see David Lampton, 41.
44. Ibid.
45. Bullock, 61.
46. Federal Regulation 67, No. 238, 2002.

47. M. Allison Wit, "Closed Borders and Closed Minds," *Journal of Educational Controversy*, Western Washington University e-Journal. Available at http://www.wce.wwu.edu/resources/cep/ejournal. Accessed October 24, 2011.
48. Victor Johnson, 2003. "Unintended Consequences: Unilateral Disarmament in the Battle of Ideas, Values and Briefs," *International Educator* 12 (2): 2–5.
49. Liu Jun, "Crawling My Way through the Maze of U.S. Bureaucracy," *China Daily* (April 20, 2011): 20.
50. Ibid.
51. Gerard Postiglione, "China's Hong Kong Bridge," in Cheng Li, ed., *Bridging Minds across the Pacific* (Lanham, MD: Lexington Books): 201.
52. Ibid., 202.
53. Qian Ning, 56.
54. David Lampton, 32.

NOTES TO CHAPTER 8

1. Chen Jia, "China Looks to Attract More Foreign Students," from *China Daily*, September 28, 2010. Available at: http://english.peopledaily.com.cn/90001/90776/90883/7152470.html.
2. Guo-hua Wang, "China's Higher Education Reform," from *China Currents* website: http://www.chinacurrents.com/spring_2010/cc_wang.htm.
3. "Formation of China's Ivy League Hailed," October 30, 2009. Available from *People's Daily* Online website: http://english.people.com.cn/90001/90776/90882/6794654.html.
4. "Greetings on the Occasion of the Tsinghua University Centennial Celebration," a speech by Yale president Richard C. Levin in Beijing, China, April 23, 2011. Available from Yale website: http://communications.yale.edu/president/speeches/2011/04/23/greetings-occasion-tsinghua-university-centennial-celebration.
5. Over the past few decades, the Chinese have been gently nudging Westerners towards a more accurate pronunciation of Mandarin Chinese including *Nanjing* and *Beijing* for older Anglicized *Peking* and *Nanking*.
6. Michael Sainsbury, "China Establishes Group of Ivy League Universities," from *The Australian*, November 4, 2009, available at www.theaustralian.com.au/news/world/china.
7. Theodore Roosevelt, *The Awaking of China*. Available at Error! Hyperlink reference not valid.. Accessed January 20, 2013.
8. Tamar Lewin, "China Attracts More American Students," from the *New York Times*, November 18, 2008.
9. Jason Sweeny, "Wave of U.S. Students Studying in China," from an article by Jason Sweeney in the *San Jose Mercury News*, September 5, 2012. Available from: www.mercurynews.com/breaking-news/ci_21468531/wave-u-s-students-studying-china. Accessed February 8, 2011.
10. Ibid.
11. Lewin, "China Attracts More American Students."
12. Karin Fischer, "As White House Pushes Study Abroad in China, Educators Question the Logistics," in *The Chronicle of Higher Education*, January 19, 2011.
13. Ibid.
14. "China, U.S. to Scale Up Student Exchange Programs," May 26, 2010. Available from www.chinaassistor.com.
15. Chen Jia, "China Looks to Attract More Foreign Students," from *China Daily*, September 28, 2010.

16. Daniel Golden, "The SAT Is to America as ___ Is to China Mainland. Applicants Have to Take the Test Abroad. The U.S. College Board Wants to Change That," *Business Week,* February 3, 2011. Available from: http://www.businessweek.com/magazine/content/11_07/b4215014259071.htm.
17. Ibid.
18. "The Institute of International Education Leads Higher Education Delegation to Build Academic Partnership between China and the United States," May 15, 2011. Available from: www.iie.org.
19. Tamar Lewin, "Study Abroad Flourishes; China Attracts More American Students," in the *New York Times,* November 18, 2008.
20. "Seven Decades of Educating Global Leaders," from the Johns Hopkins University website: http://nanjing.jhu.edu/about/index.htm. Accessed January 20, 2013.
21. "China's First Sino-American University Opening in 2013," in *People's Daily,* April 6, 2012. Available at: http://english.peopledaily.com.cn/203691/7779455.html.
22. Yojana Sharma, "CHINA: Ambitious Plans to Attract Foreign Students," *University World News,* March 13, 2011, No. 162.
23. "China Needs American Education: Here's How to Bring It There," from Forbes website: http://www.forbes.com/sites/forbesleadershipforum/2012/06/20/china-needs-american-education-heres-how-to-bring-it-there.
24. Liz Gooch, "Chinese Universities Send Big Signals to Foreigners," the *New York Times,* March 11, 2012.
25. Ibid.
26. B. P. Coppola and Yi Zhou, "U.S. Education in Chinese Lockstep? Bad Move," from *The Chronicle of Higher Education,* February 5, 2012.
27. Ibid.
28. Ibid.
29. Isaac Stone Fish, "No Academic Freedom for China," *The Daily Beast,* November 21, 2011. Available from: www.thedailybeast.com/articles.
30. Ibid.
31. "China Banning U.S. Professors Elicits Silence from Colleges, August 11, 2011, from *Bloomberg* website: www.bloomberg.com/news.
32. Linda Yeung, "CHINA: Ex-premier Criticises Higher Education Reform," May 1, 2011, from *University World News* website: http://www.universityworldnews.com/article.php?story=20110429170813946
33. Ibid.
34. Gene M. Owens, "If You Have a Lemon, Make Lemonade," in *China Daily,* November18, 2006.
35. Ibid.
36. Daniel Golden, "China Says No Talking Tibet as Confucius Funds U.S. Universities," November 1, 2011, *Bloomberg.* Available from: www.bloomberg.com.
37. "Rectification of Statues," from *The Economist,* January 20, 2011. Available from website: http://www.economist.com/node/17969895.
38. Karen Fischer, "State Department Directive Could Disrupt Teaching Activities of Campus-Based Confucius Institutes," *The Chronicle of Higher Education,* May 21, 2012.
39. Karen Fischer, "State Department Hopes to 'Fix' Visa Problem without Forcing Chinese Teachers to Leave," *The Chronicle of Higher Education,* May 23, 2012. Also see the May 23, 201,2 article by Karin Fischer, "Flap over Visas Could Harm U.S.-China Exchanges, Chinese Official Warns," in *The Chronicle of Higher Education.*
40. "Chinese History According to the Confucius Institute," in *The Epoch Times.* Available from http://www.theepochtimes.com/n2/china-news/chinese-history-according-to-the-confucius-institute-255366.html.

NOTES TO CHAPTER 9

1. Keith Bradsher, "China Makes a Great Leap into Higher Education," in the *New York Times,* January 17, 2012.
2. Philip G. Altbach, *One-Third of the Globe: The Future of Higher Education in India and China* (New York: Springer Publishing, 2009).
3. Dan Thomas, "India to Overtake China in Undergraduate Mobility," *The Pie News,* June 27, 2012. Available at: http://thepienews.com/news/india-to-overtake-china-in-undergraduate-mobility.
4. Ibid.
5. Beth McMurtrie, "China Continues to Drive International Student Growth in the U.S.," *The Chronicle of Higher Education,* November 12, 2012.
6. Ibid.
7. Chris Proulx, "Five Ways Technology Will Impact Higher Education in 2013," December 11, 2012, from *Forbes* website: www.forbes.com/sites/groupthink.
8. Laura Pappano, "Massive Open Online Courses Are Multiplying at a Rapid Pace," November 4, 2012. The *New York Times* website: www.nytimes.com/2012/11/04/education/edlife/index.html.
9. Ibid.
10. U.S. Department of State, July 20, 2011, "Musician will.i.am to Support the 100,000 Strong Initiative Concert in Beijing to Celebrate U.S.-China Educational and Cultural Exchanges." Available at: http://www.state.gov/r/pa/prs/ps/2011/07/169362.htm.
11. Andreas Lorenz, "Redder than Red: An American Portrait of China's Next Leader," Spiegel Online International, December 5, 2010. Available from website: http://www.spiegel.de/international/world/redder-than-red-an-american-portrait-of-china-s-next-leader-a-732972.html.
12. "Chinese Press for More Civil Liberties," *Washington Post,* January 9, 2013.
13. Ibid.
14. Masahiko Aoki and Jingllian, 2012. *The Chinese Economy: A New Transition* (New York: Palgrave Macmillan).
15. Ibid.
16. Ibid.
17. Dexter Roberts, "The End of China's One-child Policy?" *Businessweek,* April 19, 2012.
18. Ibid.
19. Sarah Butrimowicz, "Can China Successfully Educate Its Future Workforce?" From *Time World,* February 9, 2012.
20. Ibid.
21. Ibid.
22. Ibid.
23. Ibid.
24. Bruce Drake, "American, Chinese Publics Increasingly Wary of the Other," Pew Research Center, 2012.
25. "China Publishes Its 10-Year Plan," *The Chronicle of Higher Education,* July 29, 2010. Available at: http://chronicle.com/blogs/global/china-officially-publishes-its-10-year-education-plan/25870.
26. "China's New National Education Plan Aims to Build a Country with Rich Human Resources," July 30, 2010. China's Ministry of Education website: www.moe.edu.cn.
27. The World Bank, "China 2030, Building a Modern, Harmonious and Creative High-Income Society." Available at: www.worldbank.org. Accessed May 30, 2012.

28. The Colbert Nation, 2005. Available at: http://www.colbertnation.com/the-colbert-report-videos/24039/october-17–2005.

Bibliography

Allen, Raymond B., "Communists Should Not Teach in American Colleges," in *Educational Forum* (vol. 13, no. 4, 1994).
Altbach, Philip G., *One-Third of the Globe: The Future of Higher Education in India and China* (New York: Springer Publishing, 2009).
Altbach, Philip G., and Umakoshi, Toru, *Asian Universities* (Johns Hopkins University Press, 2004).
American Council Institute of Pacific Relations (Volume III–7, April 6, 1934): 1.
Aoki, Masahito, and Wu, Jinglian, *The Chinese Economy: A New Transition* (New York: Palgrave Macmillan).
Baoyan Cheng, "U.S.-China Educational Exchange: State, Society and Intercultural Relations" (review), in *China Review International* (vol. 16, no. 4, 2009): 536–541.
Barde, Robert, "An Alleged Wife," in *The U.S. National Archives and Records Administration* (Spring 2004, vol. 36, no. 1).
Barrett, Walter, *The Old Merchants of New York City* (New York: Carleton, 1863).
Beiler, Stacey, *Patriots or Traitors?* (Armonk, NY: M.E. Sharpe, 2004).
Bevis, Teresa Brawner, and Lucas, Christopher J., *International Students in American Colleges and Universities: A History* (New York: Palgrave Macmillan, 2007).
Bishop, Morris, *A History of Cornell* (Ithaca, NY: Cornell University Press, 1962).
Brubacher, John S., and Willis, Rudy, *Higher Education in Transition: A History of American Colleges and Universities 1636–1976*, 3rd ed. (New York: Harper & Row, 1976).
Chan, Itty, "Women of China: From the Three Obediences to Half-the-Sky," in *Journal of Research and Development in Education* (vol. 10, no. 4, 1977).
Cheng, C. Y. Seymour, "A Plea for Justice," in *Chinese Student Monthly* (June 1927).
Cheng Li, *Bridging Minds across the Pacific* (Lanham, MD: Lexington Books, 2005).
Chiang Yung-chen, "Chinese Students in America in the Early Twentieth Century," in *Chinese Students in History* (vol. 36, no. 3, Spring 2003).
Chu, T. K., "150 Years of Chinese Students in America," in *Harvard China Review* (Spring 2004).
Clyde, Paul H., *United States Policy toward China: Diplomatic and Public Documents* (Durham, NC: Duke University Press, 1940).
Conger, Sarah, *Letters from China* (Chicago: A.C. McClurg and Company, 1909), 373.

Coppola, B. P., and Zhou, Yi, "U.S. Education in Chinese Lockstep? Bad Move," *The Chronicle of Higher Education,* February 5, 2012.

Cosans, Christopher, *Owen's Ape and Darwin's Bulldog* (Bloomington: Indiana University Press, 2009).

Cott, Kenneth, "Mexican Diplomacy and the Chinese Issue, 1876–1910," in *Hispanic American Historical Review* (Volume 67, Number 1, February 1987): 69.

Dalong Li, "The Central Kingdom and the Realm Under Heaven Coming to Mean the Same: The Process of the Formation of Territory in Ancient China," in *Frontiers of History in China* (vol. 3, no. 3, 2008): 323–352.

Daniels, Roger, *Asian America* (Seattle: University of Washington Press, 1988).

De Bary, William, and Lufrano, Richard, *Sources of Chinese Tradition: From 1600 through the Twentieth Century* (New York: Columbia University Press, 2000).

Debus, Allen G., *The French Paracelsians* (Cambridge, UK: Cambridge University Press, 1991).

Dongziao Zin, *Crossing Borders* (Lanham, MD: University Press of America, 2009).

Dupree, A. Hunter, *Asa Gray, 1810–1888* (Cambridge: Belknap Press of Harvard University, 1959).

Fairbank, John King, "Patterns behind the Tientsin Massacre," in *Harvard Journal of Asiatic Studies* (vol. 20, no. 3–4, December 1957): 480–511.

Fairbank, John, and Goldman, Merle, *China: A New History* (Cambridge: Belknap Press of Harvard University, 2006).

Fischer, Karen, "State Department Directive Could Disrupt Teaching Activities of Campus-Based Confucius Institutes," *The Chronicle of Higher Education,* May 21, 2012.

Fischer, Karen, "State Department Hopes to 'Fix' Visa Problem without Forcing Chinese Teachers to Leave," *The Chronicle of Higher Education*, May 23, 2012.

Franze, Michael, *The Taiping Rebellion: History and Documents, Volume 2, Documents and Comments* (Seattle: University of Washington Press, 1971): 313–320.

Fryer, John, "Chinese Education, Past, Present and Future," in *Current Chinese Readings* (XVIII, 1897): 381–382.

Fu Xi, *The I Ching or Book of Changes* (Princeton University Press, 1967).

Galicich, Anna, *The German Americans* (New York: Chelsea House, 1989).

Geiger, Roger L., "The Era of Multipurpose Colleges in American Higher Education, 1850–1890," in *History of Higher Education Annual* (vol. 15, 1995): 56.

Gray, Jack, *Rebellions and Revolutions: China from the 1800s to the 1980s* (Oxford: Oxford University Press, 1990): 39–92.

Gulliver Katrina, "Sophia Chen Zen and Westernized Chinese Feminism", in *Journal of Chinese Overseas* (4.2 2008), 258–274.

Hayhoe, Ruth, *China's Universities 1895–1995: A Century of Conflict* (New York: Garland Publishing, 1996).

Hofstadter, Richard, and Smith, Wilson, eds., *American Higher Education: A Documentary History* (Chicago: Chicago University Press, 1961).

Huebener, *The Germans in America* (Philadelphia: Chilton Company, 1962).

Hu Shi, "Women's Place in History," in Li Yu-ning, ed., *Chinese Women through Chinese Eyes* (Armonk and London: M.E. Sharpe, Inc. 1992).

Johnson, Victor, "Unintended Consequences: Unilateral Disarmament in the Battle of Ideas, Values and Briefs," in *International Educator* (12, 2): 2–5.

Jung, Carl, foreword in Fu Xi, *The I Ching or Book of Changes* (Princeton University Press, 1967).

Keenan, Barry, *The Dewey Experiment in China: Educational Reform and Political Power in the Early Republic* (Cambridge and London: Harvard University Press, 1977).
Keenan, George, *American Diplomacy, 1900–1950* (Chicago: University of Chicago Press, 1951), 21–37.
Kuhn, Philip A., *Rebellion and Its Enemies in Late Imperial China* (Cambridge: Harvard University Press, 1970).
LaFargue, *China's First Hundred* (Pullman, WA: Washington State University Press, 1987).
Lampton, David M., *A Relationship Restored* (Washington, DC: National Academy Press, 1986).
Laufer, Berthold, "Modern Chinese Collections in Historical Light: With Especial Reference to the American Museum's Collection Representative of Chinese Culture a Decade Ago," in *American Museum Journal* 12 (April 1912): 137.
Liu Yu-sheng, *The Crisis of Chinese Consciousness* (Madison: University of Wisconsin Press, 1979).
Lucas, Christopher J., *American Higher Education* (New York: St. Martin's Press, 1994).
Mattingly, Paul H., "The Political Culture of America's Antebellum Colleges," in *History of Higher Education Annual* (vol. 17, 1997): 73–95.
McClain, Charles J., *In Search of Equality: The Chinese Struggle against Discrimination in Nineteenth-Century America* (Berkeley: University of California Press, 1994).
McElroy, Robert, "Tsing Hua, a Monument of Friendship," in *Chinese Student Monthly* (vol. 18, no. 2, December 1922).
Franz Michael, *The Taiping Rebellion: History and Documents, Volume 2, Documents and Comments* (Seattle: University of Washington Press, 1971).
McMurtrie, Beth, "China Continues to Drive International Student Growth in the U.S.", *The Chronicle of Higher Education*, November 12, 2012.
Miller, Stuart Creighton, "The American Trader's Image, 1785–1840," in *The Unwelcome Immigrant: The American Image of the Chinese, 1785–1882* (Berkeley: University of California Press, 1969).
Mills Brothers and Company, *Auction Catalog,* June 5, 1832, reprint of New York auction items (Boston: Childs Gallery, 1968).
Mo Bo, "I Was a Teenage Red Guard," in *New Internationalist* (April 1987, No. 170).
Monroe, Paul, *China: A Nation in Evolution* (Chatauqua, NY: Chatauqua Press, 1927).
Morison, Samuel Eliot, *The Founding of Harvard College* (Cambridge: Harvard University Press, 1935).
Morison, Samuel Eliot, *Three Centuries of Harvard 1636–1936* (Cambridge: Harvard University Press, 1936).
Narendra, Barbara L., "Benjamin Silliman and the Peabody Museum," in *Discovery* 14, 1979: 13–29.
Needham, Joseph, *Science and Civilization in China* (Cambridge, UK: Cambridge University Press, 1954).
Nevius, John, *China and the Chinese* (Philadelphia: Presbyterian Board of Publication, 1882): 354–361.
New England's First Fruits, 1640, in *Collections of the Massachusetts Historical Society*, 1792 (vol. 1): 242–248.
Peffer, Nathaniel, "The Returned Students," in the *Chinese Students' Monthly* 18 (April 6, 1922): 4.
Phelps, William Lyon, *Chinese Schoolmates* (New York: Oxford University Press, 1939).

Pott, L. F. Hawk, "China's Method of Revising Her Educational System," in *Annals of the American Academy of Political and Social Science* (vol. 39, January 1912): 83–86.
Qian Gang and Hu Jingcao, *Liumei Youtong: Chinese Educational Mission Students* (Shanghai: Wenhui Publishing, 1985).
Qian Ning, *Chinese Students Encounter America* (Seattle and London: University of Washington Press, 2002).
Reaves, Joseph A., *Taking in a Game: A History of Baseball in Asia* (University of Nebraska Press, 2002).
Reclus, Elisse, "Formosa," in *East Asia Volume II: Chinese Empire, Corea and Japan* (New York: D. Appleton, 1884).
Reed, Linda A. Education in the People's Republic of China and U.S.-China Educational Exchanges, 1988 (Washington, D.C.: NAFSA National Association for Foreign Student Affairs, 1988).
Rhoades, Edward J. M., "In the Shadow of Yung Wing," *Pacific Historical Review* (vol. 74, no. 1, February 2005): 19–58.
Rhoads, Edward J. M., Stepping Forth into the World (Hong Kong: Hong Kong University Press, 2011).
Roosevelt, Theodore, *The Awakening of China* (New York: Board of Foreign Missions of the Reformed Church of America, 1908).
Rowe, William T., *China's Last Empire* (Cambridge: Harvard University Press, 1979).
Rudolph, Frederick, *The American College and University* (Athens and London: University of Georgia Press, 1990).
Russell, Bertrand, *The Problem of China* (Rockville, MD: Arc Manor, 2007).
Schiff, Judith Ann, "When East Meets West," in *Yale Alumni Magazine* (November/December 2004).
Schrecker, Ellen, *The Age of McCarthyism* (Boston: St. Martin's Press, 1994).
Seaburg, Carl, and Stanley Patterson, Stanley, *Merchant Prince of Boston, Colonel T.H. Perkins, 1764–1854* (Cambridge: Harvard University Press, 1971).
Shih-Shan Henry Tsai, *The Chinese Experience in America* (Bloomington: Indiana University Press, 1986).
Shunshin Chin, *The Taiping Rebellion* (Armonk, NY: East Gate Book, 2001).
Smith, Arthur H., *Chinese Characteristics* (New York: Fleming H. Revell Company, 1894, originally published in Shanghai, 1890), 316–330.
Smith, Arthur, *China and America Today* (New York: Fleming H. Revell Company, 1907).
Spence, Jonathan D., *God's Chinese Son: The Taiping Heavenly Kingdom of Hong Xiuquan* (New York: W.W. Norton and Company, 1996).
Spence, Jonathan D., *The Search for Modern China* (New York and London: W.W. Norton, 1999).
Stiefel, Tina, *The Intellectual Revolution of Twelfth Century Europe* (New York: St. Martin's Press, 1985).
Stiffler, Douglas, "Resistance to the Sovietization of Higher Education in China," in *Universities Under Dictatorship*, eds. John Connelly and Michael Gruttner (University Park: Pennsylvania University Press, 2005): 213–245.
Swisher, *China's Management of the American Barbarians: A Study of Sino-American Relations* (New Haven: Yale University Press, 1951).
Teng Ssu-yu and Fairbank, John King, eds., *China's Response to the West: Documentary Survey, 1839–1923* (Cambridge: Harvard University Press, 1979).
Thaddeus T'ui-Chieh Hang, "Why Chinese Civilization Has Not Discovered Modern Sciences," in *Cultural Heritage and Contemporary Change,* Series III, Asia (vol. 9, 1995): 123–130.

Thomas, John N., *Asian Scholars and American Politics* (University of Washington Press, 1974).
Vogel, Ezra F., *Deng Xiaoping and the Transformation of China* (Cambridge: Belknap Press of Harvard University).
Wang, Jessica Ching Sze, *John Dewey in China*, in SUNY Series in Chinese Philosophy and Culture (Albany: State University of New York Press, 2007): 13–30.
Wang, Y. C., *Chinese Intellectuals and the West, 1872–1949*, (Chapel Hill: University of North Carolina Press, 1966).
Xin Fuliang, "The Basic Line of Thinking in Shanghai's Efforts to Attract Overseas Chinese Intellect", *Chinese Education and Society* 34 (no. 3, May/June 2001): 65–77.
Yeili Ye, *Seeking Modernity in China's Name: Chinese Students in the United States* (Stanford, CA: Stanford University Press, 2001).
Yojana Sharma, "CHINA: Ambitious Plans to Attract Foreign Students," *University World News*, March 13, 2011, No. 162.
Youzhong Sun, "The Trans-Pacific Experience of John Dewey," in *The Japanese Journal of American Studies* (no. 18, 2007).
Yung Wing, *My Life in China and America* (New York: Henry Holt and Company, 1909).
Zhou Hongyu and Chen Jingrong, "Paul Monroe and Education of Modern China," in *Educational Journal*, vol. 35, no. 1, 2007.

NEWSPAPERS AND MAGAZINES

"A Breech of National Faith," *Harper's Weekly*, March 9, 1879, 182.
Bradsher, Keith, "China Makes a Great Leap into Higher Education," *New York Times*, January 17, 2012.
Chen Jia, "China Looks to Attract More Foreign Students," from *China Daily*, September 28, 2010.
"China's Backward Step: The Recall of the Students in This Country," *New York Times*, September 2, 1881, 5.
"China's Educational Mission: Why the Scheme Is Abandoned—An Illiberal Spirit Predominant," *New York Times*, July 16, 1881, 5.
"Chinese Make Strong Protest," *San Francisco Chronicle*, April 30, 1906.
"Chinese Press for More Civil Liberties," *Washington Post*, January 9, 2013.
Cushing, Honorable Caleb, "China and the Chinese," *New York Herald*, November 1, vol. XI, no. 281, 1845, 1.
Draper, John, "The Heathen Chinee," *Harper's Weekly*, March 29, 1879, 246–247.
Gooch, Liz, "Chinese Universities Send Big Signals to Foreigners," *New York Times*, March 11, 2012.
Karin Fischer, "As White House Pushes Study Abroad in China, Educators Question the Logistics," in *The Chronicle of Higher Education*, January 19, 2011.
Kawakami, Kiyoshi K., "The Life Story of Dr. Yung Wing," *New York Times Saturday Review of Books*, March 12, 1910, 4.
Lin, Rosanne, "Talents Oppressed," in *China Daily*, April 18, 2002.
Liu Jun, "Crawling My Way through the Maze of U.S. Bureaucracy," *China Daily*, April 20, 2011, 20.
Lewin, Tamar, "Study Abroad Flourishes: China Attracts More American Students," *New York Times*, November 18, 2008.

Owens, Gene M., "If You Have a Lemon, Make Lemonade," in *China Daily*, November 18, 2006.
Reid, Gilbert, "Graduates of Our Colleges in High Posts in China," *New York Times*, October 16, 1910, SM12.
Roberts, Dexter, "The End of China's One-Child Policy?" *Businessweek*, April 19, 2012.
"The Tien-Tsin Massacre," *New York Times*, September 17, 1870.
"To Show China How to Run Her Schools," *New York Times*, September 11, 1921.
Vogel, Ezra F., "But Deng Is the Leader to Celebrate," *New York Times*, October 3, 2009.

WEB SOURCES

Beja, Jean-Philippe, "Liu Xiaobo: Living in Truth and Paying the Price,", December 10, 2010, from Amnesty International website: takeaction@amnestyusa.org.
"China Banning U.S. Professors Elicits Silence from Colleges," from Bloomberg, www.bloomberg.com/news.2011-08-11/china-banning-u-s-professors-elicits-silence-from-colleges.html.
"China Looks to Attract More Foreign Students,", *New York Times*, September 30, 2010, http://english.peopledaily.com.cn/90001/90776/90883/7152470.html.
"China Needs American Education: Here's How to Bring It There", from *Forbes* website: http://www.forbes.com/sites/forbesleadershipforum/2012/06/20/china-needs-american-education-heres-how-to-bring-it-there.
"China's New National Education Plan Aims to Build a Country with Rich Human Resources," July 30, 2010, Ministry of Education. Available at: www.moe.edu.cn.
"China Publishes Its 10-Year Plan," *The Chronicle of Higher Education*, July 29, 2010. Available from http://chronicle.com/blogs/global/china-officially-publishes-its-10-year-education-plan/25870.
"China's First Sino-American University Opening in 2013," in *People's Daily*, April 6, 2012. Available at: http://english.peopledaily.com.cn/203691/7779455.html.
"China's New National Education Plan Aims to Build a Country with Rich Human Resources," July 30, 2010. Available from China's Ministry of Education website, www.moe.edu.cn.
Chinese Educational Mission Connections, www.cemconnections.org. "Chinese History According to the Confucius Institute," in *The Epoch Times*, http://www.theepochtimes.com/n2/china-news/chinese-history-according-to-the-confucius-institute-255366.html.
Courtney, Steve, "Rising Power in the East: Joe Twichell, Mark Twain and the Chinese Educational Mission, 1872–1881." Available at www.ahcc.org. Accessed July 12, 2012.
Fish, Isaac Stone, "No Academic Freedom for China," from *The Daily Beast*, http://www.thedailybeast.com/articles/2011/11/21/no-academic-freedom-for-china.html.
"Formation of China's Ivy League Hailed," October 30, 2009. Available from *People's Daily*. Available at: http://english.people.com.cn/90001/90776/90882/6794654.html.
Golden, Daniel, "China Says No Talking Tibet as Confucius Funds U.S. Universities,"
November 1, 2011, *Bloomberg*. Available from: www.bloomberg.com.

Golden, Daniel, "The SAT Is to America as _____ Is to China," February 3, 2011. Available from *Businessweek*, http://www.businessweek.com/magazine/content/11_07_/b4215014259071.htm.
Guo-hua Wang, "China's Higher Education Reform," *China Current* 2010, http://www.chinacurrents.com/spring_2010/cc_want.htm.
Haddad, J. R., *The Romance of China: Excursion and China in United States Cultures, 1776–1976*. Program by the American Historical Association and Columbia University Press. Available from: http://www.gutenberg.org, accessed November 1, 2012.
"The Institute of International Education Leads Higher Education Delegation to Build Academic Partnership between China and the United States," May 15, 2011. Available at: www.iie.org.
Kao, Timothy, "Yung Wing and Young Chinese Students in America (1872–1881)," from The Chinese Students Memorial Society website, www.120students.org.
Levin, Richard C., "Greetings on the Occasion of the Tsinghua University Centennial Celebration," April 23, 2011, Beijing, China. Available from http://communications.yale.edu/president/speeches/2011/04/23/greetings-occasional-tsinghua-university-centennial-celebration.
Lorenz, Andreas, "Redder than Red: An American Portrait of China's Next Leader," Spiegel Online International, December 5, 2010. Available at: http://www.spiegel.de/international/world/redder-than-red-an-american-portrait-of-china-s-next-leader-a-732972.html.
"Musician will.i.am to Support the 100,000 Strong Initiative Concert in Beijing to Celebrate U.S.-China Educational and Cultural Exchanges," U.S. Department of State website, http://www.state.gov/r/pa/prs/ps/2011/07/169362.htm.
Owens, Gene M., "If You Have a Lemon, Make Lemonade," in *China Daily*, November 18, 2006.
Pappano, Laura, "Massive Open Online Courses are Multiplying at a Rapid Pace," November 4, 2012, *New York Times* website, www.nytimes.com/2012/11/04/education/edlife/index.html.
Proulx, Chris, "Five Ways Technology Will Impact Higher Education in 2013," from *Forbes*, December 11, 2012. Available from www.forbes.com/sites/groupthink.
Roosevelt, Theodore, "The Awaking of China," available from http://www.theodore-roosevelt.com/images/research/treditorials/o157.pdf.
Sainsbury, Michael, "China Establishes Group of Ivy League Universities," from *The Australian*, November 4, 2009. Available at: www.theaustralian.com.au/news/world/china.
"Seven Decades of Educating Global Leaders," from the Johns Hopkins University website: http://nanjing.jhu.edu/about/index.htm. Accessed January 20, 2013.
Soren, Rottman, "A Portrait of Sophie Zhu, Long-Time Friend of Yale-China," in Yale-China website, http://www.yalechina.org/articles/pdf/Sophie%20Xhu%20Article.pdf.
Suping Lu, "Chinese Exclusion Acts: A Brief History of United States Legislation Aimed at Chinese Immigrants," April 2008, vol. 3, no. 2. Available in Readex, www.readex.com. Accessed October 1, 2012.
Thomas, Dan, "India to Overtake China in Undergraduate Mobility," *The Pie News*, June 27, 2012. Available at: http://thepienews.com.
U.S. Department of State, July 20, 2011, "Musician will.i.am to Support the 100,000 Strong Initiative Concert in Beijing to Celebrate U.S.-China Educational and Cultural Exchanges." Available at: http://www.state.gov/r/pa/prs/ps/2011/07/169362.htm.

Wit, M. Allison, "Closed Borders and Closed Minds," *Journal of Educational Controversy*, Western Washington University e-journal. Available at: http://www.wce.wwu.edu/resources/cep/ejournal. Accessed October 24, 2011.

The World Bank, "China 2030, Building a Modern, Harmonious and Creative High-Income Society." Available from: www.worldbank.org. Accessed May 30, 2012.

Yeung, Linda, "CHINA: Ex-premier Criticises Higher Education Reform," May 1, 2011, *University World News*. Available at: http://www.universityworldnews.com/article.php?story=20110429170813946.

The Yung Wing Project website, http://ywproject.x10.mx/index.htm. Accessed July 12, 2012.

Index

A
Academia Sinica 103
academic freedom: at Tsinghua School, 103; in the 1950s, 157; C9 League, 166; impact on US-China university collaborations, 166–169; Communist Party response, 181
Acculturation: CEM students adapt to 19th century New England, 48, 52; early publications, 90; indemnity students, 93; financial, 94; special issues after 1979, 142–144. *See also* Test of English as a Foreign Language
Adelhard of Bath, 2
Afong Moy, 20
Alcock, Rutherford, 34, 35
Alexander, Lamar, 158
American Civil War, 9, 33, 45
American Journal of Science and Arts, The, 6, 7
American Revolutionary War, 4–5; colleges at the time of, 9
Angell, James B., 59, 100
anti-American boycott (1905), 86–87, 191
Asylum Hill Church, 62
attitudes: Americans' toward Chinese, 19–21; early Chinese impressions of Americans, 21

B
barbarians, 29–31
Barbour Scholarships, 98–99
Barnard, A.P., 8
Barnes, Brigadier General, 33
Bartlett family, 50, 61
Bartlett, Fanny, 50, 61–62, 67, 70
Bashan Steamship Conference, 137
Beida. *See* Beijing University (Beida)
Beijing University (Peking University): sports 92; first woman professor, 98; female Students, 99; and China Foundation Board, 102; and Hu Shi, 103; noted students, 105; alliance of "new intellectuals", 107; and John Dewey,108; and Mao Zedong, 112; and the Soviet model, 118; big character posters, 128; CIES lecturers, 140; founding of, 155
big character posters, 121, 128, 130, 214
Boston Latin School, 5
Boxer Indemnity Scholarship program, 68; and Tsinghua School, 68, 91–93; Tong Shaoyi, 75, 80, 82–84; first remission, 87–88, 191; Liang Chang, 87; Roosevelt and, 74, 85–88; and former CEM students, 89; indemnity students, 89–91, 93, 97, 104–105, 114; female indemnity scholars, 97–99, 21; and University of Michigan, 100; second remission, 102–103, 192; and John Dewey, 107; after 1930, 113
Boxer Protocol, 85,191
Boxer Rebellion (Uprising), 74, 82–85, 187, 191; indemnity and penalties, 84, 86–87, 94, 102
British East India Company, 17
Brothers in Unity, 26
Brown, Samuel Robbins, 24–26
Brus, Wlodzimierz, 136
Buddhism, 12–13

Bureau of Foreign Affairs, 31
Burlingame-Seward Treaty, 37, 40, 46, 58–59
Burlingame, Anson, 22, 33–36, 41, 45, 58, 191
Bush, George W., 151, 181

C
C-9 League, 156, 157, 192
California gold rush, 19
Campbell, A. A., 25
Cantonese Clique, 75
Canton-Hankow Railway, 77
Canton-Kowloon Railway, 75
Carnagie Endowment, xiv
Carnes brothers, Nathanial and Frederick; 16, 17, 20
Carter, Jimmy, 132–135, 191, 192, 214
Carver, Mary Low, 10
Ch'ien Hsun, 15
Chang Poling, 105
Chang Shi Kwei, 32
charity schools, 5
Chen Bichen, 15
Chen Hegin, 104
Chen Hengzhe, 97, 114
Chen Xuanling, 2
Chiang Kaishek, 76, 122, 192
Ch'ien Mu, 122
Chin Lan Pin, 41, 48, 50, 56, 57, 59, 63
China Area Aid Act, 119
China Daily, 77, 151, 167
China Educational Association for International Exchange, 139
China Foundation for the Promotion of Education and Culture, The, 102, 113, 192
Chinatowns, 58, 72
Chinese Academy of Engineering, xii
Chinese Academy of Sciences, xii, 103, 133, 142
Chinese Educational Commmission, 54–55
Chinese Educational Mission, 41–44, first dispatch, 45–47, 191; host families, 48; social and academic adjustment, 49–51; nicknames, 53; at Centennial Exhibition, 54; Hell House (CEM Headquarters), 54–56; final dispatches, 56; recall of, 56–63, 191; CEM student achievements, 63–77; Li Hongzhang and, 44, 56, 84; and indemnity funds, 89; critics of, 110–112
Chinese Exclusion Act, 59, 79, 85, 90, 191
Chinese Students Monthly, 87, 100, 101, 107
Chinese Students' Alliance, 98, 99, 100, 192
Chinese University Development Project, 138
Christianity: and development of sciences, 2–3, 5; and Yung Wing, 23, 25; CEM students and, 49, 61; sponsors of education, 80; anti-Christian movement, 82–83; Chinese Students' Christian Association, 98; National Christian Council of China, 99
Chronicle of Higher Education, 165, 170, 171
Chung Mun-Yew, 53
Chung, Connie, xiii
civil service examinations, 2, 13, 31, 84, 91
Cixi, Empress Dowager (Tzu Hsi), 15, 64, 81–84
Clemens, Samuel, 52, 54–55, 59, 85
Clinton, Bill, 148, 192
Clinton, Hillary, 159–160, 178–179, 193
College of Foreign Languages, 31
Columbia Teachers College, 104–105, 109, 115, 184
Columbia University 4, 6, 8–9, 14, 60, 70, 74, 97, 102–104, 133, 147, 156–157, 167, 169–170, 175, 177, 195
Committee on Friendly Relations Among Foreign Students, 102
Committee on Scholarly Communication with the Peoples' Republic of China (CSCPRC), 132–133, 138
Communist Party xii, 98, 101–104, 117–118, 121–122, 124, 127–128, 131, 147, 155, 168–172, 180–181
Confucius, 3, 81, 169; Confucianism, 12–14
Confucius Institutes, 167–172, 186–188, 195
Congregationalists, 9, 49

coolies (laborers), 46, 47, 51, 52, 58, 79
Coordinated Interagency Partnership Regulating International Students (CIPRIS), 150
Cornell University, 9, 98, 100, 103, 156, 176
Council on International Educational Exchange (CIEE), 140–141
Cultural Revolution, 127–131, 133–134, 143, 147, 168, 180, 182, 192
curricular change, 7–10. *See also* Yale Report
Cushing, Caleb, 20

D

Dana, James Dwight, 6
Daoism (Taoism), 1, 3
Day, Jeremiah, 7, 25
De Miranda, Francisco, 26
Deng Xiaoping, xiv, 96, 132–136, 139–140, 152, 155, 192
Dewey, John, 102–110, 112, 192
Ding Maoying, 99
Distinguished Scholar Exchange Program, 135
Duke University, 163, 166, 177
Dunster, Henry, 4
Dwight, Timothy, 6

E

Eaton, Amos, 6
Eaton, Nathanial, 4
Emerson, Ralph Waldo, 8

F

Fairbank, John King, xvi, 124
Fang Lizhi, 2
Fareed Zakaria, xiii–xiv
female education: in early America, 10; in early China, 13–15. *See also* literacy
First All-China Conference on Higher Education, 124
Five Year Plan, 124, 125, 137
football, 8, 53, 67
foot-binding, 11, 20, 28
Ford Foundation, 122, 150, 179
Foreign Aid Appropriation Act, 119
foreign students (international students), xiii–xiv; in America, 10, 26–27; work restrictions, 93; tracking and immigration, 150–151; enrollments, 173; host institutions, 175; English language training, 145; in China, 158–159, 160, 163, 186
Formosa. *See* Taiwan
Franklin, Benjamin, 7
Freeman Awards for Study in Asia, 161
Frelinghuysen, T.F., 54
Fryer, John, 37, 80
Fulbright Program, 99, 115–116
Fulbright, William J., 115
Fuzhou (Foochow) Naval College and Torpedo School, 64, 66, 71

G

Gang of Four, 128
Garden of Perfect Brightness, 29
Gatling gun, 51
German immigrants, 8; gymnasium movement, 8
Golden Shield, xii
Gong Qinwang, 35
Goodman, Allan E., 158–159, 175. *See also* Institute of International Education
Gordon, Charles "Chinese", 20
Grant, Ulysses, 54
Gray, Asa, 7
Great Leap Forward, 125–127
Great Republic, 46
Green Card Party, 148
Guangming Daily, 124
Guangxu, 21, 81, 82, 84
Guangzhou (Canton), 16, 18, 26, 28, 44, 46, 52, 68, 75, 77, 94, 145, 180
Guomindang (Nationalists), 102–103 117–118, 122–123, 132, 192
Gutzlaff, Mrs., 23–24

H

haigui, xii, xvii
Han dynasty, 30, 81; scholar-gentry 29; ethnicity 180
Hanban, 168–172, 179
Harper's Weekly, 51, 58, 59
Hart, Robert, 34
Hartford Courant, 53
Harvard Girl, xi
Harvard University, xi, 4–9, 34, 99, 105, 155, 156, 163, 177, 181; Harvard College 3, 53, 78
Harvard, Reverend John, 4
Hay, John, 84, 86–87
He Zhao-wu, 1–2

Hitchcock, Edward, 6
Ho Chieh (He Jie), 105
Hong Kong, xvii, 25, 27–28, 31, 77–78, 94, 122–123, 145, 152–153, 161, 163–164, 167, 208, 210
Hong Xiuquan, 28, 128
Hopkins-Nanjing Center, 163, 166
Hsu Chi-yu, 15
Hu Jintao, 168
Hu Shi (Hu Shih), 14, 98, 102–103, 107, 108, 114
Hume, Edward, 95
Hundred Flowers campaign, 125, 192
Huntress, 25

I
Illegal Immigration Reform and Immigrant Responsibility Act (IIRIRA), 150–151, 192
Immigration Act of 1924, 151
Immigration Act of 1952, 151
Imperial Customs Translating Department, 28
Imperial Palace, 29, 84
Institute of International Education (IIE), 96–97, 115, 119, 123, 140, 152–153, 158–159, 161–162, 173, 175–176, 179
Institute of Pacific Relations, 98, 101, 113–114
International Academics Partnership Program (IAPP), 161
Ivy League: American, xi, 8–9, 175, 177, 181; Chinese "Ivy League" (C9 League), 156, 162

J
Japan: educational ties with China, 30, 106, 111, 164; military conflicts, 64–65, 79–80, 83–84, 89, 117, 154; and Kang Youwei, 82; coal stations, 46; student enrollments in the US, 101; tension over US immigration laws, 114; and Taiwan, 123; and China's economy, 136–137
Jefferson, Thomas, 7
Jeme Tien Yau, 65–68
Jiang Qing, 128
Johns Hopkins School of Nursing, 95
Johns Hopkins University, 157
Johns-Hopkins University-Nanjing Center for Chinese and American Studies, 162, 166

Jung, Karl, 2
junks, 20, 38, 64

K
Kaiping mines, 64, 70
Kang Youwei, 80, 82
Kiang Nan Arsenal, 37–38
Kissinger, Henry, xiv
Koo, V.K. Wellington, 100, 102
Korean War, 119, 171–172, 192

L
Ladies' Association of Savannah, The, 26
LaFargue, Thomas, 43, 69, 77
Lampton, David, xvi, 149–150, 153
Lane, John W., 54
legations (pre-embassies), 83, 86
Legge, Dr. James, 26
Levin, Richard C., 157
Li Gui, 53
Li Hongzhang, 19, 22, 29–31, 44, 52, 58, 63–64, 84–85, 112
Li Sien Lan, 32
Li Ta-chao, 108
Liang Cheng, 65, 73–74, 87–88
Liang Dunyan, 61–62, 65, 67, 75, 89
Liang Yu Ho, 75–76
Lieberman, Joe, 158
Lin Zexu, 18
Lincoln, Abraham, 34
literacy, 13; female literacy in China, 14; and Mao Zedong, 118
literati, 12–15
Liu Kunyiin, 21
Liu Xiaobo, 147
Liu Yangdong, 159
Luk Wing Chuan, 65, 70–71

M
Macy, Reverend William Allen, 27
Manchu, 10–11, 29, 50, 65, 67, 76, 82, 89
Mao Zedong, 96, 108–109, 116–121, 123, 125–132, 135–136, 140, 155, 168, 172, 192
Marxism, 101, 108, 125, 130, 180
Massachusetts Institute of Technology (MIT), xvi, 60, 157, 177
May Fourth Movement, 103, 107, 108
McCarthy, Joseph, 114, 120–121, 170
McLean, John, 6
migrant students, 183–185
Miner, Luella, 85

Ministry of Education, 89, 103, 138–140, 142, 154, 156, 159, 163, 176, 186
Missionaries (Christian), xi, 19–20, 25, 29–30, 39, 95, 100, 118, 187, 191; German, 82; antimissionary movement and Boxer Uprising, 82–84; and immigration 85, 119
Mo Bo, 129, 130
Monroe, Paul, 102, 105, 109–110
Monson Academy, 25, 26
massive open online course (MOOC), 176–178
Morrison Society School, 24, 206

N

NAFSA: Association of International Educators, 115, 142, 176
Nancy Pelosi, xv
Nanjing (Nanking), 29, 68, 99, 102, 105, 124, 141, 192, 216. *See also* Treaty of Nanjing and Nanjing University
Nanjing University, 142, 155, 157, 162, 166
National Outline for Medium and Long-term Education Reform and Development, 2010–2020, 160, 193
National Science Foundation, 137, 142, 150
National Stadium, xiv
Nationalists. *See* Guomindang
Needham, Joseph, 1
New Asia College, 122
New England's First Fruits, 3
New York Daily Advertiser, 20
New York Herald, 20
New York Sun, 20
New York Times, xiv, 45, 61, 63, 75, 89, 109, 134, 145, 158, 174, 177
New York University, 104, 163, 166, 175; New York University Shanghai, 163, 193, 196
Nian Rebellion, 30
Nixon, Richard, 120, 133, 192
Northrup, B.G. (Birdsey), 48, 54

O

Obama, Barak, 159, 176, 178–179, 185, 193
Obama, Michelle, 159
Olympic games, xv

Olyphant brothers, 25–26
100,000 Strong Initiative, 159–162, 178–179, 193
one-child policy, xi, 143, 182–183
opium, 15, 17, 20, 28, 59, 77
Opium Wars, i, ix, xvi, 15, 17–20, 22, 30, 34, 191
Orientals baseball team, 53, 61, 66, 67, 72
Ou Ngoh Liang, 56
Ouyang King, 65, 71–72
Overall Plan for the Reform of the Economic System, 137

P

Paun Min Chung, 61
Peiyang University. *See* Tianjin University
People's Daily, 130, 149
Phelps, William Lyon, 53–54
Porter, Noah, 44, 48, 59–60
Press, Frank, 134
Princeton University, 4, 6–9, 102, 156, 166, 177
Project 211, 156, 192
Project 985, 149, 156, 192
Putnam Machine Company, 33

Q

Qian Ning, 143
Qing Dynasty, xi–xii, xv, xvii, 10–11, 15, 18, 28–32, 34, 38, 45, 53, 57, 66, 68, 77–79, 81–83, 85, 90, 94, 107, 128, 154, 188, 191
Qinghua College. *See* Tsinghua College
queues, 11, 50, 51, 52, 53, 62, 77

R

railroads, 10, 21; in China, 66–67, 70, 75–76, 78, 83
Red Guards, 128–131, 180
Rhoads, Edward J. M., xvi
Ritchie, A. A., 25
Rockefeller Foundation, 112
Rockefeller, John D., Jr., 109
Rockhill, William, 86–87
Rogers, William Barton, 7
Roosevelt, Theodore, 73–74, 79, 85–89, 158
Root, Elihu, 97
Rudolph, Frederick, 3
Rugh, Dr. Dwight, 122
Russell, Bertrand, 12, 109, 112
Russia, 67–68, 83, 85, 102. *See also* Soviet Union

234 Index

Russo-Japanese War, 73

S
Sacred Book of Imperial Edicts, 42
Scholastic Achievement Test (SAT), 161
Scherer, Frances, 95–96
School of Western Language and Science, 31
Seelye, Julius, 54
Self-Strengthening Movement; 45, 64, 66, 70, 79–81, 191
Seward, George F., 46
Seward, William, 34–35, 37, 191
Shanghai, xii, xv–xvi, 28, 32–33, 39, 42, 44–46, 62–63, 72–73, 76, 80, 87, 90, 93, 95–96, 98, 107, 112, 128, 140–141, 145–146, 148–149, 157, 163, 166, 193
Shanghai-Nanking (Nanjing) Railroad, 76
Sheffield Scientific School, 6
Shortrede, Andrew, 25
Shu Xincheng, 110–112
Sik, Ota, 136
Silliman, Benjamin, 6
Sino-Japanese War, 96, 154, 172
Sisters of Charity, 40
Smith, Arthur H., 22, 84, 87–88
Society for the Promotion of Collegiate and Theological Education in the West, 9
Song Dynasty, 1, 14, 81
Soviet Union,123–124, 127, 133, 135. *See also* Russia
Student and Exchange Visitor Information System (SEVIS), 151
Sun Yat Sen, 76–77, 93, 102, 152, 192

T
Taiping Rebellion 19, 28–32, 128, 191
Taiwan 103, 117, 119, 123, 134, 153, 161, 170, 192
Tang Shaoyi, 65, 67, 74–76, 89
Tao Xingzhi, 104
Taoism. *See* Daoism
tea trade, 11, 15–16, 18–21, 25, 31–32, 66; tea drinking in America, 16, 21
Thousand Foreign Experts, 164, 193
Three Gorges Dam, xv
Tiananmen Square, 117, 118, 130, 132, 147–148, 166–167, 170, 192
Tianjin, 75 -76, 95, 105; Tianjin Naval Academy, 64; Tianjin Medical School, 64; Tianjin (Peiyang) University, 80, 154–155
Tibet, xv, 75, 162, 166, 170
Ticknor, George, 7
Tierong "Sophie" Zhu, 95–96
Ting Yih Chang, 38, 40
Test of English as a Foreign Language (TOEFL), 145
Tong Shao Yi. *See* Tang Shaoyi
transcontinental railroads, 19, 21
Treaty of (Tianjin) Tientsin, 30, 35
Treaty of Nanjing, 30, 191
Tsinghua School/College (1911–1928), 68, 70, 77, 89, 91–93, 98–99; female students, 97 Tsinghua University 99, 102–103, 112, 117, 156–157, 162–163, 167, 180, 182, 192
Tsinghua Middle School 130
Tsinghuapper, 92
Tsung Li Yamun, 60
Twichell, J.H., 52, 54, 59, 62
Tymme, Thomas, 2

U
United Nations Educational, Scientific and Cultural Organization (UNESCO), 140, 186
United States Military Academy at West Point, 57
United States-China Consultation on People-to-People Exchange, 159–160, 176, 179
United States-China Cultural Engagement Act, 158, 193
University of Illinois, 88, 175
University of Michigan, 34, 59, 98–100, 144, 146, 157, 165, 175, 196
University of Virginia, 7, 26

V
Vance, Cyrus, 134

W
Wang, Y.C., xvi, 12, 30, 111–112
War of Resistance against Japan, 117
Washington, George, 34–35
Wayland, Francis, 8
Weibo, 167, 183
Wen Jaibo, 158
Wen Seang, 38–39
Wen's Book of Mother Indoctrination, 14

Index 235

William and Mary, College of , 4, 7
Williams, Samuel Wells, 78
Wong Chin (Wang Jin), 104
Wong Foon, 25
Wong Kai-kah, 62, 65, 72–73; letter to Mrs. Bartlett 197–199
Wong Shing, 25–26
Woo Tsze Tung, 56–57, 59, 63
Woo, Y.T., 50, 65, 68–70
Woodcock, Leonard, 134
World Bank, 137–138, 186
World War I, 96
World War II, xiii, 27, 106, 122
Wu Jinglian, 136
Wu Yifang, 98

X

Xi Jinping, 179–181, 193
Xinhua, xv, 153, 164
Xinjiang 13, 166
Xu Jiyu, 34–35

Y

Yale College, 4,6; Yale University, 9, 24–26, 33, 39, 41, 48, 52–53, 59, 61, 66, 68, 72, 74, 76, 78, 94, 96, 122, 141, 156–157, 163, 188; Yale Report, 7–8

Yale-China Association, 96, 114, 121–122, 141; Yale-in-China 94–95
Yali Middle School, 95–96, 114, 121–122
Yan Mei, 15
Yeh Tingshien (Yi Ding Xin), 104
yellow peril, 21, 55, 88
Yiting Liu, xi
Young, John Russell, 54
Young Men's Christian Association (YMCA), 90, 92–93, 113
Yu Ching Sung (Yu Qing Song), 105
Yuan Shikai, 74–76, 87
Yung Wing, 22–33, 37–63, 78–80, 112, 188–189, 191
Yung, Mary Kellogg, 63

Z

Zbigniew Brzezinski, 134
Zeng Guofan, 22, 29, 31–32, 37–38, 40–41, 45, 57
Zeng Liashun, 26, 41
Zeng Pu, 50
Zhang Xiuqin, 160, 176
Zhang Zhidong, 21, 68, 81
Zhang, Charles, xvi
Zhong Juncheng, 50
Zhu Rongji, 167